THE WOUND AND THE BOW

BOOKS BY EDMUND WILSON

I THOUGHT OF DAISY

AXEL'S CASTLE

THE TRIPLE THINKERS

TO THE FINLAND STATION

THE WOUND AND THE BOW

THE SHOCK OF RECOGNITION

MEMOIRS OF HECATE COUNTY

EUROPE WITHOUT BAEDEKER

CLASSICS AND COMMERCIALS

THE SHORES OF LIGHT

FIVE PLAYS

RED, BLACK, BLOND AND OLIVE

A PIECE OF MY MIND

THE AMERICAN EARTHQUAKE

APOLOGIES TO THE IROQUOIS

WILSON'S NIGHT THOUGHTS

PATRIOTIC GORE

THE COLD WAR AND THE INCOME TAX

O CANADA

THE BIT BETWEEN MY TEETH

A PRELUDE

THE DUKE OF PALERMO AND OTHER PLAYS

THE DEAD SEA SCROLLS: 1947-1969

The Wound and the Bow

SEVEN STUDIES
IN LITERATURE
BY
EDMUND WILSON

OHIO UNIVERSITY PRESS

ATHENS

Library of Congress Cataloging-in-Publication Data

Wilson, Edmund, 1895-1972.
   The wound and the bow : seven studies in literature / by
Edmund Wilson.
      p.   cm.
   Originally published: New York : Oxford University Press,
c1941.
   ISBN 0-8214-1189-6 (pbk. : alk. paper)
   1. Suffering in literature.   2. Literature–History and criticism.
I. Title.
PN56.S742W55   1997
809'.93353–dc21
                                                          96-51164
                                                          CIP

CONTENTS

A large part of the material in this book has appeared in a different form in *The Atlantic Monthly* and *The New Republic*.

INTRODUCTION

by Janet Groth

THE WOUND AND THE BOW brings together seven wonderful
essays on the delicate theme of the relation between art
and suffering by one of America's greatest literary and social critics, Edmund Wilson. This welcome reissue – one of
several for this title – testifies to the value publishers put
on it and to a reluctance among them ever to let it stay out
of print for very long.

The subjects treated – Dickens and Kipling, Edith
Wharton and Ernest Hemingway, Joyce and Sophocles, and,
perhaps most surprisingly, Jacques Casanova – reveal the
range and diversity of Edmund Wilson's interests, his historical grasp, his learning, and his intellectual curiosity.

When it was first published, in 1941, Wilson was already
a celebrated figure with significant critical contributions to
his credit. His first such work, *Axel's Castle*, published in
1931, had introduced the reading public in America and
Britain to the modernist movement embracing W. B. Yeats,
T. S. Eliot, Paul Valéry, Proust, Joyce, and Gertrude Stein,
all of whom Wilson linked to the Symbolist poets of nineteenth-century France. His clear explanation of the symbolic method underlying the sometimes difficult and
forbidding works of these authors provides what has been
called "an indispensable map to the literature of the 20th
century," a "way in" to that – for many – inaccessible country of the Waste Land, of Dublin on Bloomsday and of
Combray by Swann's Way and the Guermantes Way.

Yet, as important as the historical background and explication of symbolism undoubtedly are, it is the vivid portraits of the artists Wilson draws in *Axel's Castle* which tend to establish the book in readers' minds and in their affections. Wilson has already begun his practice of acting the role, in his criticism, of the sympathetic mediator. He pictures for us the newlyweds, Mr. and Mrs. W. B. Yeats, huddled over a table as, employing Mrs. Yeats' mystical technique of automatic writing, they eagerly await "metaphors for poetry." And he gives us a poignant glimpse of the dying Marcel Proust, propped up on his deathbed, working feverishly to complete proofs of the final version of *The Remembrance of Things Past*, sustained in his task by the moral fiber which, Wilson says, he had inherited from his Jewish grandmother, and by pails of iced beer, which he had sent up from the Ritz.

In other words, Wilson was already establishing himself in America, as Matthew Arnold had done a generation before in England, as the successor to their French critical models, Michelet, Taine, and Sainte-Beuve. Like them, Wilson approached his critical analyses of literary artists by "creating the creators themselves" in dramatic fashion before us. And he was continuing the practice he had described in his dedication to *Axel's Castle* of writing literary criticism as "a history of man's ideas and imaginings in the setting of the conditions which have shaped them."

When *The Wound and the Bow* first came out, the notice in the *New York Times* was typical of the warm reception it received, calling it a work "in the best tradition of literary criticism" and praising the way it combines "exact information with shrewd and searching penetration into the personal life of the artist." Even reviewers puzzled about the relation of the essays to its title admired the work as a whole. One reviewer, complaining that "at times the jigsaw pieces fit together neatly; at others, a discernible gap appears," nevertheless found the essays themselves "stimulating and excellent." The *Times*, which thought them "arbitrarily integrated into one volume," goes on to praise the collection in the glowing terms cited above and proclaim it "by far the most interesting criticism of the year." Alfred Kazin confessed "I happen to admire Mr. Wilson's work so passionately I would find even his laundry notes interesting." David Daiches wished "these essays had been longer." And Morton Zabel found it "a book that illuminates the problems of criticism in a remarkable way." Oddly, *Time*, while recommending it to "all students of serious literature," did not see Wilson's reputation being "bolstered" by it. But the *Yale Review*, which thought it lacked humor (though others had derived great pleasure from its wit), said its "solid virtues will advance his fame as one of the best literary critics now writing." Yale got it right.

Just what is "the wound" and what "the bow" of the title? The image comes from the myth of Philoctetes, about which Sophocles wrote a little-known play that is the subject of Wilson's last essay in this volume. Philoctetes is a Greek archer who suffers a wound in his foot, a snakebite; the persistent, malodorous eruptions from this wound render him so disgusting to his fellows that he is exiled to a lonely island. But when it is clear that both the archer and his invincible bow are essential to victory over Troy, he is persuaded – by a sympathetic mediator named Neoptolemus – to come out of exile and wield his bow for the benefit of his country. As I have noted elsewhere, the entire myth is generally taken as Wilson's metaphorical way of saying that great gifts and great suffering often conspire in the formation of the artist. What has not always been seen so clearly is that the essay may also stand as Wilson's metaphorical statement of the artist's, and the critic's, function in society. The general failure to recognize this may have arisen from a general failure to recognize Neoptolemus as the critic-figure in Wilson's version of the tale. Yet the importance Wilson ascribes to Neoptolemus is unmistakable when he asks, in his concluding paragraph: "How then is the gulf to be got over between the ineffective plight of the bowman and his proper use of the bow, between his ignominy and his destined glory?" Wilson's answer is most instructive in its suggestion of a paradigm for sympathetic criticism: "Only by the intervention of one who is guileless enough to treat him, not as a monster, nor yet as a magical property which is wanted for accomplishing some end, but simply as another man, whose suffering elicits his sympathy and whose courage and pride he admires." By taking the risk, involving himself, and keeping faith with Philoctetes, Neoptolemus, says Wilson, "dissolves Philoctetes' stubbornness and thus cures him and sets him free, and saves the campaign as well."

Not until Leon Edel, in his introductory portrait of Edmund Wilson in *The Twenties*, identified Neoptolemus with Wilson himself did the full implications of Wilson's essay become evident. Edel points out that "Neoptolemus, in this recreation, becomes a kind of archetypal critic, as Philoctetes represents the archetypal artist; he reflects, even more than the archer, the image and vocation of Edmund Wilson."

Returning to the myth from this perspective, we can imagine Wilson making the point, through the artist-figure Philoctetes, not only that genius and suffering may be inextricably entwined, but also that the artist must remain engaged or run the risk of losing, at least to a degree, his artistic power. We can also see Wilson's suggestion, by means of Neoptolemus, that the critic's function is twofold: first, to treat the artist with "sympathetic imagination" (Edel's phrase, incidentally, for Wilson's critical approach), while holding him always to his highest abilities; and second, to become his champion and mediator with the rest of society.

Early commentators tended to make Wilson's wound and bow allusion into a simplistic connection between art and neurosis. Lionel Trilling alone seemed to understand that the wound, in Wilson's presentation, is an attendant circumstance of talent, not the cause. It is easy to overstate Wilson's case. Just last spring, however, the *New York Times* reported on a study in the *New England Journal of Medicine* that does indeed document a high degree of connection between genius and some form of mental or physical dysfunction. And Wilson certainly does believe, with Joyce (whose "I bleed by the black stream / For my torn bough" is Wilson's chosen epigram for this volume), that art is born out of suffering and, often, heroic struggle on the part of the artist, and that we understand it the better for knowing something of that struggle. Thus, in these seven essays, he brings forward – like a sympathetic mediator arguing before the Greeks on behalf of Philoctetes – the stories of Dickens' childhood trauma in the blacking factory, of Kipling's six-year abandonment by his parents, of Edith Wharton's unhappy marriage, Casanova's illegitimacy, Joyce's near-blindness, and Hemingway's ambivalence toward women and his compensating machismo.

The Wound and the Bow did not bring forth a new body of literary theory nor a new school of literary criticism. Wilson's contributions were, rather, the animating and reanimating of the reputations of the artists he treated in it and the often successful search for the sources of their literary artistry and craftsmanship.

This reissue provides a forceful reminder that another of Wilson's critical functions was his role, as his friend F. Scott Fitzgerald put it, as the "literary conscience of my generation." The essays on Kipling and Hemingway, especially, suggest that one of the permanent contributions of this book is its forthright statements about the credo of intellectual honesty that must underlie any successful artistic work. His chastisements of these writers for allowing ego or politics to distort their rendering of people and society are clearer statements of artistic values than we have seen in a long while. Wilson's role as a moral barometer, it would seem, is one he continues to fulfill.

Turning briefly to the essays themselves, the first thing one notices, aside from the pleasure to be found in their prose, is Wilson's easy command of his subjects. He seems to have read not only all of Dickens but all of the critical and biographical writing on Dickens as well. For a specialist in Dickens studies this would be a matter of course, but for Wilson, who was forced to depend for a living upon the publication of articles, such extensive preparation is a mark of his integrity as a journalist-critic.

His reward in the case of "The Two Scrooges" was the satisfaction of seeing his ambitious aim largely met. He set out to change the popular, and the academic, perception of Dickens as a cozy, comic writer, a mere entertainer, to universal acknowledgment of his status as one of the serious masters of the novel and a great social prophet. He accomplished, years after Dickens' lifetime, what William Dean Howells achieved for the reputation of Mark Twain while he lived. For, to all intents and purposes, and notwithstanding a perceptive essay by George Orwell that appeared at about the same time, modern criticism of Dickens begins with this essay of Wilson's. It is still an admirable place for the modern reader to get to know Dickens.

If Wilson had similar hopes of changing the modern perception of Kipling, he was to be disappointed. The Kipling read today is largely still the writer of the *Jungle Books* and *Kim* and perhaps "The Man Who Would Be King." But anyone who wants to understand the process by which a writer of so fine a gift could diminish his talent in jingoistic pursuits will find, in this essay, a sympathetic and thoroughly compelling account of an artist whose bow was rendered defective by his inability to deal with the traumas of his life. Wilson writes a stunning indictment of that defect: "Kipling has committed one of the most serious sins against his calling which are possible for an imaginative writer. He has resisted his own sense of life and discarded his own moral intelligence." Wilson hints at a Pyrrhic victory of sorts when, in his last years, at the price of losing his only son, Kipling was finally brought to stop glorifying war as a stirring patriotic adventure. In an elegiac mood Wilson concludes, "certainly these last stories of Kipling are among

the most moving he wrote." He finds in them "quite another Kipling. His prophets have an altered message. . . .
His soldiers are no longer so cocky, so keen to kill inferior
peoples, so intent on the purposes of the Empire."

"Uncomfortable Casanova" is a somewhat anomalous but
fascinating look at a social misfit whose bow consists of his
rock-bottom honesty, in his *Memoirs* (just being printed in
English in their entirety), with regard to the inconvenient
truths of his life as the bastard son of an actress, a person
without caste in a highly caste-ridden society, and a man
whose life of sexual exploits and seductions has become
legendary but of which he gives an account that by no means
places him in an advantageous light.

The relative weakness of "Justice to Edith Wharton" may
spring from Wilson's failure in this case to follow his own
professional standards in terms of thoroughness of preparation. He admits "I have read only one of Mrs. Wharton's
novels written since *Old New York*," and then goes on to
give that one novel – *Twilight Sleep* – a drubbing. But to do
Wilson himself justice, even though he is much less sure-
footed in delineating Mrs. Wharton's "wound" than we have
seen him be in the case of Dickens and Kipling, the essay
does represent considerable accomplishment.

For ten years, until Diana Trilling entered the lists, Wilson's was the only voice arguing for recognition of the social as well as literary significance of Wharton's work. Irving
Howe included both of their essays in the Wharton volume
he edited for the Twentieth Century Views series in 1962,
acknowledging that, even then, justice to Edith Wharton,
in the sense of readily granted praise and proportionate
academic attention, was still largely justice deferred. Though
R. W. B. Lewis' biography and Cynthia Wolff's critical ap-
preciation in the seventies advanced the cause, not until
the eighties and nineties brought feminist critical attention
to Wharton has there been full treatment of her work.

If Wilson did not achieve his aim of establishing Wharton in the forefront of American writers of the early years

of the century, it may be partly because the "wound" to which he attributes her special acuteness of perception in this period (i.e., that she was suffering from problems deriving from her unhappy marriage) is somewhat unconvincing. Equally dubious is Wilson's conjecture that the reason her work falls off, in his view, after 1917 is that, free of her marriage, she becomes better adjusted through a happy resettlement in Paris. If we had only the following sentence to go by, we could indeed find cause to label Wilson a sexist (which would hardly distinguish him from other male critics of the period in which he wrote): "It is sometimes true of women writers – less often, I believe, of men – that a manifestation of something like genius may be stimulated by some exceptional emotional strain, but will disappear when the stimulus has passed." He claims that men develop their artistic talent independent of "the vicissitudes of [their] emotional experience" and goes on to cite Henry James to Wharton's disadvantage. He seems to have forgotten his own argument in the Kipling essay that it was just those vicissitudes which were destroying his work. But we need not pillory Wilson on the strength (or weakness) of this one reflection. The case to be made for him as a male evolved beyond his time is well documented in his Hemingway essay, which I will come to shortly.

In addition to having led the long unheeded cry for reevaluation of her work, Wilson's lasting contribution to the Wharton critical heritage by means of this essay is the notice he takes in it of her artistic use of setting. At first when he calls attention to her personal interest in the subject of the decorative arts, and when he calls her "the poet of interior decoration," one suspects he may be speaking tongue in cheek, but his harrowing report of Undine Spragg's little boy among the velvets and brocades of the grand *hôtel* where he is left to wander recalls the Marxian sympathy with which he enters into Dickens' Victorian interiors. We see that he respects and admires Edith Wharton no less than he does Dickens for the hatred with which they describe the decor-heavy, soulless materialism of their respective societies. Of Dickens he says, "It is necessary to see him as a man in order to appreciate him as an artist – to exorcise the spell which has bewitched him into a stuffy piece of household furniture and to give him his proper rank as the poet of the portièred and upholstered world who saw clearest through the coverings and curtains." Of Wharton he notes: "in the case of Edith Wharton, the *décors* become the agents of tragedy. . . . The people . . . are pursued by them as by spirits of doom and ultimately crushed by their accumulation."

One aspect of Wilson's writing that may seem odd to readers today is his addition of a kind of postscript, both to this essay and to the Hemingway and Joyce essays, in which he attempts to emend his views in light of later publications. This is in keeping with his unembarrassed humanistic belief that intellectual discourse is a dynamic affair and that each individual intellect must always be open to self-correction and emendation in the presence of new data. In the face of so much present-day noncomprehension of this point it is perhaps necessary to insist that there is a difference between changing one's mind after considering new evidence and engaging in dishonest "waffling."

Though Wilson had available less biographical support for the genesis of Hemingway's "wound" than the recent biographies of Kenneth Lynn and others would have supplied, Wilson is once more very acute in his description of the wound and its effect on Hemingway's bow. He knows only that "The emotion which principally comes through in *Francis Macomber* and *The Snows of Kilimanjaro* . . . is a growing antagonism to women." After a startling inventory of instances of such antagonism Wilson condemns this attitude as morally "trashy" and shows that it disfigures Hemingway's work. It is impossible to read Wilson's scorn for Hemingway's sexism in this short essay and not feel that these are attitudes toward women which he himself, at least consciously, rejects.

This essay is also notable for the clarity of its discussion of the leftist political pressures being exerted upon writers like Hemingway in the thirties and for the mastery with which Wilson draws distinctions between valuable Marxian ideals and the abhorrent events perpetrated in Marx's name by the Stalinist regime.

"The Dream of H. C. Earwicker" stands apart from the other essays in this set by being a gloss, and an excellent one, on a single, difficult novel, *Finnegans Wake*. Only by implication – Wilson's implication that both the strengths and the weaknesses of Joyce's prose style in the novel are attributable in some measure to his physical wound, i.e., his dwindling eyesight – does the essay fit his overall theme.

With the addition to the concept of "the wound" provided by the social maladjustment of Casanova and the physical disability of Joyce, Wilson conveys a much more complex idea of the biographical occasion that may stimulate artistic expression than would a conception that sees it in terms of neurosis alone.

It would be superfluous and very probably harmful to its largely implied meanings to add further interpretive comment on Wilson's "Philoctetes." But we should note that here, too, in the very essay on Sophocles' play in which he elucidates it, Wilson is applying the concept of "the wound and the bow" to Sophocles himself. He undertakes to turn the cool classicist back into a suffering human being. "Somewhere," he insists, "even in the fortunate Sophocles there had been a sick and raving Philoctetes." He does so, not in any reductive spirit, but, rather, to increase our knowledge of the artist. That increase of knowledge, Wilson believes, will increase our understanding, and so increase our pleasure. Why, though, place the cornerstone of the volume last rather than first? Readers of *Axel's Castle* will remember that only in the final chapter of that work, too, did the meaning of the title become clear. In both cases, Wilson did it, I believe, so that the issues raised by the individual essays would reverberate in the reader's mind, creating indirectly the thematic retroactive link rather than a simple one-to-one relationship. Emily Dickinson says the poet must tell the truth, but tell it at a slant – and that is sometimes the case with the master critic too, when dealing with any generalization about so complex a structure as the human mind.

I bleed by the black stream
For my torn bough!

JAMES JOYCE

THE WOUND AND THE BOW

DICKENS: THE TWO SCROOGES

To the Students of English 354,
University of Chicago, Summer, 1939

OF ALL THE great English writers, Charles Dickens has received in his own country the scantiest serious attention from either biographers, scholars, or critics. He has become for the English middle class so much one of the articles of their creed — a familiar joke, a favorite dish, a Christmas ritual — that it is difficult for British pundits to see in him the great artist and social critic that he was. Dickens had no university education, and the literary men from Oxford and Cambridge, who have lately been sifting fastidiously so much of the English heritage, have rather snubbingly let him alone. The Bloomsbury that talked about Dostoevsky ignored Dostoevsky's master, Dickens. What happens when the London of Lytton Strachey does take Dickens up is shown in Hugh Kingsmill's book, *The Sentimental Journey,* in which the man who was called by Taine 'the master of all hearts' is made into one of those Victorian scarecrows with ludicrous Freudian flaws — so infantile, pretentious, and hypocritical as to deserve only a perfunctory sneer.

Since Forster's elaborate memoir, which even in the supplemented edition of Ley has never been a real biography, no authoritative book about Dickens has been published. Some of the main facts about his life have till recently been kept from the public, and now that they have finally

3

come out they have usually been presented either by dod-
dering Dickens-fanciers or through the medium of garru-
lous memoirs. Mr. Ralph Straus and Mr. T. A. Jackson
have recently published studies of Dickens — the one from
the psychological, the other from the Marxist, point of
view — which attempt a more searching treatment; but
though they contain some valuable insights, neither is
really first-rate, for neither handles surely enough or carries to fundamental findings the line which it undertakes.
The typical Dickens expert is an old duffer who, as Mr.
Straus has said, is primarily interested in proving that
Mr. Pickwick stopped at a certain inn and slept in a certain bed.

As for criticism, there has been in English one admirable critic of Dickens, George Gissing, whose prefaces
and whose book on Dickens not only are the best thing on
Dickens in English but stand out as one of the few really
first-rate pieces of literary criticism produced by an Englishman of the end of the century. For the rest, you have
mainly G. K. Chesterton, who turned out in his books on
Dickens some of the best work of which he was capable
and who said some excellent things, but whose writing
here as elsewhere is always melting away into that peculiar
pseudo-poetic booziness which verbalizes with large con-
ceptions and ignores the most obtrusive actualities. Chesterton celebrated the jolly Dickens; and Bernard Shaw off-
set this picture by praising the later and gloomier Dickens
and insisting on his own debt to the author of *Little Dorrit*
at a time when it was taken for granted that he must de-
rive from such foreigners as Ibsen and Nietzsche.

Chesterton asserted that time would show that Dickens
was not merely one of the Victorians, but incomparably
the greatest English writer of his time; and Shaw coupled
his name with that of Shakespeare. It is the conviction of
the present writer that both these judgments were justified. Dickens — though he cannot of course pretend to the

rank where Shakespeare has few companions — was nevertheless the greatest dramatic writer that the English had had since Shakespeare, and he created the largest and most varied world. It is the purpose of this essay to show that we may find in Dickens' work today a complexity and a depth to which even Gissing and Shaw have hardly, it seems to me, done justice — an intellectual and artistic interest which makes Dickens loom very large in the whole perspective of the literature of the West.

I

The father of Charles Dickens' father was head butler in the house of John Crewe (later Lord Crewe) of Crewe Hall, Member of Parliament for Chester; and the mother of his father was a servant in the house of The Marquess of Blandford in Grosvenor Square, who was Lord Chamberlain to the Household of George III. This grandmother, after her marriage, became housekeeper at Crewe Hall, and it is assumed that it was through the patronage of her employer that her son John Dickens was given a clerkship in the Navy Pay Office.

John Dickens began at £70 a year and was in time increased to £350. But he had always had the tastes of a gentleman. He was an amiable fellow, with an elegant manner and a flowery vein of talk, who liked to entertain his friends and who could not help creating the impression of a way of life beyond his means. He was always in trouble over bills.

When Charles, who had been born (February 7, 1812) at Portsmouth and had spent most of his childhood out of London at Portsmouth, Portsea and Chatham, who had had a chance to go to the theater and to read the *Arabian Nights* and the eighteenth-century novelists, and had been taught by a tutor from Oxford, came up to London at the age of nine to join his parents, who had been obliged to return there, he was terribly shocked to find them, as a consequence of his father's debts, now living in a little back garret in one of the poorest streets of Camden Town. On February 20, 1824, when Charles was twelve, John Dickens was arrested for debt and taken to the Marshalsea Prison, announcing, as he left the house: 'The sun has set upon me forever!' At home the food began to run low; and they had to pawn the household belongings till all but two rooms were bare. Charles even had to carry his books, one by one, to the pawnshop. It was presently decided that the boy should go to work at six shillings a week for a cousin who manufactured blacking; and through six months, in a rickety old house by the river, full of dirt and infested with rats, he pasted labels on blacking bottles, in the company of riverside boys who called him 'the little gentleman.' He wanted terribly to go on with his schooling, and couldn't grasp what had happened to him. The whole of the rest of the family moved into the Marshalsea with his father; and Charles, who had a lodging near them, went to the jail after work every evening and ate breakfast with them every morning. He was so ashamed of the situation that he would never allow his companion at the blacking warehouse, whose name was Bob Fagin, to go with him to the door of the prison, but would take leave of him and walk up the steps of a strange house and pretend to be going in. He had had a kind of nervous fits in his earlier childhood, and now these began to recur. One day at work he was seized with such an acute spasm that he had to lie down on some straw on the floor, and the boys who worked with him spent half the day applying blacking bottles of hot water to his side.

John Dickens inherited a legacy in May and got out of jail the twenty-eighth; but he let Charles keep on working in the warehouse. The little boys did their pasting next to the window in order to get the light, and people used to stop to look in at them because they had become so quick and skilful at it. This was an added humiliation for Charles; and one day when John Dickens came there, he wondered how his father could bear it. At last — perhaps, Dickens thought, as a result of what he had seen on this visit — John quarreled with Charles's employer, and took the boy out of the warehouse and sent him to school.

These experiences produced in Charles Dickens a trauma from which he suffered all his life. It has been charged by some of Dickens' critics that he indulged himself excessively in self-pity in connection with these hardships of his childhood; it has been pointed out that, after all, he had only worked in the blacking warehouse six months. But one must realize that during those months he was in a state of complete despair. For the adult in desperate straits, it is almost always possible to imagine, if not to contrive, some way out; for the child, from whom love and freedom have inexplicably been taken away, no relief or release can be projected. Dickens' seizures in his blacking-bottle days were obviously neurotic symptoms; and the psychologists have lately been telling us that lasting depressions and terrors may be caused by such cuttings-short of the natural development of childhood. For an imaginative and active boy of twelve, six months of despair are quite enough. 'No words can express,' Dickens wrote of his first introduction to the warehouse, in a document he gave to Forster, 'the secret agony of my soul as I sunk into this companionship; compared these every day associates with those of my happier childhood; and felt my early hopes of growing up to be a learned and distinguished man crushed in my breast. The deep remembrance of the sense I had of being utterly neglected and hopeless; of the shame I felt in my position; of the misery it was to my young heart to believe that, day by day, what I had learned, and thought, and delighted in, and raised my fancy and my emulation up by, was passing away from me, never to be brought back any more; cannot be written. My whole nature was so penetrated with the grief and humiliation of such considerations, that even now, famous and caressed and happy, I often forget in my dreams that I have a dear wife and children; even that I am a man; and wander desolately back to that time of my life.'

He never understood how his father could have abandoned him to such a situation. 'I know my father,' he once told Forster, 'to be as kind-hearted and generous a man as ever lived in the world. Everything that I can remember of his conduct to his wife, or children, or friends, in sickness or affliction is beyond all praise. By me, as a sick child, he has watched night and day, unweariedly and patiently, many nights and days. He never undertook any business, charge or trust that he did not zealously, conscientiously, punctually, honorably discharge. His industry has always been untiring. He was proud of me, in his way, and had a great admiration of [my] comic singing. But, in the case of his temper, and the straitness of his means, he appeared to have lost utterly at this time the idea of educating me at all, and to have utterly put from him the notion that I had any claim upon him, in that regard, whatever.' And Charles never forgave his mother for having wanted to keep him working in the warehouse even after his father had decided to take him out. 'I never afterwards forgot,' he wrote of her attitude at this time. 'I never shall forget, I never can forget.'

Of those months he had never been able to bring himself to speak till, just before conceiving *David Copperfield*, he wrote the fragment of autobiography he sent to Forster; and, even after he had incorporated this material in an altered form in the novel, even his wife and children were never to learn about the realities of his childhood till they read about it after his death in Forster's *Life*. But the work of Dickens' whole career was an attempt to digest these early shocks and hardships, to explain them to himself, to justify himself in relation to them, to give an intelligible and tolerable picture of a world in which such things could occur.

Behind the misfortune which had humiliated Charles was the misfortune which had humiliated his father. John Dickens was a good and affectionate man, who had done the best he was able within the limits of his personality and who had not deserved to be broken. But behind these undeserved misfortunes were sources of humiliation perhaps more disturbing still. The father of Charles Dickens' mother, also a £350-a-year clerk in the Navy Pay Office, with the title of Conductor of Money, had systematically, by returning false balances, embezzled funds to the amount of £5689 3s. 3d. over a period of seven years; and when the fraud was discovered, had fled. And the background of domestic service was for an Englishman of the nineteenth century probably felt as more disgraceful than embezzlement. Certainly the facts about Dickens' ancestry were kept hidden by Dickens himself and have, so far as I know, only been fully revealed in the memoir by Miss Gladys Storey, based on interviews with Mrs. Perugini, Dickens' last surviving daughter, which was published in England in the summer of 1939.

But all these circumstances are worth knowing and bearing in mind, because they help us to understand what Dickens was trying to say. He was less given to false moral attitudes or to fear of respectable opinion than most of the great Victorians; but just as through the offices of his friends and admirers his personal life has been screened from the public even up to our own day, in a way that would have been thought unjustified in the case of a Keats or a Byron of the earlier nineteenth century, so the meaning of Dickens' work has been obscured by that element of the conventional which Dickens himself never quite outgrew. It is necessary to see him as a man in order to appreciate him as an artist — to exorcise the spell which has bewitched him into a stuffy piece of household furniture and to give him his proper rank as the poet of that portièred and upholstered world who saw clearest through the coverings and the curtains.

II

If one approaches his first novel, *Pickwick Papers,* with these facts of Dickens' biography in mind, one is struck by certain features of the book which one may not have noticed before.

Here the subject has been set for Dickens. He was supposed to provide some sort of text for a series of comic sporting plates by Seymour — something in the vein of Surtees' *Jorrocks.* As soon, however, as Dickens' scheme gives him a chance to get away from the sporting plates and to indulge his own preoccupations, the work takes a different turn.

There are in *Pickwick Papers,* especially in the early part, a whole set of interpolated short stories which make a contrast with the narrative proper. These stories are mostly pretty bad and deserve from the literary point of view no more attention than they usually get; but, even allowing here also for an element of the conventional and popular, of the still-thriving school of Gothic horror, we are surprised to find rising to the surface already the themes which were to dominate his later work.

The first of these interludes in *Pickwick* deals with the death of a pantomime clown, reduced through drink to the direst misery, who, in the delirium of his fever, imagines that he is about to be murdered by the wife whom he has been beating. In the second story, a worthless husband also beats his wife and sets an example of bad conduct to his son; the boy commits a robbery, gets caught and convicted — in prison remains obdurate to his mother's attempts to soften his sullen heart; she dies, he repents, it is too late; he is transported, returns after seventeen years and finds no one to love or greet him; he stumbles at last upon his father, now a sodden old man in the workhouse; a scene of hatred and violence ensues; the father, filled with terror, strikes the son across the face with a stick, the son seizes the father by the throat, and the old man bursts a blood-vessel and falls dead. The third story is a document by a madman, which, like the delirium of the dying clown, gives Dickens an opportunity to exploit that vein of hysterical fancy which was to find fuller scope in *Barnaby Rudge* and which was there to figure for him the life of the imagination itself. The narrator has lived in the knowledge that he is to be the victim of hereditary insanity. At last he feels that he is going mad, but at the same moment he inherits money: men fawn upon him and praise him now, but he secretly rejoices in the sense that he is not one of them, that he is fooling them. He marries a girl, who loves another but who has been sold to him by her father and brothers; seeing his wife languish away and coming to understand the situation, fearing also lest she may hand on the family curse, he tries to kill her in her sleep with a razor; she wakes up but dies of the shock. When one of her brothers comes to reproach him, the madman throws him down and chokes him; runs amuck and is finally caught.

But it is in *The Old Man's Tale About the Queer Client* (Chapter XXI) that Dickens' obsessions appear most plainly. Here at the threshold of Dickens' work we are confronted with the Marshalsea Prison. A prisoner for debt, a 'healthy, strong-made man, who could have borne almost any fatigue of active exertion,' wastes away in his confinement and sees his wife and child die of grief and want. He swears to revenge their deaths on the man who has put him there. We have another long passage of delirium, at the end of which the prisoner comes to, to learn that he has inherited his father's money. At a seaside resort where he has been living, he sees a man drowning one evening: the father of the drowning man stands by and begs the ex-prisoner to save his son. But when the wronged man recognizes his father-in-law, the scoundrel who sent him to prison and who allowed his own daughter and grandson to die, he retaliates by letting the boy drown; then, not content with this, he buys up, at 'treble and quadruple their nominal value,' a number of loans which have been made to the old man. These loans have been arranged on the understanding that they are renewable up to a certain date; but the wronged man, taking advantage of the fact that the agreement has never been put on paper, proceeds to call them in at a time when his father-in-law has 'sustained many losses.' The old man is dispossessed of all his property and finally runs away in order to escape prison; but his persecutor tracks him down to a 'wretched lodging' — note well: 'in Camden Town' — and there finally reveals himself and announces his implacable intention of sending his persecutor to jail. The old man falls dead from shock, and the revenger disappears.

In the meantime, the same theme has been getting under way in the main current of the comic novel. Mr. Pickwick has been framed by Dodson and Fogg, and very soon — another wronged man — he will land in the debtors' prison, where a good many of the other characters will join him and where the whole book will deepen with a new dimension of seriousness. The hilarity of the scene in court, in which Mr. Pickwick is convicted of trifling with Mrs. Bardell's affections — a scene openly borrowed from *Jorrocks* but wonderfully transformed by Dickens, and as brilliant as the story of the fiendish revenge on the fiendish father-in-law is bathetic — may disguise from the reader the significance which this episode had for Dickens. Here Dickens is one of the greatest of humorists: it is a laughter which is never vulgar but which discloses the vulgarity of the revered — a laughter of human ecstasy that rises like the phœnix from the cinders to which the dismal denizens of the tribunals have attempted to reduce decent human beings. It represents, like the laughter of Aristophanes, a real escape from institutions.

I shall make no attempt to discuss at length the humor of the early Dickens. This is the aspect of his work that is best known, the only aspect that some people know. In praise of Dickens' humor, there is hardly anything new to say. The only point I want to make is that the humor of Dickens does differ from such humor as that of Aristophanes in being unable forever to inhabit an empyrean of blithe intellectual play, of charming fancies and biting good sense. Dickens' laughter is an exhilaration which already shows a trace of the hysterical. It leaps free of the prison of life; but gloom and soreness must always drag it back. Before he has finished *Pickwick* and even while he is getting him out of jail and preparing to unite the lovers, the prison will close in again on Dickens. While he is still on the last instalments of *Pickwick,* he will begin writing *Oliver Twist* — the story of a disinherited boy, consigned to a workhouse which is virtually a jail and getting away only to fall into the hands of a gang of burglars, pickpockets and prostitutes.

And now we must identify the attitudes with which Dickens' origins and his early experiences had caused him to meet mankind. The ideal of *Pickwick Papers* is a kindly retired business man, piloted through a tough and treacherous world by a shrewd servant of watchful fidelity, who perfectly knows his place: Mr. Pickwick and Sam Weller. But this picture, though real enough to its creator, soon gives way to the figure of a parentless and helpless child — a figure of which the pathos will itself be eclipsed by the horror of the last night in the condemned cell of a betrayer of others to the gallows, and by the headlong descent into hell of a brute who clubs his girl to death and who, treed like a cat by the pursuing mob, hangs himself in trying to escape.

III

Edmund Yates described Dickens' expression as 'blunt' and 'pleasant,' but 'rather defiant.'

For the man of spirit whose childhood has been crushed by the cruelty of organized society, one of two attitudes is natural: that of the criminal or that of the rebel. Charles Dickens, in imagination, was to play the rôles of both, and to continue up to his death to put into them all that was most passionate in his feeling.

His interest in prisons and prisoners is evident from the very beginning. In his first book, *Sketches by Boz,* he tells how he used to gaze at Newgate with 'mingled feelings of awe and respect'; and he sketches an imaginary picture of a condemned man's last night alive, which he is soon to elaborate in *Oliver Twist*. Almost the only passage in *American Notes* which shows any real readiness on Dickens' part to enter into the minds and feelings of the people among whom he is traveling is the fantasy in which he imagines the effects of a sentence of solitary confinement in a Philadelphia jail. He visited prisons wherever he went, and he later found this cruel system imitated in the jail at Lausanne. Dickens was very much gratified when the system was finally abandoned as the result of the prisoners' going mad just as he had predicted they would. He also wrote a great deal about executions. One of the vividest things in *Pictures from Italy* is a description of a guillotining; and one of the most impressive episodes in *Barnaby Rudge* is the narration — developed on a formidable scale — of the hanging of the leaders of the riots. In 1846, Dickens wrote letters to the press in protest against capital punishment for murderers, on the ground among other grounds that this created sympathy for the culprits; in 1849, after attending some executions in London with Forster, he started by writing to *The Times* an agitation which had the effect of getting public hangings abolished. Even in 1867, in the course of his second visit to America, 'I have been tempted out,' Dickens wrote Forster, 'at three in the morning to visit one of the large police station-houses, and was so fascinated by the study of a horrible photograph-book of thieves' portraits that I couldn't put it down.'

His interest in the fate of prisoners thus went a good deal farther than simple memories of the debtors' prison or notes of a court reporter. He identified himself readily with the thief, and even more readily with the murderer. The man of powerful will who finds himself opposed to society must, if he cannot upset it or if his impulse to do so is blocked, feel a compulsion to commit what society regards as one of the capital crimes against itself. With the antisocial heroes of Dostoevsky, this crime is usually murder or rape; with Dickens, it is usually murder. His obsession with murderers is attested by his topical pieces for *Household Words*; by his remarkable letter to Forster on the performance of the French actor Lemaître in a play in which he impersonated a murderer; by his expedition, on his second visit to America, to the Cambridge Medical School for the purpose of going over the ground where Professor Webster had committed a murder in his laboratory and had continued to meet his courses with parts of the body under the lid of his lecture-table. In Dickens' novels, this theme recurs with a probing of the psychology of the murderer which becomes ever more convincing and intimate. Leaving the murderers of the later Dickens till we come to his later books, we may, however, point out here that the crime and flight of Jonas Chuzzlewit already show a striking development beyond the cruder crime and flight of Sikes. The fantasies and fears of Jonas are really, as Taine remarked, the picture of a mind on the edge of insanity. What is valid and impressive in this episode is the insight into the consciousness of a man who has put himself outside human fellowship — the moment, for example, after the murder when Jonas is 'not only fearful *for* himself but *of* himself' and half-expects, when he returns to his bedroom, to find himself asleep in the bed.

At times the two themes — the criminal and the rebel — are combined in a peculiar way. *Barnaby Rudge* — which from the point of view of Dickens' comedy and character-drawing is the least satisfactory of his early books — is, up to *Martin Chuzzlewit*, the most interesting from the point of view of his deeper artistic intentions. It is the only one of these earlier novels which is not more or less picaresque and, correspondingly, more or less of an improvisation (though there is a certain amount of organization discernible in that other somber book, *Oliver Twist*); it was the only novel up to that time which Dickens had been planning and reflecting on for a long time before he wrote it: it is first mentioned in 1837, but was not written till 1841. Its immediate predecessor, *The Old Curiosity Shop,* had been simply an impromptu yarn, spun out — when Dickens discovered that the original scheme of *Master Humphreys Clock* was not going over with his readers — from what was to have been merely a short story; but *Barnaby Rudge* was a deliberate attempt to find expression for the emotions and ideas that possessed him.

The ostensible subject of the novel is the anti-Catholic insurrection known as the 'Gordon riots' which took place in London in 1780. But what is obviously in Dickens' mind is the Chartist agitation for universal suffrage and working-class representation in Parliament which, as a result of the industrial depression of those years, came to a crisis in 1840. In Manchester the cotton mills were idle, and the streets were full of threatening jobless men. In the summer of 1840 there was a strike of the whole North of England, which the authorities found it possible to put down only by firing into the working-class crowds; this

was followed the next year by a brickmakers' strike,
which ended in bloody riots. Now the immediate occasion
for the Gordon riots had been a protest against a bill
which was to remove from the English Catholics such
penalties and disabilities as the sentence of life imprisonment for priests who should educate children as Catholics
and the disqualifications of Catholics from inheriting property; but the real causes behind the demonstration have
always remained rather obscure. It seems to indicate an
indignation more violent than it is possible to account for
by mere anti-Catholic feeling that churches and houses
should have been burnt wholesale, all the prisons of London broken open, and even the Bank of England attacked,
and that the authorities should for several days have done
so little to restrain the rioters; and it has been supposed
that public impatience at the prolongation of the American War, with a general desire to get rid of George III,
if not of the monarchy itself, must have contributed to the
fury behind the uprising.

This obscurity, at any rate, allowed Dickens to handle
the whole episode in an equivocal way. On the surface he
reprobates Lord George Gordon and the rioters for their
fanatical or brutal intolerance; but implicitly he is exploiting to the limit certain legitimate grievances of the
people: the neglect of the lower classes by a cynical eighteenth-century aristocracy, and especially the penal laws
which made innumerable minor offenses punishable by
death. The really important theme of the book — as Dickens shows in his preface, when he is discussing one of the
actual occurrences on which the story is based — is the
hanging under the Shop-lifting Act of a woman who has
been dropped by her aristocratic lover and who has forged
notes to provide for her child. This theme lies concealed,
but it makes itself felt from beginning to end of the book.
And as *Pickwick*, from the moment it gets really under
way, heads by instinct and, as it were, unconsciously

straight for the Fleet prison, so *Barnaby Rudge* is deliberately directed toward Newgate, where, as in *Pickwick*
again, a group of characters will be brought together; and
the principal climax of the story will be the orgiastic burning of the prison. This incident not only has nothing to
do with the climax of the plot, it goes in spirit quite
against the attitude which Dickens has begun by announcing. The satisfaction he obviously feels in demolishing the
sinister old prison, which, rebuilt, had oppressed him in
childhood, completely obliterates the effect of his right-
minded references in his preface to 'those shameful tu-
mults,' which 'reflect indelible disgrace upon the time in
which they occurred, and all who had act or part in them.'
In the end, the rioters are shot down and their supposed
instigators hanged; but here Dickens' *parti pris* emerges
plainly: 'Those who suffered as rioters were, for the most
part, the weakest, meanest and most miserable among
them.' The son of the woman hanged for stealing, who
has been one of the most violent of the mob and whose
fashionable father will do nothing to save him, goes to the
scaffold with courage and dignity, cursing his father and
'that black tree, of which I am the ripened fruit.'

Dickens has here, under the stimulus of the Chartist
agitation, tried to give his own emotions an outlet through
an historical novel of insurrection; but the historical episode, the contemporary moral, and the author's emotional
pattern do not always coincide very well. Indeed, perhaps
the best thing in the book is the creation that most runs
away with the general scheme that Dickens has attempted. Dennis the hangman, although too macabre to
be one of Dickens' most popular characters, is really one
of his best comic inventions, and has more interesting
symbolic implications than Barnaby Rudge himself. Dennis is a professional executioner, who has taken an active
part in the revolt, apparently from simple motives of sadism. Knowing the unpopularity of the hangman, he makes

an effort to keep his identity a secret; but he has found this rather difficult to do, because he sincerely loves his profession and cannot restrain himself from talking about it. When the mob invades Newgate, which Dennis knows so well, he directs the liberation of the prisoners; but in the end he slips away to the condemned cells, locks them against the mob and stands guard over the clamoring inmates, cracking them harshly over the knuckles when they reach their hands out over the doors. The condemned are his vested interest, which he cannot allow the rebels to touch. But the momentum of the mob forces the issue, breaks through and turns the criminals loose. When we next encounter Dennis, he is a stool pigeon, turning his former companions in to the police. But he is unable to buy immunity in this way; and he is finally hanged himself. Thus this hangman has a complex value: he is primarily a sadist who likes to kill. Yet he figures as a violator as well as a protector of prisons. In his rôle of insurgent, he attacks authority; in his rôle of hangman, makes it odious. Either way he represents on Dickens' part a blow at those institutions which the writer is pretending to endorse. There is not, except in a minor way, any other symbol of authority in the book.

The formula of *Barnaby Rudge* is more or less reproduced in the other two novels of Dickens that deal with revolutionary subjects — which, though they belong to later periods of Dickens' work, it is appropriate to consider here. In *Hard Times* (1854), he manages in much the same way to deal sympathetically with the working-class protest against intolerable industrial conditions at the same time that he lets himself out from supporting the trade-union movement. In order to be able to do this, he is obliged to resort to a special and rather implausible device. Stephen Blackpool, the honest old textile worker, who is made to argue the cause of the workers before the vulgar manufacturer Bounderby, refuses to join the union because he has promised the woman he loves that he will do nothing to get himself into trouble. He thus finds himself in the singular position of being both a victim of the blacklist and a scab. The trade-union leadership is represented only — although with a comic fidelity, recognizable even today, to a certain type of labor organizer — by an unscrupulous spellbinder whose single aim is to get hold of the workers' pennies. Old Stephen, wandering away to look for a job somewhere else, falls into a disused coal-pit which has already cost the lives of many miners, and thus becomes a martyr simultaneously to the employers and to the trade-union movement. In *A Tale of Two Cities* (1859), the moral of history is not juggled as it is in *Barnaby Rudge,* but the conflict is made to seem of less immediate reality by locating it out of England. The French people, in Dickens' picture, have been given ample provocation for breaking loose in the French Revolution; but once in revolt, they are fiends and vandals. The vengeful Madame Defarge is a creature whom — as Dickens implies — one would not find in England, and she is worsted by an Englishwoman. The immediate motive behind *A Tale of Two Cities* is no doubt, as has been suggested and as is intimated at the beginning of the last chapter, the English fear of the Second Empire after Napoleon III's Italian campaign of 1859: Dickens' impulse to write the book closely followed the attempt by Orsini to assassinate Napoleon III in the January of '58. But there is in this book as in the other two — though less angrily expressed — a threat. If the British upper classes, Dickens seems to say, will not deal with the problem of providing for the health and education of the people, they will fall victims to the brutal mob. This mob Dickens both sympathizes with and fears.

Through the whole of his early period, Dickens appears to have regarded himself as a respectable middle-class man.

If Sam Weller, for all his outspokenness, never oversteps his rôle of valet, Kit in *The Old Curiosity Shop* is a model of deference toward his betters who becomes even a little disgusting.

When Dickens first visited America, in 1842, he seems to have had hopes of finding here something in the nature of that classless society which the foreign 'fellow travelers' of yesterday went to seek in the Soviet Union; but, for reasons both bad and good, Dickens was driven back by what he did find into the attitude of an English gentleman, who resented the American lack of ceremony, was annoyed by the American publicity, and was pretty well put to rout by the discomfort, the poverty and the tobacco-juice which he had braved on his trip to the West. Maladjusted to the hierarchy at home, he did not fit in in the United States even so well as he did in England: some of the Americans patronized him, and others were much too familiar. The mixed attitude — here seen at its most favorable to us — which was produced when his British ideas intervened to rein in the sympathy which he tended to feel for American innovations, is well indicated by the passage in *American Notes* in which he discusses the factory-girls of Lowell. These girls have pianos in their boarding-houses and subscribe to circulating libraries, and they publish a periodical. 'How very preposterous!' the writer imagines an English reader exclaiming. 'These things are above their station.' But what is their station? asks Dickens. 'It is their station to work,' he answers. 'And they *do* work. . . . For myself, I know no station in which, the occupation of today cheerfully done and the occupation of tomorrow cheerfully looked to, any one of these pursuits is not most humanizing and laudable. I know no station which is rendered more endurable to the person in it, or more safe to the person out of it, by having ignorance for its associates. I know no station which has a right to monopolize the means of mutual instruction, improvement and rational entertainment; or which has even continued to be a station very long after seeking to do so.' But he remarks that 'it is pleasant to find that many of [the] Tales [in the library] are of the Mills, and of those who work in them; that they inculcate habits of self-denial and contentment, and teach good doctrines of enlarged benevolence.' The main theme of *Nicholas Nickleby* is the efforts of Nicholas and his sister to vindicate their position as gentlefolk.

But there is also another reason why these political novels of Dickens are unclear and unsatisfactory. Fundamentally, he was not interested in politics. As a reporter, he had seen a good deal of Parliament, and he had formed a contemptuous opinion of it which was never to change to the end of his life. The Eatanswill elections in *Pickwick* remain the type of political activity for Dickens; the seating of Mr. Veneering in Parliament in the last of his finished novels is hardly different. The point of view is stated satirically in Chapter XII of *Bleak House,* in which a governing-class group at a country house are made to discuss the fate of the country in terms of the political activities of Lord Coodle, Sir Thomas Doodle, the Duke of Foodle, the Right Honorable William Buffy, M.P., with his associates and opponents Cuffy, Duffy, Fuffy, etc., while their constituents are taken for granted as a certain large number of supernumeraries, who are to be occasionally addressed, and relied upon for shouts and choruses, as on the theatrical stage.' A little later (September 30, 1855), he expresses himself explicitly in the course of a letter to Forster: 'I really am serious in thinking — and I have given as painful consideration to the subject as a man with children to live and suffer after him can honestly give to it — that representative government is become altogether a failure with us, that the English gentilities and subserviences render the people unfit for it, and that

the whole thing has broken down since that great seven-
teenth-century time, and has no hope in it.'

In his novels from beginning to end, Dickens is making
the same point always: that to the English governing
classes the people they govern are not real. It is one of the
great purposes of Dickens to show you these human actualities who figure for Parliament as strategical counters
and for Political Economy as statistics; who can as a rule
appear only even in histories in a generalized or idealized
form. What does a workhouse under the Poor Laws look
like? What does it feel like, taste like, smell like? How
does the holder of a post in the government look? How
does he talk? what does he talk about? how will he treat
you? What is the aspect of the British middle class at each
of the various stages of its progress? What are the good
ones like and what are the bad ones like? How do they
affect you, not merely to meet at dinner, but to travel with,
to work under, to live with? All these things Dickens can
tell us. It has been one of the principal functions of the
modern novel and drama to establish this kind of record;
but few writers have been able to do it with any range at
all extensive. None has surpassed Dickens.

No doubt this concrete way of looking at society may
have serious limitations. Dickens was sometimes actually
stupid about politics. His lack of interest in political tactics
led him, it has sometimes been claimed, to mistake the
actual significance of the legislation he was so prompt to
criticize. Mr. T. A. Jackson has pointed out a characteristic example of Dickens' inattention to politics in his report
of his first trip to America. Visiting Washington in 1842,
he registers an impression of Congress very similar to his
impressions of Parliament ('I may be of a cold and insensible temperament, amounting in iciness, in such matters'); and he indulges in one of his gushings of sentiment
over 'an aged, gray-haired man, a lasting honor to the land

that gave him birth, who has done good service to his country, as his forefathers did, and who will be remembered scores upon scores of years after the worms bred in its corruption are so many grains of dust — it was but a week since this old man had stood for days upon his trial before this very body, charged with having dared to assert the infamy of that traffic which has for its accursed merchandise men and women, and their unborn children. Now this aged gray-haired man, Mr. Jackson reminds us, was none other than John Quincy Adams, who, far from being on his trial, was actually on the verge of winning in his long fight against a House resolution which had excluded petitions against slavery, and who was deliberately provoking his adversaries for purposes of propaganda. Dickens did not know that the antislavery cause, far from being hopeless, was achieving its first step toward victory. (So on his second visit to America — when, however, he was ill and exhausted — his interest in the impeachment of Andrew Johnson seems to have been limited to 'a misgiving lest the great excitement . . . will damage our receipts' from his readings.) Yet his picture of the United States in 1842, at a period of brave boastings and often squalid or meager realities, has a unique and permanent value. Macaulay complained that Dickens did not understand the Manchester school of utilitarian economics which he criticized in *Hard Times*. But Dickens' criticism does not pretend to be theoretical: all he is undertaking to do is to tell us how practising believers in Manchester utilitarianism behave and how their families are likely to fare with them. His picture is strikingly collaborated by the autobiography of John Stuart Mill, who was brought up at the fountainhead of the school, in the shadow of Bentham himself. In Mill, choked with learning from his childhood, overtrained on the logical side of the mind, and collapsing into illogical despair when the lack began to make itself felt of the elements his education had neglected, the tragic moral of the system of Gradgrind is pointed with a sensational obviousness which would be regarded as exaggeration in Dickens.

This very distrust of politics, however, is a part of the rebellious aspect of Dickens. Dickens is almost invariably *against* institutions: in spite of his allegiance to Church and State, in spite of the lip-service he occasionally pays them, whenever he comes to deal with Parliament and its laws, the courts and the public officials, the creeds of Protestant dissenters and of Church of England alike, he makes them either ridiculous or cruel, or both at the same time.

IV

In the work of Dickens' middle period — after the murder in *Martin Chuzzlewit* — the rebel bulks larger than the criminal.

Of all the great Victorian writers, he was probably the most antagonistic to the Victorian Age itself. He had grown up under the Regency and George IV; had been twenty-five at the accession of Victoria. His early novels are freshened by breezes from an England of coaching and village taverns, where the countryside lay just outside London; of an England where jokes and songs and hot brandy were always in order, where every city clerk aimed to dress finely and drink freely, to give an impression of open-handedness and gallantry. The young Dickens of the earliest preserved letters, who invites his friends to partake of 'the rosy,' sounds not unlike Dick Swiveller. When Little Nell and her grandfather on their wanderings spend a night in an iron foundry, it only has the effect of a sort of Nibelungen interlude, rather like one of those surprise grottoes that you float through when you take the little boat that threads the tunnel of the 'Old Mill' in an amusement park — a luridly lighted glimpse on the same level, in Dickens' novel, with the waxworks, the perform-

ing dogs, the dwarfs and giants, the village church. From
this point it is impossible, as it was impossible for Dickens,
to foresee the full-length industrial town depicted in *Hard
Times*. In that age the industrial-commercial civilization
had not yet got to be the norm; it seemed a disease which
had broken out in spots but which a sincere and cheerful
treatment would cure. The typical reformers of the period
had been Shelley and Robert Owen, the latter so logical a
crank, a philanthropist so much all of a piece, that he
seems to have been invented by Dickens — who insisted
that his Cheeryble brothers, the philanthropic merchants
of *Nicholas Nickleby*, had been taken from living originals.

But when Dickens begins to write novels again after
his return from his American trip, a new kind of character appears in them, who, starting as an amusing buffoon,
grows steadily more unpleasant and more formidable. On
the threshold of *Martin Chuzzlewit* (1843-45: the dates
of its appearance in monthly numbers), you find Pecksniff, the provincial architect; on the threshold of *Dombey
and Son* (1846-48), you find Dombey, the big London
merchant; and before you have got very far with the
idyllic *David Copperfield* (1849-50), you find Murdstone,
of Murdstone and Grimby, wine merchants. All these figures stand for the same thing. Dickens had at first imagined that he was pillorying abstract faults in the manner
of the comedy of humors: Selfishness in *Chuzzlewit*,
Pride in *Dombey*. But the truth was that he had already
begun an indictment against a specific society: the self-
important and moralizing middle class who had been making such rapid progress in England and coming down like
a damper on the bright fires of English life — that is, on
the spontaneity and gaiety, the frankness and independence, the instinctive human virtues, which Dickens admired and trusted. The new age had brought a new kind
of virtues to cover up the flourishing vices of cold avarice

and harsh exploitation; and Dickens detested these virtues.

The curmudgeons of the early Dickens — Ralph Nick-leby and Arthur Gride, Anthony and Jonas Chuzzlewit (for *Martin Chuzzlewit* just marks the transition from the early to the middle Dickens) — are old-fashioned money-lenders and misers of a type that must have been serving for decades in the melodramas of the English stage. In Dickens their whole-hearted and outspoken meanness gives them a certain cynical charm. They are the bad uncles in the Christmas pantomime who set off the jolly clowns and the good fairy, and who, as everybody knows from the beginning, are doomed to be exposed and extin-guished. But Mr. Pecksniff, in the same novel with the Chuzzlewits, already represents something different. It is to be characteristic of Pecksniff, as it is of Dombey and Murdstone, that he does evil while pretending to do good. As intent on the main chance as Jonas himself, he pre-tends to be a kindly father, an affectionate relative, a pious churchgoer; he is the pillar of a cathedral town. Yet Pecksniff is still something of a pantomime comic whom it will be easy enough to unmask. Mr. Dombey is a more difficult problem. His virtues, as far as they go, are real: though he is stupid enough to let his business get into the hands of Carker, he does lead an exemplary life of a kind in the interests of the tradition of his house. He makes his wife and his children miserable in his devotion to his mercantile ideal, but that ideal is at least for him serious. With Murdstone the ideal has turned sour: the respect-able London merchant now represents something sinister. Murdstone is not funny like Pecksniff; he is not merely a buffoon who masquerades: he is a hypocrite who believes in himself. And where Dombey is made to recognize his error and turn kindly and humble in the end, Mr. Murd-stone and his grim sister are allowed to persist in their course of working mischief as a matter of duty.

In such a world of mercenary ruthlessness, always justified by rigorous morality, it is natural that the exploiter of others should wish to dissociate himself from the exploited, and to delegate the face-to-face encounters to someone else who is paid to take the odium. Karl Marx, at that time living in London, was demonstrating through these middle years of the century that this system, with its falsifying of human relations and its wholesale encouragement of cant, was an inherent and irremediable feature of the economic structure itself. In Dickens, the Mr. Spenlow of *David Copperfield,* who is always blaming his mean exactions on his supposedly implacable partner, Mr. Jorkins, develops into the Casby of *Little Dorrit,* the benignant and white-haired patriarch who turns over the rack-renting of Bleeding Heart Yard to his bull-terrier of an agent, Pancks, while he basks in the admiration of his tenants; and in *Our Mutual Friend,* into Fledgeby, the moneylender who makes his way into society while the harmless old Jew Riah is compelled to play the cruel creditor.

With Dickens' mounting dislike and distrust of the top layers of that middle-class society with which he had begun by identifying himself, his ideal of middle-class virtue was driven down to the lower layers. In his earlier novels, this ideal had been embodied in such patrons and benefactors as Mr. Pickwick, the retired business man; the substantial and warmhearted Mr. Brownlow, who rescued Oliver Twist; and the charming old gentleman, Mr. Garland, who took Kit Nubbles into his service. In *David Copperfield* the lawyer Wickfield, who plays a rôle in relation to the hero somewhat similar to those of Brownlow and Garland, becomes demoralized by too much port and falls a victim to Uriah Heep, the upstart Pecksniff of a lower social level. The ideal — the domestic unit which preserves the sound values of England — is located by Dickens through this period in the small middle-class household: Ruth Pinch and her brother in *Martin Chuz-*

zlewit; the bright hearths and holiday dinners of the *Christmas Books;* the modest home to which Florence Dombey descends from the great house near Portland Place, in happy wedlock with the nephew of Sol Gills, the ships'-instrument-maker.

It is at the end of *Dombey and Son,* when the house of Dombey goes bankrupt, that Dickens for the first time expresses himself explicitly on the age that has come to remain:

'The world was very busy now, in sooth, and had a deal to say. It was an innocently credulous and a much ill-used world. It was a world in which there was no other sort of bankruptcy whatever. There were no conspicuous people in it, trading far and wide on rotten banks of religion, patriotism, virtue, honor. There was no amount worth mentioning of mere paper in circulation, on which anybody lived pretty handsomely, promising to pay great sums of goodness with no effects. There were no shortcomings anywhere, in anything but money. The world was very angry indeed; and the people especially who, in a worse world, might have been supposed to be bankrupt traders themselves in shows and pretences, were observed to be mightily indignant.'

And now — working always through the observed interrelations between highly individualized human beings rather than through political or economic analysis — Dickens sets out to trace an anatomy of that society. *Dombey* has been the first attempt; *Bleak House* (1852-53) is to realize this intention to perfection; *Hard Times,* on a smaller scale, is to conduct the same kind of inquiry.

For this purpose Dickens invents a new literary *genre* (unless the whole mass of Balzac is to be taken as something of the sort): the novel of the social group. The young Dickens had summed up, developed and finally outgrown the two traditions in English fiction he had found: the picaresque tradition of Defoe, Fielding and Smollett, and the sentimental tradition of Goldsmith and Sterne. People like George Henry Lewes have complained of Dickens' little reading; but no artist has ever absorbed his predecessors — he had read most of them in his early boyhood — more completely than Dickens did. There is something of all these writers in Dickens and, using them, he has gone beyond them all. In the historical novel *Barnaby Rudge* — a detour in Dickens' fiction — he had got out of Scott all that Scott had to give him. He was to profit in *Hard Times* by Mrs. Gaskell's industrial studies. But in the meantime it was Dickens' business to create a new tradition himself.

His novels even through *Martin Chuzzlewit* had had a good deal of the looseness of the picaresque school of *Gil Blas,* where the episodes get their only unity from being hung on the same hero, as well as the multiple parallel plots, purely mechanical combinations, that he had acquired from the old plays — though he seems to have been trying more intensively for a unity of atmosphere and feeling. But now he is to organize his stories as wholes, to plan all the characters as symbols, and to invest all the details with significance. *Dombey and Son* derives a new kind of coherence from the fact that the whole novel is made to center around the big London business house: you have the family of the man who owns it, the manager and his family, the clerks, the men dependent on the ships that export its goods, down to Sol Gills and Captain Cuttle (so *Hard Times* is to get its coherence from the organism of an industrial town).

In *Bleak House,* the masterpiece of this middle period, Dickens discovers a new use of plot, which makes possible a tighter organization. (And we must remember that he is always working against the difficulties, of which he often complains, of writing for monthly instalments, where everything has to be planned beforehand and it is impossible, as he says, to 'try back' and change anything, once it has been printed.) He creates the detective story which is also a social fable. It is a *genre* which has lapsed since Dickens. The detective story — though Dickens' friend Wilkie Collins preserved a certain amount of social satire — has dropped out the Dickensian social content; and the continuators of the social novel have dropped the detective story. These continuators — Shaw, Galsworthy, Wells — have of course gone further than Dickens in the realistic presentation of emotion; but from the point of view of dramatizing social issues, they have hardly improved upon *Bleak House*. In Shaw's case, the Marxist analysis, with which Dickens was not equipped, has helped him to the tighter organization which Dickens got from his complex plot. But in the meantime it is one of Dickens' victories in his rapid development as an artist that he should succeed in transforming his melodramatic intrigues of stolen inheritances, lost heirs and ruined maidens — with their denunciatory confrontations that always evoke the sound of fiddling in the orchestra — into devices of artistic dignity. Henceforth the solution of the mystery is to be also the moral of the story and the last word of Dickens' social 'message.'

Bleak House begins in the London fog, and the whole book is permeated with fog and rain. In *Dombey* the railway locomotive — first when Mr. Dombey takes his trip to Leamington, and later when it pulls into the station just at the moment of Dombey's arrival and runs over the fugitive Carker as he steps back to avoid his master — figures as a symbol of that progress of commerce which Dombey himself represents; in *Hard Times* the uncovered coal-pit into which Stephen Blackpool falls is a symbol for the abyss of the industrial system, which swallows up lives in its darkness. In *Bleak House* the fog stands for Chancery, and Chancery stands for the whole web of clotted antiquated institutions in which England stifles and decays. All the principal elements in the story – the young people, the proud Lady Dedlock, the philanthropic gentleman John Jarndyce, and Tom-all-Alone's, the rotting London slum – are involved in the exasperating Chancery suit, which, with the fog-bank of precedent looming behind it like the Great Boyg in *Peer Gynt,* obscures and impedes at every point the attempts of men and women to live natural lives. Old Krook, with his legal junkshop, is Dickens' symbol for the Lord Chancellor himself; the cat that sits on his shoulder watches like the Chancery lawyers the caged birds in Miss Flite's lodging; Krook's death by spontaneous combustion is Dickens' prophecy of the fate of Chancery and all that it represents.

I go over the old ground of the symbolism, up to this point perfectly obvious, of a book which must be still, by the general public, one of the most read of Dickens' novels, because the people who like to talk about the symbols of Kafka and Mann and Joyce have been discouraged from looking for anything of the kind in Dickens, and usually have not read him, at least with mature minds. But even when we think we do know Dickens, we may be surprised to return to him and find in him a symbolism of a more complicated reference and a deeper implication than these metaphors that hang as emblems over the door. The Russians themselves, in this respect, appear to have learned from Dickens.

Thus it is not at first that we recognize all the meaning of the people that thrive or survive in the dense atmosphere of *Bleak House* – an atmosphere so opaque that the somnolent ease at the top cannot see down to the filth at the bottom. And it is an atmosphere where nobody sees clearly what kind of race of beings is flourishing between the bottom and the top. Among the middle ranks of this society we find persons who appear with the pretension of representing Law or Art, Social Elegance, Philanthropy, or Religion – Mr. Kenge and Mr. Vholes, Harold

Skimpole, Mr. Turveydrop, Mrs. Pardiggle and Mrs. Jellyby, and Mr. and Mrs. Chadband — side by side with such a sordid nest of goblins as the family of the money-lender Smallweed. But presently we see that all these people are as single-mindedly intent on selfish interests as Grandfather Smallweed himself. This gallery is one of the best things in Dickens. The Smallweeds themselves are artistically an improvement on the similar characters in the early Dickens: they represent, not a theatrical convention, but a real study of the stunted and degraded products of the underworld of commercial London. And the two opposite types of philanthropist: the moony Mrs. Jellyby, who miserably neglects her children in order to dream of doing good in Africa, and Mrs. Pardiggle, who bullies both her children and the poor in order to give herself a feeling of power; Harold Skimpole, with the graceful fancy and the talk about music and art that ripples a shimmering veil over his systematic sponging; and Turveydrop, the Master of Deportment, that parody of the magnificence of the Regency, behind his rouge and his padded coat and his gallantry as cold and as inconsiderate as the Chadbands behind their gaseous preachments. Friedrich Engels, visiting London in the early forties, had written of the people in the streets that they seemed to 'crowd by one another as if they had nothing in common, nothing to do with one another, and as if their only agreement were the tacit one that each shall keep to his own side of the pavement, in order not to delay the opposing streams of the crowd, while it never occurs to anyone to honor his fellow with so much as a glance. The brutal indifference, the unfeeling isolation of each in his private interest, becomes the more repellent the more these individuals are herded together within a limited space.' This is the world that Dickens is describing.

Here he makes but one important exception: Mr. Rouncewell, the ironmaster. Mr. Rouncewell is an ambitious son of the housekeeper at Chesney Wold, Sir Leicester Dedlock's country house, who has made himself a place in the world which Sir Leicester regards as beyond his station. One of the remarkable scenes of the novel is that in which Rouncewell comes back, quietly compels Sir Leicester to receive him like a gentleman and asks him to release one of the maids from his service so that she may marry Rouncewell's son, a young man whom he has christened Watt. When Lady Dedlock refuses to release the maid, Rouncewell respectfully abandons the project, but goes away and has the insolence to run against Sir Leicester's candidate in the next parliamentary election. (This theme of the intervention of the industrial revolution in the relations between master and servant has already appeared in *Dombey and Son* in the admirable interview between Dombey and Polly Toodles, whom he is employing as a wetnurse for his motherless child. Polly's husband, who is present, is a locomotive stoker and already represents something anomalous in the hierarchy of British society. When the Dombeys, who cannot accept her real name, suggest calling Polly 'Richards,' she replies that if she is to be called out of her name, she ought to be paid extra. Later, when Dombey makes his railway journey, he runs into Polly's husband, who is working on the engine. Toodles speaks to him and engages him in conversation, and Dombey resents this, feeling that Toodles is somehow intruding outside his own class.)

But in general the magnanimous, the simple of heart, the amiable, the loving and the honest are frustrated, subdued, or destroyed. At the bottom of the whole gloomy edifice is the body of Lady Dedlock's lover and Esther Summerson's father, Captain Hawdon, the reckless soldier, adored by his men, beloved by women, the image of the old life-loving England, whose epitaph Dickens is now writing. Captain Hawdon has failed in that world, has perished as a friendless and penniless man, and has been

buried in the pauper's graveyard in one of the foulest
quarters of London, but the loyalties felt for him by the
living will endure and prove so strong after his death that
they will pull that world apart. Esther Summerson has
been frightened and made submissive by being treated as
the respectable middle class thought it proper to treat an
illegitimate child, by one of those Puritanical females
whom Dickens so roundly detests. Richard Carstone has
been demoralized and ruined; Miss Flite has been driven
insane. George Rouncewell, the brother of the ironmaster,
who has escaped from Sir Leicester's service to become a
soldier instead of a manufacturer and who is treated by
Dickens with the sympathy which he usually feels for his
military and nautical characters, the men who are doing
the hard work of the Empire, is helpless in the hands of
moneylenders and lawyers. Caddy Jellyby and her husband, young Turveydrop, who have struggled for a decent
life in a poverty partly imposed by the necessity of keeping
up old Turveydrop's pretenses, can only produce, in that
society where nature is so mutilated and thwarted, a sickly
defective child. Mr. Jarndyce himself, the wise and generous, who plays in *Bleak House* a rôle very similar to that
of Captain Shotover in Bernàrd Shaw's *Heartbreak House*
(which evidently owes a good deal to *Bleak House*), is an
eccentric at odds with his environment, who, in his efforts
to help the unfortunate, falls a prey to the harpies of
philanthropy.

   With this indifference and egoism of the middle class,
the social structure must buckle in the end. The infection
from the poverty of Tom-all-Alone's will ravage the man-
sions of country gentlemen. Lady Dedlock will inevitably
be dragged down from her niche of aristocratic idleness to
the graveyard in the slum where her lover lies. The idea
that the highest and the lowest in that English society of
shocking contrasts are inextricably tied together has already appeared in the early Dickens — in Ralph Nickleby

and Smike, for example, and in Sir John Chester and
Hugh — as a sort of submerged motif which is never given
its full expression. Here it has been chosen deliberately
and is handled with immense skill so as to provide the
main moral of the fable. And bound up with it is another
motif which has already emerged sharply in Dickens.
Dickens has evidently in the course of his astonishing rise,
found himself up against the blank and chilling loftiness
— what the French call *la morgue anglaise* — of the English upper classes: as we shall see, he developed a pride of
his own, with which he fought it to his dying day. Pride
was to have been the theme of *Dombey:* the pride of Edith
Dombey outdoes the pride of Dombey and levels him to
the ground. But in *Bleak House,* the pride of Lady Dedlock, who has married Sir Leicester Dedlock for position,
ultimately rebounds on herself. Her behavior toward the
French maid Hortense is the cause of her own debase-
ment. For where it is a question of pride, a high-tempered
girl from the South of France can outplay Lady Dedlock:
Hortense will not stop at the murder which is the logical
upshot of the course of action dictated by her wounded
feelings. Dickens is criticizing here one of the most un-
assailable moral props of the English hierarchical system.

Between *Dombey and Son* and *Bleak House,* Dickens
published *David Copperfield.* It is a departure from the
series of his social novels. Setting out to write the autobiography of which the fragments appear in Forster's *Life,*
Dickens soon changed his mind and transposed this material into fiction. In the first half of *David Copperfield,* at
any rate, Dickens strikes an enchanting vein which he had
never quite found before and which he was never to find
again. It is the poem of an idealized version of the loves
and fears and wonders of childhood; and the confrontation
of Betsey Trotwood with the Murdstones is one of Dickens' most successful stagings of the struggle between the

human and the anti-human, because it takes place on the plane of comedy rather than on that of melodrama. But *Copperfield* is not one of Dickens' deepest books: it is something in the nature of a holiday. David is too candid and simple to represent Dickens himself; and though the blacking warehouse episode is utilized, all the other bitter circumstances of Dickens' youth were dropped out when he abandoned the autobiography.

v

With *Little Dorrit* (1855-57), Dickens' next novel after *Bleak House* and *Hard Times,* we enter a new phase of his work. To understand it, we must go back to his life.

Dickens at forty had won everything that a writer could expect to obtain through his writings: his genius was universally recognized; he was fêted wherever he went; his books were immensely popular; and they had made him sufficiently rich to have anything that money can procure. He had partly made up for the education he had missed by traveling and living on the Continent and by learning to speak Italian and French. (Dickens' commentary on the continental countries is usually not remarkably penetrating; but he did profit very much from his travels abroad in his criticism of things in England. Perhaps no other of the great Victorian writers had so much the consciousness that the phenomena he was describing were of a character distinctively English.) Yet from the time of his first summer at Boulogne in 1853, he had shown signs of profound discontent and unappeasable restlessness; he suffered severely from insomnia and, for the first time in his life, apparently, worried seriously about his work. He began to fear that his vein was drying up.

I believe that Forster's diagnosis — though it may not go to the root of the trouble — must here be accepted as correct. There were, he intimates, two things wrong with Dickens: a marriage which exasperated and cramped him and from which he had not been able to find relief, and a social maladjustment which his success had never straightened out.

The opportunities of the young Dickens to meet eligible young women had evidently been rather limited. That he was impatient to get married, nevertheless, is proved by his announcing his serious intentions to three girls in close succession. The second of these was Maria Beadnell, the original of Dora in *David Copperfield* and, one supposes, of Dolly Varden, too, with whom he fell furiously in love, when he was eighteen and she nineteen. Her father worked in a bank and regarded Charles Dickens, the stenographer, as a young man of shabby background and doubtful prospects; Maria, who seems to have been rather frivolous and silly, was persuaded to drop her suitor — with the result for him which may be read in the letters, painful in their wounded pride and their backfiring of a thwarted will, which he wrote her after the break. This was one of the great humiliations of Dickens' early life he was at that time twenty-one) and, even after he had liquidated it in a sense by depicting the futilities of David's marriage with Dora, the disappointment still seems to have troubled him and Maria to have remained at the back of his mind as the Ideal of which he had been cheated.

He lost very little time, however, in getting himself a wife. Two years after his rejection by Maria Beadnell, he was engaged to the daughter of George Hogarth, a Scotchman, who, as the law agent of Walter Scott and from having been mentioned in the *Noctes Ambrosianae*, was invested with the prestige of having figured on the fringes of the Edinburgh literary world. He asked Dickens to write for the newspaper which he was editing at that time in London, and invited the young man to his house. There Dickens found two attractive daughters, and he married the elder, Catherine, who was twenty. But the

other daughter, Mary, though too young for him to marry
— she was only fifteen when he met her — had a strange
hold on Dickens' emotions. When, after living with the
Dickenses for a year after their marriage, she suddenly
died in Dickens' arms, he was so overcome by grief that
he stopped writing *Pickwick* for two months and insisted
in an obsessed and morbid way on his desire to be buried
beside her: 'I can't think there ever was love like I bear
her. . . . I have never had her ring off my finger day or
night, except for an instant at a time, to wash my hands,
since she died. I have never had her sweetness and excellence absent from my mind so long.' In *The Old Curiosity
Shop,* he apotheosized her as Little Nell. What basis this
emotion may have had in the fashionable romanticism of
the period or in some peculiar psychological pattern of
Dickens', it is impossible on the evidence to say. But this
passion for an innocent young girl is to recur in Dickens'
life; and in the meantime his feeling for Mary Hogarth
seems to indicate pretty clearly that even during the early
years of his marriage he did not identify the Ideal with
Catherine.

Catherine had big blue eyes, a rather receding chin and
a sleepy and languorous look. Beyond this, it is rather difficult to get a definite impression of her. Dickens' terrible
gallery of shrews who browbeat their amiable husbands
suggests that she may have been a scold; but surely Dickens himself was no Joe Gargery or Gabriel Varden. We do
not know much about Dickens' marriage. We know that,
with the exception of his sister-in-law Georgina, Dickens
grew to loathe the Hogarths, who evidently lived on him
to a considerable extent; and we must assume that poor
Catherine, in both intellect and energy, was a good deal
inferior to her husband. He lived with her, however,
twenty years, and, although it becomes clear toward the
end that they were no longer particularly welcome, he
gave her during that time ten children.

And if Dickens was lonely in his household, he was
lonely in society, also. He had, as Forster indicates, at-
tained a pinnacle of affluence and fame which made him
one of the most admired and most sought-after persons in
Europe without his really ever having created for himself
a social position in England, that society *par excellence*
where everybody had to have a definite one and where
there was no rank reserved for the artist. He had gone
straight, at the very first throw, from the poor tenement,
the prison, the press table, to a position of imperial supremacy over the imaginations of practically the whole
literate world; but in his personal associations, he cultivated the companionship of inferiors rather than — save,
perhaps, for Carlyle — of intellectual equals. His behavior
toward Society, in the capitalized sense, was rebarbative to
the verge of truculence; he refused to learn its patter and
its manners; and his satire on the fashionable world comes
to figure more and more prominently in his novels. Dickens is one of the very small group of British intellectuals
to whom the opportunity has been offered to be taken up
by the governing class and who have actually declined
that honor.

His attitude — which in the period we have been discussing was still that of the middle-class 'Radical' opposing
feudal precedent and privilege: Mr. Rouncewell, the iron-
master, backed against Sir Leicester Dedlock — is illustrated by the curious story of his relations with Queen
Victoria. In 1857, Dickens got up a benefit for the family
of Douglas Jerrold, in which he and his daughters acted.
The Queen was asked to be one of the sponsors; and, since
she was obliged to refuse any such request for fear of being obliged to grant them all, she invited Dickens to put
on the play at the palace. He replied that he 'did not feel
easy as to the social position of my daughters, etc., at a
Court under those circumstances,' and suggested that the
Queen might attend a performance which should be given

for her alone. She accepted, and sent backstage between the acts asking Dickens to come and speak to her. 'I replied that I was in my Farce dress, and must beg to be excused. Whereupon she sent again, saying that the dress "could not be so ridiculous as that," and repeating the request. I sent my duty in reply, but again hoped Her Majesty would have the kindness to excuse my presenting myself in a costume and appearance that were not my own. I was mighty glad to think, when I woke this morning, that I had carried the point.' The next year he was approached on behalf of the Queen, who wanted to hear him read the *Christmas Carol*; but he expressed his 'hope that she would indulge me by making one of some audience or other — for I thought an audience necessary to the effect.' It was only in the last year of his life — and then only on what seems to have been the pretext on the Queen's part that she wanted to look at some photographs of the battlefields of the Civil War which Dickens had brought back from America — that an interview was finally arranged. Here the record of Dickens' lecture manager, George Dolby, supplements the account given by Forster. Dickens told Dolby that 'Her Majesty had received him most graciously, and that, as Court etiquette requires that no one, in an ordinary interview with the sovereign, should be seated, Her Majesty had remained the whole time leaning over the head of a sofa. There was a little shyness on both sides at the commencement, but this wore away as the conversation proceeded.' When Victoria regretted that it had not been possible for her ever to hear Dickens read, he replied that he had made his farewell to the platform; when she said that she understood this, but intimated that it would be gracious on Dickens' part so far to forget his resolve as to give her the pleasure of hearing him, he insisted that this would be impossible. Not impossible, perhaps, said the Queen, but inconsistent, no doubt — and she knew that he was the most consistent of men. Yet they parted on very good terms: she invited him to her next levee and his daughter to the drawing-room that followed. If there is some stickling for his dignity on Dickens' part here, there is evidently also some scruple on the Queen's.

To be caught between two social classes in a society of strict stratifications — like being caught between two civilizations, as James was, or between two racial groups, like Proust — is an excellent thing for a novelist from the point of view of his art, because it enables him to dramatize contrasts and to study interrelations which the dweller in one world cannot know. Perhaps something of the sort was true even of Shakespeare, between the provincial bourgeoisie and the Court. Dostoevsky, who had a good deal in common with Dickens and whose career somewhat parallels his, is a conspicuous example of a writer who owes his dramatic scope at least partly to a social maladjustment. The elder Dostoevsky was a doctor and his family origins were obscure, so that his social position was poor in a Russia still predominantly feudal; yet he bought a country estate and sent his sons to a school for the children of the nobility. But the family went to pieces after the mother's death: the father took to drink and was murdered by his serfs for his cruelty. Dostoevsky was left with almost nothing, and he slipped down into that foul and stagnant underworld of the Raskólnikovs and Stavrógins of his novels. Dickens' case had been equally anomalous: he had grown up in an uncomfortable position between the upper and the lower middle classes, with a dip into the proletariat and a glimpse of the aristocracy through their trusted upper servants. But this position, which had been useful to him as a writer, was to leave him rather isolated in English society. In a sense, there was no place for him to go and belong; he had to have people come to him.

And in the long run all that he had achieved could not make up for what he lacked. *Little Dorrit* and *Great Expectations* (1860-61), which follows it after *A Tale of*

Two Cities, are full of the disillusion and discomfort of this period of Dickens' life. The treatment of social situations and the treatment of individual psychology have both taken turns distinctly new.

Dickens now tackles the Marshalsea again, but on a larger scale and in a more serious way. It is as if he were determined once for all to get the prison out of his system. The figure of his father hitherto has always haunted Dickens' novels, but he has never known quite how to handle it. In Micawber, he made him comic and lovable; in Skimpole, he made him comic and unpleasant — for, after all, the vagaries of Micawber always left somebody out of pocket, and there is another aspect of Micawber — the Skimpole aspect he presented to his creditors. But what kind of person, really, had John Dickens been in himself? How had the father of Charles Dickens come to be what he was? Even after it had become possible for Charles to provide for his father, the old man continued to be a problem up to his death in 1851. He got himself arrested again, as the result of running up a wine bill; and he would try to get money out of his son's publishers without the knowledge of Charles. Yet Dickens said to Forster, after his father's death: 'The longer I live, the better man I think him'; and *Little Dorrit* is something in the nature of a justification of John.

Mr. Dorrit is 'a very amiable and very helpless middle-aged gentleman . . . a shy, retiring man, well-looking, though in an effeminate style, with a mild voice, curling hair, and irresolute hands — rings upon the fingers in those days — which nervously wandered to his trembling lip a hundred times in the first half-hour of his acquaintance with the jail.' The arrival of the Dorrit family in prison and their gradual habituation to it are done with a restraint and sobriety never displayed by Dickens up to now. The incident in which Mr. Dorrit, after getting used to accepting tips in his rôle of the Father of the Marshalsea,

suddenly becomes insulted when he is offered copper half-
pence by a workman, has a delicacy which makes up in
these later books for the ebb of Dickens' bursting exuber-
ance. If it is complained that the comic characters in these
novels, the specifically 'Dickens characters,' are sometimes
mechanical and boring, this is partly, perhaps, for the reason that they stick out in an unnatural relief from a surface that is more quietly realistic. And there are moments
when one feels that Dickens might be willing to abandon
the 'Dickens character' altogether if it were not what the
public expected of him. In any case, the story of Dorrit is
a closer and more thoughtful study than any that has gone
before of what bad institutions make of men.

But there is also in *Little Dorrit* something different
from social criticism. Dickens is no longer satisfied to
anatomize the organism of society. The main symbol here
is the prison (in this connection, Mr. Jackson's chapter is
the best thing that has been written on *Little Dorrit*); but
this symbol is developed in a way that takes it beyond the
satirical application of the symbol of the fog in *Bleak
House* and gives it a significance more subjective. In the
opening chapter, we are introduced, not to the debtors'
prison, but to an ordinary jail for criminals, which, in the
case of Rigaud and Cavalletto, will not make the bad man
any better or the good man any worse. A little later, we
are shown an English business man who has come back
from many years in China and who finds himself in a
London – the shut-up London of Sunday evening – more
frightening, because more oppressive, than the thieves'
London of *Oliver Twist*. ' "Heaven forgive me," said he,
"and those who trained me. How I have hated this day!"
There was the dreary Sunday of his childhood, when he
sat with his hands before him, scared out of his senses by
a horrible tract which commenced business with the poor
child by asking him, in its title, why he was going to
Perdition?' At last he gets himself to the point of going to

see his mother, whom he finds as lacking in affection and as gloomy as he could have expected. She lives in a dark and funereal house with the old offices on the bottom floor, one of the strongholds of that harsh Calvinism plus hard business which made one of the mainstays of the Victorian Age; she lies paralyzed on 'a black bier-like sofa,' punishing herself and everyone else for some guilt of which he cannot discover the nature. The Clennam house is a jail, and they are in prison, too. So are the people in Bleeding Heart Yard, small tenement-dwelling shopkeepers and artisans, rack-rented by the patriarchal Casby; so is Merdle, the great swindler-financier, imprisoned, like Kreuger or Insull, in the vast scaffolding of fraud he has contrived, who wanders about in his expensive house — itself, for all its crimson and gold, as suffocating and dark as the Clennams' — afraid of his servants, unloved by his wife, almost unknown by his guests, till on the eve of the collapse of the edifice he quietly opens his veins in his bath.

At last, after twenty-five years of jail, Mr. Dorrit inherits a fortune and is able to get out of the Marshalsea. He is rich enough to go into Society; but all the Dorrits, with the exception of the youngest, known as 'Little Dorrit,' who has been born in the Marshalsea itself and has never made any pretensions, have been demoralized or distorted by the effort to remain genteel while tied to the ignominy of the prison. They cannot behave like the people outside. And yet that outside world is itself insecure. It is dominated by Mr. Merdle, who comes, as the story goes on, to be universally believed and admired — is taken up by the governing class, sent to Parliament, courted by lords. The Dorrits, accepted by Society, still find themselves in prison. The moral is driven home when old Dorrit, at a fashionable dinner, loses control of his wits and slips back into his character at the Marshalsea: ' "Born here," he repeated, shedding tears. "Bred here. Ladies and gentlemen, my daughter. Child of an unfortunate father, but — ha — always a gentleman. Poor, no doubt, but — hum — proud."' He asks the company for 'Testimonials,' which had been what he had used to call his tips. (Dr. Manette, in *A Tale of Two Cities,* repeats this pattern with his amnesic relapses into the shoemaking he has learned in prison.) Arthur Clennam, ruined by the failure of Merdle, finally goes to the Marshalsea himself; and there at last he and Little Dorrit arrive at an understanding. The implication is that, prison for prison, a simple incarceration is an excellent school of character compared to the dungeons of Puritan theology, of modern business, of money-ruled Society, or of the poor people of Bleeding Heart Yard who are swindled and bled by all of these.

The whole book is much gloomier than *Bleak House,* where the fog is external to the characters and represents something removable, the obfuscatory elements of the past. The murk of *Little Dorrit* permeates the souls of the people, and we see more of their souls than in *Bleak House.* Arthur Clennam, with his broodings on his unloving mother, who turns out not to be his real mother (a poor doomed child of natural impulse, like Lady Dedlock's lover), is both more real and more depressing than Lady Dedlock. Old Dorrit has been spoiled beyond repair: he can never be rehabilitated like Micawber. There is not even a villain like Tulkinghorn to throw the odium on a predatory class: the official villain Blandois has no organic connection with the story save as a caricature of social pretense. (Though the illustrations suggest that he may have been intended as a sort of cartoon of Napoleon III, whose régime Dickens loathed — in which case the tie-up between Blandois and the Clennams may figure a close relationship between the shady financial interests disguised by the flashy façade of the Second Empire and the respectable business interests of British merchants, so inhuman behind their mask of morality. Blandois is crushed in the end by the collapse of the Clennams' house, as people were already predicting that Napoleon would be by that of his own.) The rôle of the Court of Chancery is more or less played by the Circumlocution Office and the governing-class family of Barnacles — perhaps the most brilliant thing of its kind in Dickens: that great satire on all aristocratic bureaucracies, and indeed on all bureaucracies, with its repertoire of the variations possible within the bureaucratic type and its desolating picture of the emotions of a man being passed on from one door to another. But the Circumlocution Office, after all, only influences the action in a negative way.

The important thing to note in *Little Dorrit* — which was originally to have been called *Nobody's Fault* — is that the fable is here presented from the point of view of imprisoning states of mind as much as from that of oppressive institutions. This is illustrated in a startling way by *The History of a Self-Tormentor,* which we find toward the end of the book. Here Dickens, with a remarkable pre-Freudian insight, gives a sort of case history of a woman imprisoned in a neurosis which has condemned her to the delusion that she can never be loved. There is still, to be sure, the social implication that her orphaned childhood and her sense of being slighted have been imposed on her by the Victorian attitude toward her illegitimate birth. But her handicap is now simply a thought-pattern, and from that thought-pattern she is never to be liberated.

Dickens' personal difficulties make themselves felt like an ache at the back of *Little Dorrit* — in which he represents his hero as reflecting: 'Who has not thought for a moment, sometimes? — that it might be better to flow away monotonously, like the river, and to compound for its insensibility to happiness with its insensibility to pain.' The strain of his situation with his wife had become particularly acute the year that the book was begun. Dickens had been very much excited that February to get a letter from

Maria Beadnell, now married. The readiness and warmth
of his response shows how the old Ideal had lighted up
again. He was on the point of leaving for Paris, and during his absence he looked forward eagerly to seeing her:
he arranged to meet her alone. The drop in the tone of his
letters after this meeting has taken place is blighting to
poor Mrs. Winter. He had found her banal and silly, with
the good looks of her girlhood gone. He put her into his
new novel as Flora Finching, a sort of Dora Spenlow vul-
garized and transmogrified into a kind of Mrs. Nickleby
— that is, into another version of Dickens' unforgiven
mother. It seems clear that the type of woman that Dickens is chiefly glorifying during the years from *Martin
Chuzzlewit* through *Little Dorrit*: the devoted and self-
effacing little mouse, who hardly aspires to be loved, derives from Georgina Hogarth, his sister-in-law. Georgina,
who had been eight when Dickens was married, had come
to womanhood in the Dickens household. Dickens grew
fond of her, explaining that his affection was due partly
to her resemblance to her dead sister. She gradually took
over the care of the children, whom Dickens complained
of their mother's neglecting; and became the real head of
the household — creating a situation which is reflected in
these heroines of the novels. The virtues of Ruth Pinch
are brought out mainly through her relation to her brother
Tom; Esther Summerson, who keeps house for Mr. Jarndyce but does not suspect that he wants to marry her, is
suspended through most of *Bleak House* in a relation to
him that is semi-filial; Little Dorrit is shown throughout in
a sisterly and filial relation, and Arthur Clennam, before
he figures as a lover, plays simply, like Mr. Jarndyce, the
rôle of a protective and elderly friend. In the love of Little
Dorrit and Clennam, there seems to be little passion, but
a sobriety of resignation, almost a note of sadness: they
'went down,' Dickens says at the end, "into a modest life
of usefulness and happiness,' one of the objects of which

was to be 'to give a mother's care . . . to Fanny's [her sister's] neglected children no less than to their own.'

These children of Dickens' — he now had nine — were evidently giving him anxiety. He used to grumble about their lack of enterprise; and it would appear from Mrs. Perugini's story, which trails off in a depressing record of their failures and follies and untimely deaths, that in general they did not turn out well. The ill-bred daughter and worthless son of Dorrit probably caricature Dickens' fears. Surely the Dorrits' travels on the Continent caricature the progress of the Dickenses. Old Dorrit's rise in the world is no rescue at the end of a fairy tale, as it would have been in one of the early novels. The point of the story is that this rise can be only a mockery: the Dorrits will always be what the Marshalsea has made them.

The theme of *Little Dorrit* is repeated in *Great Expectations* (1860-61). This second of Dickens' novels in which the hero tells his own story is like an attempt to fill in some of the things that have been left out of *David Copperfield*. The story is the reverse of the earlier one. David was a gentleman by birth, who by accident became a wage slave. Pip is a boy out of the blacksmith's shop, who by accident gets a chance to become a gentleman. He straightway turns into a mean little snob.

The formula of *Bleak House* is repeated, too. The solution of the puzzle is again Dickens' moral, here more bitterly, even hatefully, delivered. Pip owes his mysterious income to the convict whom, in his childhood, he befriended on the marshes. Abel Magwitch himself had been a wretched tinker's boy, who had 'first become aware of [himself] a-thieving turnips for a living.' Later he had been exploited by a gentlemanly rotter turned crook, who had left Magwitch to take the rap when they had both fallen into the hands of the law. The poor rascal had been impressed by the advantage that his companion's social status — he had been to the public school — had given him in the eyes of the court; and when Magwitch later prospered in New South Wales, he decided to make a gentleman of Pip. Thus Pip finds himself in a position very similar to Lady Dedlock's: the money that chains him to Magwitch will not merely associate him with a poverty and ignorance more abject than that from which he has escaped, but will put him under obligations to an individual who represents to him the dregs of the underworld, a man with a price on his head. Not only this; but the proud lady here — who has known Pip in his first phase and scorns him because she thinks him a common village boy — turns out to be the daughter of Magwitch and of a woman who has been tried for murder and who is now employed in the humble capacity of housekeeper by the lawyer who got her off.

The symbol here is the 'great expectations' which both Pip and Estella entertain: they figure (Mr. T. A. Jackson has here again put his finger on the point) the Victorian mid-century optimism. Estella and Pip have both believed that they could count upon a wealthy patroness, the heiress of a now disused brewery, to make them secure against vulgarity and hardship. But the patroness vanishes like a phantom, and they are left with their leisure-class habits and no incomes to keep them up. They were originally to lose one another, too: the tragedies in Dickens' novels are coming more and more to seem irremediable. Estella was to marry for his money a brutal country squire, and Pip was never to see her again except for one brief meeting in London. Here is the last sentence of the ending that Dickens first wrote: 'I was very glad afterwards to have had the interview; for, in her face, and in her voice, and in her touch, she gave me the assurance that suffering had been stronger than Miss Havisham's teaching, and had given her a heart to understand what my heart used to be.'

This was to have been all, and it was perfect in tone

and touch. But Bulwer Lytton made Dickens change it to the ending we now have, in which Estella's husband gets killed and Pip and she are united. Dickens was still a public entertainer who felt that he couldn't too far disappoint his audience.

In *Little Dorrit* and *Great Expectations,* there is, therefore, a great deal more psychological interest than in Dickens' previous books. We are told what the characters think and feel, and even something about how they change. And here we must enter into the central question of the psychology of Dickens' characters.

The world of the early Dickens is organized according to a dualism which is based – in its artistic derivation – on the values of melodrama: there are bad people and there are good people, there are comics and there are characters played straight. The only complexity of which Dickens is capable is to make one of his noxious characters become wholesome, one of his clowns turn into a serious person. The most conspicuous example of this process is the reform of Mr. Dombey, who, as Taine says, 'turns into the best of fathers and spoils a fine novel.' But the reform of Scrooge in *A Christmas Carol* shows the phenomenon in its purest form.

We have come to take Scrooge so much for granted that he seems practically a piece of Christmas folklore; we no more inquire seriously into the mechanics of his transformation than we do into the transformation of the Beast in the fairy tale into the young prince that marries Beauty. Yet Scrooge represents a principle fundamental to the dynamics of Dickens' world and derived from his own emotional constitution. It was not merely that his passion for the theater had given him a taste for melodramatic contrasts; it was rather that the lack of balance between the opposite impulses of his nature had stimulated an appetite for melodrama. For emotionally Dickens *was* unstable. Allowing for the English restraint, which masks what the Russian expressiveness indulges and perhaps over-expresses, and for the pretenses of English biographers, he seems almost as unstable as Dostoevsky. He was capable of great hardness and cruelty, and not merely toward those whom he had cause to resent: people who patronized or intruded on him. On one occasion, in the presence of other guests, he ordered Forster out of his house over some discussion that had arisen at dinner; he was certainly not gentle with Maria Winter; and his treatment of Catherine suggests, as we shall see, the behavior of a Renaissance monarch summarily consigning to a convent the wife who has served her turn. There is more of emotional reality behind Quilp in *The Old Curiosity Shop* than there is behind Little Nell. If Little Nell sounds bathetic today, Quilp has lost none of his fascination. He is ugly, malevolent, perverse; he delights in making mischief for its own sake; yet he exercises over the members of his household a power which is almost an attraction and which resembles what was known in Dickens' day as 'malicious animal magnetism.' Though Quilp is ceaselessly tormenting his wife and browbeating the boy who works for him, they never attempt to escape: they admire him; in a sense they love him.

So Dickens' daughter, Kate Perugini, who had destroyed a memoir of her father that she had written, because it gave 'only half the truth,' told Miss Gladys Storey, the author of *Dickens and Daughter*, that the spell which Dickens had been able to cast on his daughters was so strong that, after he and their mother had separated, they had refrained from going to see her, though he never spoke to them about it, because they knew that he did not like it, and would even take music lessons in a house just opposite the one where she was living without daring to pay her a call. 'I loved my father,' said Mrs. Perugini, 'better than any man in the world — in a different way of course. . . . I loved him for his faults.' And she added, as she rose and walked to the door: 'my father was a wicked man — a very wicked man.' But from the memoirs of his other daughter Mamie, who also adored her father and seems to have viewed him uncritically, we hear of his colossal Christmas parties, of the vitality, the imaginative exhilaration, which swept all the guests along. It is Scrooge bursting in on the Cratchits. Shall we ask what Scrooge would actually be like if we were to follow him beyond the frame of the story? Unquestionably he would relapse when the merriment was over — if not while it was still going on — into moroseness, vindictiveness, suspicion. He would, that is to say, reveal himself as the victim of a manic-depressive cycle, and a very uncomfortable person.

This dualism runs all through Dickens. There has always to be a good and a bad of everything: each of the books has its counterbalancing values, and pairs of characters sometimes counterbalance each other from the casts of different books. There has to be a good manufacturer, Mr. Rouncewell, and a bad manufacturer, Mr. Bounderby; a bad old Jew, Fagin, and a good old Jew, Riah; an affable lawyer who is really unscrupulous, Vholes, and a kindly lawyer who pretends to be unfeeling, Jaggers; a malicious dwarf, Quilp, and a beneficent dwarf, Miss Mowcher (though Dickens had originally intended her to be bad); an embittered and perverse illegitimate daughter, Miss Wade, the Self-Tormentor, and a sweet and submissive illegitimate daughter, Esther Summerson. Another example of this tendency is Dickens' habit, noted by Mr. Kingsmill, of making the comic side of his novels a kind of parody on the sentimental side. Pecksniff is a satire on that domestic sentiment which wells up so profusely in Dickens himself when it is a question of a story for the Christmas trade; the performances of the Vincent Crummleses provide a burlesque of the stagy plot upon which *Nicholas Nickleby* is based.

Dickens' difficulty in his middle period, and indeed more or less to the end, is to get good and bad together in one character. He had intended in *Dombey and Son* to make Walter Gay turn out badly, but hadn't been able to bring himself to put it through. In *Bleak House,* however, he had had Richard Carstone undergo a progressive demoralization. But the real beginnings of a psychological interest may be said to appear in *Hard Times,* which, though parts of it have the crudity of a cartoon, is the first novel in which Dickens tries to trace with any degree of plausibility the processes by which people become what they are. We are given a certain sympathetic insight into what has happened to the Gradgrind children; and the conversion of Mr. Gradgrind is very much better prepared for than that of Mr. Dombey. In *Great Expectations* we see Pip pass through a whole psychological cycle. At first, he is sympathetic, then by a more or less natural process he turns into something unsympathetic, then he becomes sympathetic again. Here the effects of both poverty and riches are seen from the inside in one person. This is for Dickens a great advance; and it is a development which, if carried far enough, would end by eliminating the familiar Dickens of the lively but limited stage characters, with their tag lines and their unvarying make-ups.

The crisis of Dickens' later life had already come before *Great Expectations.* That 'old unhappy loss or want of something' which he makes David Copperfield feel after his marriage to Dora had driven him into a dream of retreating to the monastery of the Great St. Bernard, where it had been his original idea to have the whole of *Little Dorrit* take place. But he had ended by resorting to another order which, in mimicking the life of men, may remain almost as impenetrably cut off from it as the monks of the St. Bernard themselves. Dickens embarked upon a series of theatricals, which, though undertaken originally as benefits, took on a semi-professional character and came to look more and more like pretexts for Dickens to indulge his appetite for acting.

He had written Forster of 'the so happy and yet so un-happy existence which seeks its realities in unrealities, and finds its dangerous comfort in a perpetual escape from the disappointment of heart around it.' But now the pressure of this disappointment was to drive him into a deeper ad-diction to that dangerous comfort of unrealities. It was as if he had actually to embody, to act out in his own person, the life of his imagination. He had always loved acting: as a child, he had projected himself with intensity into the characters of the plays he had seen. He had always loved amateur theatricals and charades. He used to say that it relieved him, if only in a game, to throw himself into the personality of someone else. His whole art had been a kind of impersonation, in which he had exploited this or that of his impulses by incorporating it in an imaginary person rather than — up to this point, at any rate — exploring his own personality. The endings of his early novels, in which the villain was smashingly confounded and the young juvenile got the leading woman, had been the conven-tional dénouements of Drury Lane. Whole scenes of *Barnaby Rudge* had been high-flown declamations in a blank verse which connects Dickens almost as closely with the dramatic tradition of Shakespeare as with the fictional tradition of Fielding. Dickens admitted that he found it difficult, whenever he became particularly serious, to re-frain from falling into blank verse; and though his prose, like everything else in his art, underwent a remarkable development, tightening up and becoming cleaner, he never quite got rid of this tendency. The scene in which Edith Dombey turns upon and unmasks Mr. Carker, with its doors arranged for exits and entrances, its suspense en-gineered through the presence of the servants, its set speeches, its highfalutin language, its hair-raising reversal of rôles, its interruption at the climactic moment by the

sudden sound of the bell that announces the outraged
husband — this scene, which is one of the worst in Dickens, must be one of the passages in fiction most completely
conceived in terms of the stage. In *Bleak House,* he is still
theatrical, but he has found out how to make this instinct
contribute to the effectiveness of a novel: the theatrical
present tense of the episodes which alternate with Esther
Summerson's diary does heighten the excitement of the
narrative, and the theatrical Lady Dedlock is an improvement on Edith Dombey. Yet in the novels that follow
Bleak House, this theatricalism recurs as something never
either quite eliminated from or quite assimilated by Dickens' more serious art, an element which remains unreal if
it is not precisely insincere and on which his stories sometimes run aground. Later, when he was giving his public
readings, he wrote a whole series of stories — *Somebody's
Luggage, Mrs. Lirriper, Doctor Marigold* — which were
primarily designed for public performance and in which
excellent character monologues lead up to silly little episodes in the bad sentimental taste of the period which
Dickens had done so much to popularize. Dickens had a
strain of the ham in him, and, in the desperation of his
later life, he gave in to the old ham and let him rip.

That this satisfied the deeper needs of Dickens as little
as it does those of his readers seems to be proved by what
followed. He met behind the scenes of the theater some-
time in '57 or '58 a young girl named Ellen Ternan, the
daughter of a well-known actress. When Dickens first saw
her, she was hiding behind one of the properties and crying because she had to go on in a costume that offended
her sense of modesty. Dickens reassured her. She was
eighteen, and she evidently appealed to that compassion-
ate interest in young women which had made him apothe-
osize Mary Hogarth. He saw her again and became in-
fatuated. He had been complaining to Forster that 'a sense
comes always crashing on me now, when I fall into low

spirits, as of one happiness I have missed in life, and one
friend and companion I have never made'; and it must
have seemed to him that now he had found her.

He had made an agreement with Catherine in the early
days of their marriage that if either should fall in love
with anyone else, he should frankly explain to the other.
He now told her that he was in love with Miss Ternan
and compelled her to call on the girl. Dickens conducted
the whole affair with what appears to us the worst possible
taste, though I shall show in a moment that there were
special reasons why his behavior seemed natural to him.
He arranged to have Ellen Ternan take part in his benefit
performances, and, whether by design or not, gave her
rôles which ran close enough to the real situation to offend
Mrs. Dickens. Mr. Wright, who first made this whole
episode public in 1934, believes, probably rightly, that
Sydney Carton is Dickens' dramatization of the first hopeless phase of his love. In the spring of '58, however, Dickens arranged a separation from Catherine and left her
with one of their sons in London while he removed with
the rest of the children and Georgina to the new place he
had bought at Gadshill. He published a statement in
Household Words and circulated a singular letter which
was not long in getting into print, in which he explained
that he and Catherine had nothing whatever in common
and should never have got married; defended, without
naming her, Ellen Ternan; and denounced, without naming them, as 'two wicked persons' his mother-in-law and
his sister-in-law Helen for having intimated that there
could be 'on this earth a more virtuous and spotless creature' than Ellen. It was true that he and Ellen had not
been lovers; but he now induced Ellen to be his mistress
and set her up in an establishment of her own. He wrote
her name into his last three novels as Estella Provis, Bella
Wilfer, and finally Helena Landless — her full name was
Ellen Lawless Ternan.

In order to understand what is likely to seem to us on
Dickens' part a strange and disagreeable exhibitionism, we
must remember his relation to his public. Perhaps no other
kind of writer depends so much on his audience as the
novelist. If the novelist is extremely popular, he may even
substitute his relation to his public for the ordinary human
relations. And for this reason he responds to his sales in a
way which may seem ridiculous to a writer in a different
field; yet to the novelist the rise or the drop in the number
of the people who buy his books may be felt in very much
the same way as the coolness or the passion of a loved one.
In Dickens' case, a falling-off in the popularity of his
monthly instalments would plunge him into anxiety and
depression. He had played up Sam Weller in *Pickwick*
because he saw that the character was going well, and he
sent Martin Chuzzlewit to America because he found that
interest in the story was flagging. And now it had come
to be true in a sense that his only companion in his fictional world was the public who saw him act and read his
novels. When he began, as he did that same spring, to
give regular public readings – which enabled him to live
these novels, as it were, in his own person, and to feel the
direct impact on his audience – the relation became more
intimate still. For Dickens, the public he addressed in this
statement about his marriage was probably closer than the
wife by whom he had had ten children; and now that he
had fallen in love with Ellen, instead of finding in her a
real escape from the eternal masquerade of his fiction, his
first impulse was to transport her to dwell with him in that
imaginary world itself, to make her a character in a novel
or play, and to pay court to her in the presence of his
public.

But the old sense of 'loss or want' does not seem to have
been cured by all this. 'My father was like a madman,'
says Mrs. Perugini, 'when my mother left home. This affair brought out all that was worst – all that was weakest

in him. He did not care a damn what happened to any of us. Nothing could surpass the misery and unhappiness of our home.' And this misery still hung over the household, in spite of Dickens' festive hospitality, even after the separation had been arranged. Poor Mrs. Dickens in her exile was wretched — 'Do you think he is sorry for me?' she asked Kate on one of the only two occasions when she ever heard her mother mention her father — and there was always at the back of their consciousness this sense of something deeply wrong. Kate Dickens, with more independence than Mamie, does not seem much to have liked having Miss Ternan come to Gadshill; and she finally married a brother of Wilkie Collins, without really caring about him, in order to get away from home. After the wedding, which Mrs. Dickens had not attended, Mamie found her father weeping in Kate's bedroom, with his face in her wedding dress: 'But for me,' he said to her, 'Katy would not have left home.'

This episode of Ellen Ternan has been hushed up so systematically, and the information about it is still so meager, that it is difficult to get an impression of Ellen. We do, however, know something about what Dickens thought of her from the heroines in his last books who are derived from her. Estella is frigid and indifferent: it amuses her to torture Pip, who loves her 'against reason, against promise, against peace, against hope, against happiness, against all discouragement that could be'; she marries a man she does not love for his money. Bella Wilfer up to her conversion by Mr. Boffin is equally intent upon money — which was certainly one of the things that Ellen got out of her liaison with Dickens. Both Estella and Bella are petulant, spoiled and proud. They represent, as it were, the qualities of the Edith Dombey-Lady Dedlock great lady combined with the capriciousness of Dora Spenlow — the old elements of Dickens' women simply mixed in a new way. And these novels of Dickens in which Ellen figures show perhaps more real desperation than *Little Dorrit* itself, with its closing note of modest resignation. It seems to be the general opinion that Ellen was neither so fascinating nor so gifted as Dickens thought her. After his death, she married a clergyman, and she confided to Canon Benham that she had loathed her relationship with Dickens and deeply regretted the whole affair. She had borne Dickens a child, which did not live. It may be — though we have no date — that Dickens' short story, *Doctor Marigold* (1865), which became one of his favorite readings, the monologue of a traveling 'cheap jack,' who keeps an audience entertained with his patter while his child is dying in his arms, is a reflection of this event.

In spite of the energy of a *diable au corps* which enabled him to put on his plays and to perform prodigies of walking and mountain-climbing at the same time that he was composing his complicated novels, the creative strain of a lifetime was beginning to tell heavily on Dickens. He had always felt under an obligation to maintain a standard of living conspicuously lavish for a literary man: in his statement about his separation from his wife, he boasts that he has provided for her as generously 'as if Mrs. Dickens were a lady of distinction and I a man of fortune.' And now he was compelled both by the demon that drove him and by the necessity of earning money in order to keep up the three establishments for which he had made himself responsible and to launch his sons and daughters on the world, to work frantically at his public readings. His nervous disorders persisted: he was troubled while he was writing *Great Expectations* with acute pains in the face; and he developed a lameness in his left foot, which, though he blamed it on taking walks in heavy snowstorms, was also evidently due to the burning-out of his nerves. He was maimed by it all the rest of his life. 'Twice last week,' he writes in '66, 'I was seized in a most distressing manner – apparently in the heart; but, I am persuaded, only in the nervous system.'

Three years had passed since *Great Expectations* before Dickens began another novel; he worked at it with what was for him extreme slowness, hesitation and difficulty; and the book shows the weariness, the fears and the definitive disappointments of this period.

This story, *Our Mutual Friend* (1864-65), like all these later books of Dickens, is more interesting to us today than it was to Dickens' public. It is a next number in the Dickens sequence quite worthy of its predecessors, a development out of what has gone before that is in certain ways quite different from the others. It may be said Dickens never really repeats himself: his thought makes a consistent progress, and his art, through the whole thirty-five years of his career, keeps going on to new materials and effects; so that his work has an interest and a meaning as a whole. The difficulty that Dickens found in writing *Our Mutual Friend* does not make itself felt as anything in the nature of an intellectual disintegration. On the contrary, the book compensates for its shortcomings by the display of an intellectual force which, though present in Dickens' work from the first, here appears in a phase of high tension and a condition of fine muscular training. The Dickens of the old eccentric 'Dickens characters' has here, as has often been noted, become pretty mechanical and sterile. It is a pity that the creator of Quilp and of Mrs. Jarley's waxworks should have felt himself under the necessity of fabricating Silas Wegg and the stuffed animals of Mr. Venus. Also, the complex Dickens plot has come to seem rather tiresome and childish. But Dickens has here distilled the mood of his later years, dramatized the tragic discrepancies of his character, delivered his final judgment on the whole Victorian exploit, in a fashion so impressive

that we realize how little the distractions of this period
had the power to direct him from the prime purpose of his
life: the serious exercise of his art.

As the fog is the symbol for *Bleak House* and the prison
for *Little Dorrit,* so the dust-pile is the symbol for *Our
Mutual Friend.* It dominates even the landscape of London, which has already been presented by Dickens under
such a variety of aspects, but which now appears — though
with Newgate looming over it as it did in *Barnaby Rudge*
— under an aspect that is new: 'A gray dusty withered evening in London city has not a hopeful aspect,' he writes of
the day when Bradley Headstone goes to pay his hopeless
court to Lizzie Hexam. 'The closed warehouses and offices have an air of death about them, and the national
dread of color has an air of mourning. The towers and
steeples of the many house-encompassed churches, dark
and dingy as the sky that seems descending on them, are
no relief to the general gloom; a sun-dial on a church-wall
has the look, in its useless black shade, of having failed in
its business enterprise and stopped payment for ever; melancholy waifs and strays of housekeepers and porters
sweep melancholy waifs and strays of papers and pins into
the kennels, and other more melancholy waifs and strays
explore them, searching and stooping and poking for
everything to sell. The set of humanity outward from the
City is as a set of prisoners departing from gaol, and dismal Newgate seems quite as fit a stronghold for the
mighty Lord Mayor as his own state-dwelling.'

The actual dust-pile in question has been amassed by a
dust-removal contractor, who has made out of it a considerable fortune. The collection of refuse at that time was
still in private hands, and was profitable because the
bones, rags and cinders, and even the dust itself, were valuable for various kinds of manufacture. The plot of *Our
Mutual Friend* has to do with the struggle of a number of
persons to get possession of or some share in this money.

(The other principal industry which figures in *Our Mutual Friend* is the robbing of the dead bodies in the Thames.) But the real meaning of the dust-pile is not in doubt: 'My lords and gentlemen and honorable lords,' writes Dickens, when the heap is being carted away, 'when you in the course of your dust-shoveling and cinder-raking have piled up a mountain of pretentious failure, you must off with your honorable coats for the removal of it, and fall to the work with the power of all the queen's horses and all the queen's men, or it will come rushing down and bury us alive.'

Dickens' line in his criticism of society is very clear in *Our Mutual Friend,* and it marks a new position on Dickens' part, as it results from a later phase of.the century. Dickens has come at last to despair utterly of the prospering middle class. We have seen how he judged the morality of the merchants. In *Bleak House,* the iron-master is a progressive and self-sustaining figure who is played off against parasites of various sorts; but in *Hard Times,* written immediately afterward, the later development of Rouncewell is dramatized in the exploiter Bounderby, a new kind of Victorian hypocrite, who pretends to be a self-made man. In *Little Dorrit,* the one set of characters who are comparatively healthy and cheerful still represent that middle-class home which has remained Dicken's touchstone of virtue; but even here there is a distinct change in Dickens' attitude. Mr. Meagles, the retired banker, with his wife and his beloved only daughter, become the prey of Henry Gowan, a well-connected young man of no fortune who manages to lead a futile life (the type has been well observed) between the social and artistic worlds without ever making anything of either. But the smugness and insularity, even the vulgarity, of the Meagleses is felt by Dickens as he has never felt it in connection with such people before. After all, in taking in Tattycoram, the foundling, the Meagleses could not help making her feel her position of inferiority. A little more emphasis in this direction by Dickens and the Meagleses might seem to the reader as odious as they recurrently do to her. Tattycoram herself, with her painful alternations between the extremes of affection and resentment, probably reflects the oscillations of Dickens himself at this period.

But the resentment is to get the upper hand. The Meagleses turn up now as the Podsnaps, that horrendous middle-class family, exponents of all the soundest British virtues, who however, are quite at home in a social circle of sordid adventurers and phony *nouveaux riches,* and on whom Dickens visits a satire as brutal as themselves. Gone are the high spirits that made of Pecksniff an exhilarating figure of fun — gone with the Yoho! of the stagecoach on which Tom Pinch traveled to London. The Podsnaps, the Lammles, the Veneerings, the Fledgebys, are unpleasant as are no other characters in Dickens. It comes to us as a disturbing realization that Dickens is now *afraid* of Podsnap (who, with his talk about the paramount importance of not bringing the blush to the young person's cheek, would of course have been the loudest among those who disapproved of Dickens' affair with Miss Ternan). And Fledgeby, the young moneylender of the second generation, with his peachy cheeks and slender figure, who lives in the Albany and dines out — Grandfather Smallweed is a man beside him! It is startling to find that Dickens has here even hit upon a principle which another group of commercial-patriotic rotters were later to exploit on a large scale. One of the ugliest scenes in Dickens is that in which Fledgeby ascribes his own characteristics to the gentle old Jew Riah and makes him the agent of his meanness and sharp-dealing. And not content with making Fledgeby a cur, Dickens himself shows a certain cruelty in having him ultimately thrashed by Lammle under circumstances of peculiar ignominy and then having the little dolls'

dressmaker apply plasters with pepper on them to his
wounds. This incident betrays a kind of sadism which we
never felt in Dickens' early work — when Nicholas Nickleby beat Squeers, for example — but which breaks out
now and then in these later books in a disagreeable fashion.

If the middle class has here become a monster, the gentry have taken on an aspect more attractive than we have
ever known them to wear as a class in any previous novel
of Dickens. If an increase of satiric emphasis turns the
Meagleses into the Podsnaps, so a shift from the satirical
to the straight turns the frivolous and idle young man of
good family, who has hitherto always been exhibited as
more or less of a scoundrel — James Harthouse or Henry
Gowan — into the sympathetic Eugene Wrayburn. Eugene and his friend Mortimer Lightwood, the little old
diner-out named Twemlow, the only gentleman in the
Veneerings' circle, and the Reverend Frank Milvey, 'expensively educated and wretchedly paid,' the Christian
turned social worker, are the only representatives of the
upper strata who are shown as having decent values; and
they are all the remnants of an improverished gentry.
Outside these, you find the decent values — or what
Dickens intends to be such — in an impoverished proletariat and lower middle class: the modest clerk, the old
Jew, the dolls' dressmaker, the dust-contractor's foreman,
the old woman who minds children for a living. And the
chief heroine is not Bella Wilfer, who has to be cured of
her middle-class ideals, but Lizzie Hexam, the illiterate
daughter of a Thames-side water-rat. Dickens has here, for
the first time in his novels, taken his leading woman from
the lowest class; and it will be the principal moral of *Our
Mutual Friend* that Wrayburn will have the courage to
marry Lizzie. The inevitable conjunction of the high with
the low is not here to result in a tragedy but to figure as a
fortunate affair. Nor does it involve the whole structure of
society in the same way as in the earlier novels: the me-

chanics are somewhat different. The point is made that
the Podsnap-Veneering upper scum of the successful middle class remain unaffected by what has happened and do
not seriously affect anyone else. Such people, in Dickens'
view, have by this time become completely dissociated
from anything that is admirable in English life. Simply,
Eugene Wrayburn no longer appears at the Veneerings'
parties. When they sneer at the unseemliness of his marriage, Mr. Twemlow suddenly flares up and declares with
an authority which makes everyone uncomfortable that
Eugene has behaved like a gentleman; and that is the end
of the book.

Dickens has aligned himself in *Our Mutual Friend*
with a new combination of forces. Shrinking from Podsnap and Veneering, he falls back on that aristocracy he
had so savagely attacked in his youth, but to which,
through his origins, he had always been closer than he
had to the commercial classes. After all, Sir John Chester
had had qualities of coolness, grace and ease which, when
they appear in an excellent fellow like Eugene, are infinitely preferable to Podsnap. The Chartist movement in
England had run into the sands in the fifties; but during
the sixties the trade union movement had been making
remarkable progress. Dickens had begun *Our Mutual
Friend* in the autumn of 1863, and the first number appeared the following May. In July definite steps were
taken at a meeting of French and English workers for an
'international working men's alliance,' and the Workers'
International, under the guidance of Karl Marx, was
founded at the end of September. This trend may have
influenced Dickens, for the final implication of his story
is — to state it in the Marxist language — that the de-
classed representatives of the old professional upper classes
may unite with the proletariat against the commercial
middle class.

There is, however, another element that plays an important rôle in the story: the proletarian who has educated himself to be a member of this middle class. Lizzie Hexam has a brother, whom she has induced to get an education and who, as soon as he has qualified himself to teach, drops his family even more callously than Pip did his; and the schoolmaster of Charley Hexam's school, another poor man who has advanced himself, is the villain of *Our Mutual Friend*. We are a long way here from the days when the villains and bad characters in Dickens, the Quilps and the Mrs. Gamps, could be so fascinating through their resourcefulness and vitality that, as G. K. Chesterton says, the reader is sorry at the end when they are finally banished from the scene and hopes that the discredited scoundrel will still open the door and stick his head in and make one more atrocious remark. Such figures are so much all of a piece of evil that they have almost a kind of innocence. But here Bradley Headstone has no innocence: he is perverted, tormented, confused. He represents a type which begins to appear in these latest novels of Dickens and which originally derives perhaps from those early theatrical villains, of the type of the elder Rudge or Monks in *Oliver Twist*, skulking figures with black looks and ravaged faces: a literary convention of which one would suppose it would be impossible to make anything plausible. Yet Dickens does finally succeed in giving these dark figures reality.

In Bradley Headstone's case, it is his very aspirations which have gone bad and turned the stiff and anxious schoolmaster into a murderer. He wants to marry Lizzie Hexam and he is wounded by her preference for Eugene, whose nonchalance and grace infuriate him because he knows he can never achieve them. In order to make himself a place in society, he has had rigorously to repress his passions; and now that they finally break out, it is more horrible than Bill Sikes or Jonas Chuzzlewit, because we understand Bradley as a human being. Bradley is the first murderer in Dickens who exhibits any complexity of character. And he is the first to present himself as a member of respectable Victorian society. There is a dreadful and convincing picture of the double life led by Headstone as he goes about his duties as a schoolmaster after he has decided to murder Eugene. In *Great Expectations,* the Ellen Ternan character, Estella, rejects the love of the hero. In *Our Mutual Friend,* Bella Wilfer rejects Rokesmith in much the same way — though less cruelly, and though she later marries him. But Rokesmith is a colorless character, and the real agonies of frustrated passion appear in *Our Mutual Friend* in the scene between Bradley and Lizzie. This is the kind of thing — the Carker and Edith Dombey kind of thing — that is likely to be bad in Dickens; but here it has a certain reality and a certain unpleasant power. Who can forget the tophatted schoolmaster striking his fist against the stone wall of the church?

The inference is, of course, that Bradley, if he had not been shipwrecked in this way, would have approximated as closely as possible to some sort of Murdstone or Gradgrind. But his death has a tragic symbolism which suggests a different kind of moral. In order to escape detection, he has disguised himself at the time of the murder as a disreputable waterside character who is known to have a grievance against Eugene. When the man finds out what has happened, he makes capital of it by blackmailing Bradley. Headstone finally tackles him on the edge of the deep lock of a canal, drags him into the water, and holds him under until he is drowned; but in doing so, he drowns himself. It is as if the illiterate ruffian whom he would now never be able to shake off has come to represent the brutish part of Bradley's own nature. Having failed to destroy Eugene, he destroys himself with the brute.

In *The Mystery of Edwin Drood*, the motif of Bradley Headstone is, with certain variations, repeated.

This novel, written five years later, Dickens never lived to finish, and it is supposed to have been left an enigma. We must first try to solve the enigma; and to do so we must proceed with a consciousness of the real meaning of Dickens' work. For though it is true that *Edwin Drood* had been enormously written about, it has been always from the point of view of trying to find out what Dickens intended to do with the plot. None of the more serious critics of Dickens has ever been able to take the novel very seriously. They persist in dismissing it as a detective story with good touches and promising characters, but of no interest in the development of Dickens' genius. Bernard Shaw, who is interested in the social side of Dickens, declares that it is 'only a gesture by a man three quarters dead'; and it is true, as Forster remarked, that *The Mystery of Edwin Drood* seems quite free from the social criticism which had grown more biting as Dickens grew older; but what Forster and Shaw do not see is that the psychological interest which had been a feature of Dickens' later period is carried farther in *Edwin Drood*. Like all the books that Dickens wrote under the strain of his later years, it has behind it bitter judgments and desperate emotions. Here as elsewhere the solution of the mystery was to have said something that Dickens wanted to say.

It did not, it is true, become possible to gauge the full significance of the novel until certain key discoveries had been made in regard to the plot itself; but the creation of such a character as John Jasper at this point in Dickens' development should have had its significance for any student of Dickens and should have led to a more careful consideration, in the light of certain hints supplied by Forster, of the psychological possibilities of the character.

It has remained for two American scholars to hit upon the cardinal secrets that explain the personality of Jasper. As both these discoveries have been made since the publication in 1912 of W. Roberston Nicoll's otherwise comprehensive book, *The Problem of Edwin Drood,* they have not received attention there; they are not included by Thomas Wright in the bibliography of *Edwin Drood* in his *Life of Charles Dickens,* published in 1936; and so far as I know, up to the present time, nobody who has written about Dickens has been in a position to combine these ideas. Yet what happens when one puts them together is startling: the old novel acquires a sudden new value. Just as one can revive invisible ink by holding it over a lamp or bring out three dimensions in a photograph by looking at it through certain lenses, so it is possible to recall to life the character of John Jasper as he must have been conceived by Dickens.

The most important revelation about *Edwin Drood* has been made by Mr. Howard Duffield, who published an article called *John Jasper — Strangler* in *The American Bookman* of February, 1930. Mr. Duffield has here shown conclusively that Jasper is supposed to be a member of the Indian sect of Thugs, who made a profession of ingratiating themselves with travelers and then strangling them with a handkerchief and robbing them. This brotherhood, which had been operating for centuries pretty much all over India and which had given the British government a great deal of trouble before it succeeded in putting them down during the thirties, had already attracted attention in the West. Two of the British officers who had been engaged in the suppression of the Thugs had written books about them — one of them in the form of a story, Meadows Taylor's *Confessions of a Thug,* supposed to be narrated by the Thug himself. Eugène Sue had introduced into *The Wandering Jew* a Thug strangler practicing in Europe; and an American novelist, James de Mille,

was publishing a novel called *Cord and Creese,* which
exploited the situation of an Englishman affiliated with
the Thugs, in the same year, 1869, that Dickens began
Edwin Drood. We know that Dickens' friend, Edward
Bulwer Lytton, had already thought of using this theme.
Dickens himself had mentioned the Thugs in 1857 in
connection with a garrotting epidemic in London. The
publication in 1868 of Wilkie Collins' detective story, *The
Moonstone,* in which a band of Hindu devotees commit
a secret murder in England, seems to have inspired Dickens with the idea of outdoing his friend the next year with
a story of a similar kind.

Now, we know from the statement of Sir Luke Fildes,
Dickens' illustrator in *Edwin Drood,* that Dickens intended to have Jasper strangle Drood with the long scarf
which he (Jasper) wears around his neck; and we know
from many circumstances and certain hints that the story
was to have had its roots in the East. Neville and Helena
Landless are supposed to come from Ceylon; and Mr.
Jasper, who smokes opium and sees elephants in his
trances, is described as having 'thick, lustrous, well-ar-
ranged black hair and whiskers' and a voice that sometimes sounds 'womanish' — in short, as something very
much like a Hindu. Furthermore, as Mr. Duffield had
established, John Jasper — and this explains a good deal
that has never been understood — has been trying to fulfill the ritualistic requirements for a sanctified and successful Thug murder. The Thugs were worshipers of Kali,
the Hindu goddess of destruction, and their methods had
been prescribed by the goddess. They had to commit their
crimes with the fold of cloth which was a fragment of
the gown of Kali. Kali's gown was supposed to be black,
Jasper's scarf is black. This cloth had to be worn, as Jasper's scarf is. A secret burial place had to be selected, as
Jasper selects Mrs. Sapsea's tomb, before the murder took
place. The omens had to be observed, as is done by Mr.

Jasper when he makes his nocturnal trip to the top of the
cathedral tower; the call of a rook in sight of a river was
regarded as a favorable sign, the approving word of the
goddess, and that, one finds, is precisely what Jasper hears.
The significance of the birds is planted plainly at the
beginning of Chapter II, when the Cloisterham rooks are
first mentioned: 'Whosoever has observed that sedate and
clerical bird, the rook, may perhaps have noticed that
when he wings his way homeward toward nightfall, in a
sedate and clerical company, two rooks will suddenly de-
tach themselves from the rest, will retrace their flight for
some distance, and will there poise and linger; çonveying
to mere men the fancy that it is of some occult importance
to the body politic, that this artful couple should pretend
to have renounced connection with it.' The Thug preys
exclusively on travelers: Edwin Drood is going on a journey; and when Jasper, in his second opium dream, is
heard talking to himself about the murder, it is all in terms
of a journey and a fellow traveler. The Thug is to use
exaggerated words of endearment, as Jasper does with
Drood. He is to persuade his victim to leave his lodging a
little after midnight, as Jasper has done with Drood, and
to stupefy him with a drug in his food or drink, as Jasper
has obviously done, first with Edwin and Neville, and
afterwards with Durdles.

Since Jasper is eventually to be caught, he is evidently
to have slipped up in the ritual. Mr. Duffield suggests that
Jasper's mistake has been to commit the murder without
an assistant; but he has overlooked the Thug superstition
(recorded by Edward Thornton in *Illustrations of the
History and Practices of the Thugs,* published in 1837)
that nothing but evil could come of murdering a man with
any gold in his possession. Now, Drood, unknown to
Jasper, is carrying the gold ring which Grewgious has
given him for Rosa; and we have it on Dickens' own testi-
mony to Forster that the body of Edwin Drood is to be

identified by this ring, which has survived the effects of the quicklime. True, Edwin has also been wearing the stickpin and the gold watch; but since Jasper knew about these and took care to leave them in the weir, he may have made a point of removing them after Edwin was drugged and before he was murdered.

Supplementing this interesting discovery we find a paper by Mr. Aubrey Boyd in the series of *Humanistic Studies* (Volume IX) published by Washington University, in which he shows that Jasper is also a hypnotist. Dickens had always been interested in hypnotism. Forster speaks of his first seriously studying it in 1841. He even found that he himself, with that extraordinarily magnetic personality which made it possible for him so to fascinate his audiences and which exerted, as Mrs. Perugini testifies, so irresistible a power over his family, had the ability to hypnotize people. His first experiment was performed on his wife in the course of his earlier trip to America. He had, he wrote Forster, been 'holding forth upon the subject rather luminously, and asserting that I thought I could exercise the influence, but had never tried.' 'Kate sat down, laughing, for me to try my hand upon her. . . . In six minutes, I magnetized her into hysterics, and then into the magnetic sleep. I tried again next night, and she fell into the slumber in little more than two minutes. . . . I can wake her with perfect ease; but I confess (not being prepared for anything so sudden and complete) I was on the first occasion rather alarmed.' Later, we hear of his hypnotizing John Leech in order to relieve his pain during an illness.

In the meantime, he had a strange experience, reported by Mrs. Perugini, with an Englishwoman he had met in Genoa in 1844. This lady, who was married to a Swiss printer, was afflicted with delusions that "took the form of a phantom which spoke to her, and other illusionary figures of the most hideous shapes and gory appearance, which came in a crowd, chattering one to the other as they pursued her, and after a time faded, veiling their loathsome faces as they disappeared into space.' Dickens, who at the time was suffering from a recurrence of the spasms of pain in his side which had afflicted him as a child in the blacking warehouse, hypnotized her once or twice every day and found that he could control the delusions. He seems to have become obsessed with the case: the treatment went on for months. On one occasion, 'he was in such a fever of anxiety to receive a letter from his friend concerning the state of his wife that he watched through a telescope the arrival of the mailbags into port.' He mesmerized her 'in the open country and at wayside inns where . . . they would halt for refreshment or stay the night. He mesmerized her in railway carriages — anywhere, if the moment was opportune. By degrees she became better and more serene in her mind and body.' The delusions were apparently dispelled.

It was obviously on the cards that Dickens would do something with this subject in his novels; and it ought to have given the Drood experts a lead when they encountered a reference to it in the third chapter of *Edwin Drood*. W. Robertson Nicoll, disregarding this key passage, mentions the matter in another connection: he sees that Jasper has 'willed' Crisparkle to go to the weir, where he will find the watch and stickpin of Edwin; but he does not inquire further. It remained for Mr. Boyd, who has some special knowledge of Mesmer and his writings, to recognize that Dickens has introduced the whole repertory of the supposed feats of mesmerism — called also 'animal magnetism' at the time — just as he has reproduced the practices of the Thugs. Mr. Jasper is clearly exercising 'animal magnetism,' in this case the kind known as 'malicious,' on Rosa Budd in the scene in which he accompanies her at the piano; he is exercising it on Edwin and Neville when he causes them to quarrel in his rooms. It was supposed in Dickens' time that this influence could be projected through the agency of mere sound: hence the insistent keynote in the piano scene and the swelling note of the organ that frightens Rosa in the garden. And it was also supposed to penetrate matter: hence Rosa's remark to Helena that she feels as if Jasper could reach her through a wall. It could be made to impregnate objects in such a way as to remain effective after the master of the magnetic fluid was no longer himself on the scene: Jasper has put a spell on the water in which Edwin's watch and stickpin are to be found. And it is possible, though Mr. Boyd does not suggest it, that the transmission of Jasper's influence from a distance may also explain the behavior, of which the implausible character has been noted, of the men who pursue and waylay Landless.

The revealing hint here, however, is the passage in the third chapter, of which Boyd has understood the significance and which has led him to a brilliant conjecture: 'As, in some cases of drunkenness,' writes Dickens, 'and in others of animal magnetism, there are two states of consciousness that never clash, but each of which pursues its separate course as though it were continuous instead of broken (thus, if I hide my watch when I am drunk, I must be drunk again before I can remember where), so Miss Twinkleton has two distinct and separate phases of being.' Dickens had told Forster that the originality of his idea for *Drood*, 'a very strong one, though difficult to work' (Dickens' words in a letter), was to consist (Forster's words in recounting a conversation with Dickens) 'in the review of the murderer's career by himself at the close, when its temptations were to be dwelt upon as if, not he the culprit, but some other man, were the tempted. The last chapters were to be written in the condemned cell, to which his wickedness, all elaborately elicited from him as if told of another, had brought him.'

John Jasper has, then, 'two states of consciousness'; he

is, in short, what we have come to call a dual personality.
On the principle that 'if I hide my watch when I am
drunk, I must be drunk again before I can remember
where,' it will be necessary, in order to extort his confession, to induce in him that state of consciousness, evidently not the one with which he meets the cathedral
world, that has caused him to commit the murder. The
possibility of opium, suggested by Robertson Nicoll, ought
surely to be excluded, since Wilkie Collins, in *The Moonstone,* had just made use of this device: the man who has
taken the Moonstone under the influence of laudanum,
administered to him without his knowing it, is made to
repeat his action under the influence of a second dose.
The drunkenness in which Jasper will betray himself
will not, then, be produced by a drug. Dickens must go
Collins one better. Mr. Boyd has evidently solved the
puzzle in guessing that Helena Landless is eventually to
hypnotize Jasper. In the scene at the piano, in which
Jasper is made to work upon Rosa with the effect of her
becoming hysterical, Helena maintains an attitude of
defiance and announces that she is not afraid of him. It
had already been established by J. Cuming Walters — it
was the first of the important discoveries about *Drood* —
that Datchery, the mysterious character who comes to
Cloisterham to spy on Jasper, is Helena in disguise. We
have been told, in Chapter VII, that Helena had several
times 'dressed as a boy and shown the daring of a man'
in running away from her brutal stepfather; and Dickens'
alterations in his text, both the amplifications of the written copy and the later excisions from the proofs, indicate
very clearly that he was aiming — in dealing with such
details as Helena's wig and her attempts to conceal her
feminine hands — to insinuate evidences of her real identity without allowing the reader to find it out too soon.
Helena is to get the goods on Jasper, and in the end, having no doubt acquired in India the same secret which he

had been exploiting (there may be also, as so often in Dickens, some question of a family relationship), she will put him in a trance and make him speak.

What Mr. Boyd, however, was not in a position to do was combine this idea with the Thug theme. The Thugs were all in a sense divided personalities. Colonel James L. Sleeman, in his book on the subject, emphasizes what he calls this 'Jekyll-and-Hyde' aspect of their activities. The Thugs were devoted husbands and loving fathers; they made a point — again like Mr. Jasper — of holding positions of honor in the community. And in their own eyes they were virtuous persons: they were serving the cult of the goddess. In their case, the Jekyll-and-Hyde aspect of their careers was exceptional only from the point of view of persons outside the cult. When caught, they would proudly confess to the number of lives they had taken. But in the case of Mr. Jasper, there is a respectable and cultivated Christian gentleman living in the same soul and body with a worshiper of the goddess Kali. The murder has been rehearsed in his opium dreams: he has evidently gone to the opium den for that purpose. He has kept himself under the influence of the drug all the time he has been plotting the murder. But it will not be possible to make him confess by compelling him to take opium. Helena, with her stronger will, is to accomplish this through hypnotism.

And now what has all this to do with the Dickens we already know? Why should he have occupied the last years of his life in concocting this sinister detective story?

Let us consider his situation at this period. He is still living between Gadshill and the house of his mistress Ellen Lawless Ternan, who appears now in *Edwin Drood*, identified even more plainly than before, under the name of Helena Landless. The motif of the disagreeable scene between Bradley Headstone and Lizzie Hexam is repeated

in the even more unpleasant, though theatrical and unconvincing, interview between Jasper and Rosa Budd —
Jasper presenting, like Headstone, a ghastly travesty of
the respectable Victorian. The Ellen Ternan heroine is
here frankly made an actress: Helena Landless is an im-
personator so accomplished that she can successfully play
a male character in real life; and she is even more formidable than Estella because she is to stand up to and unmask
Jasper. Her strength is to be contrasted not only with the
fatal duplicity of Jasper, but with the weakness of Drood
and Neville. All of these three men are to perish, and
Rosa is to marry Mr. Tartar, the foursquare young ex-
Navy man, bursting with good spirits, agility and a perhaps rather overdone good health.

Dickens had just finished his public appearances and
had said his farewell to the platform. The great feature
of his last series of readings had been the murder of Nancy
by Sikes, a performance which he had previously tried on
his friends and from which Forster and others had wished
to dissuade him. He was warned by a woman's doctor of
his acquaintance that 'if only one woman cries out when
you murder the girl, there will be a contagion of hysteria
all over the place.' But Dickens obviously derived from
thus horrifying his hearers some sort of satisfaction. The
scene was perhaps a symbolical representation of his behavior in banishing his wife. Certainly the murder of
Nancy had taken on something of the nature of an obsessive hallucination. Dickens' imagination had always
been subject to a tendency of this kind. It had been
pointed out by Taine that the fantasies and monomanias
of his lunatics only exaggerate characteristics which are
apparent in Dickens' whole work — the concentration on
and reiteration of some isolated aspect or detail of a person
or a place, as when Mr. Dick in *David Copperfield* is
haunted by King Charles's head. In one of the sketches of
The Uncommercial Traveller, written during these later

years, Dickens tells of having been obsessed by the image
of a drowned and bloated corpse that he had seen in the
Paris morgue, which for days kept popping up among the
people and things he encountered and sometimes compelled him to leave public places, though it eventually
drove him back to the morgue. In the case of the woman
in Italy whose delusions he attempted to dispel, one gets
the impression that these bloody visions were almost as
real to him as they were to her. And now, at the time of
these readings, he jokes about his 'murderous instincts'
and says that he goes about the street feeling as if he were
'wanted' by the police.

He threw himself at any rate into the murder scene
with a passion that became quite hysterical, as if reading
it had become at this point in his life a real means of self-
expression. At Clifton, he wrote Forster, 'we had a contagion of fainting; and yet the place was not hot. I should
think we had from a dozen to twenty ladies taken out
stiff and rigid, at various times!' At Leeds, whether in order
to intensify the effect or to avert the possible objections of
the audience, he hired a man to rise from the stalls and protest in the middle of the murder scene against daring to
read such a thing before ladies — with the result that the
people hissed him and put him out. It was the opinion of
Dickens' doctor that the excitement and strain of acting
this episode were the immediate cause of Dickens' death.
It always took him a long time to calm himself after he had
played this scene, and the doctor, who noted his pulse at
the end of each selection, saw that it invariably ran higher
then than it did after any of the other scenes. When
Dolby, the manager of Dickens' tours, tried to persuade
him to cut down on the murder, reserving it for the larger
towns, Dickens had a paroxysm of rage: 'Bounding up
from his chair, and throwing his knife and fork on his
plate (which he smashed to atoms), he exclaimed:
"Dolby! your infernal caution will be your ruin one of

these days!"' Immediately afterwards, he began to weep and told Dolby that he knew he was right. The doctors eventually compelled him to interrupt his tour and take a rest.

His son, Sir Henry Dickens, who speaks in his memoir of his father of the latter's 'heavy moods of deep depression, of intense nervous irritability, when he was silent and oppressed,' tells of an incident that occurred at a Christmas party the winter before Dickens died: 'He had been ailing very much and greatly troubled with his leg, which had been giving him much pain; so he was lying on a sofa one evening after dinner, while the rest of the family were playing games.' Dickens participated in one of these games, in which you had to remember long strings of words, contributed by the players in rotation. When it came around to Dickens, he gave a name which meant nothing to anybody: 'Warren's Blacking, 30, Strand.' He did this, says his son, who knew nothing at that time of this episode in his father's childhood, 'with an odd twinkle and strange inflection in his voice which at once forcibly arrested my attention and left a vivid impression on my mind for some time afterwards. Why, I could not, for the life of me, understand. . . . At that time, when the stroke that killed him was gradually overpowering him, his mind reverted to the struggles and degradation of his childhood, which had caused him such intense agony of mind, and which he had never been able entirely to cast from him.'

Two weeks before his death, he went to a dinner arranged by Lord and Lady Houghton in order that the Prince of Wales and the King of Belgium might meet him. Lady Houghton was a granddaughter of that Lord Crewe in whose house Dickens' grandfather had been butler. She well remembered going as a child to the housekeeper's room to hear his grandmother tell wonderful

stories. Dickens' neuritic foot was giving him such trouble
at this time that up till almost an hour before dinner he
could not be sure of going. He did finally decide to go; but
when he got to the Houghton house, he found that he
could not mount the stairs, and the Prince and the Belgian
king had to come down to meet him.

But now the Dickens who had been cut off from society has discarded the theme of the rebel and is carrying
the theme of the criminal, which has haunted him all his
life, to its logical development in his fiction. He is to explore the deep entanglement and conflict of the bad and
the good in one man. The subject of *Edwin Drood* is the
subject of Poe's *William Wilson,* the subject of *Dr. Jekyll
and Mr. Hyde,* the subject of *Dorian Gray.* It is also the
subject of that greater work than any of these, Doestoev-
sky's *Crime and Punishment.* Dostoevsky, who owed so
much to Dickens and who was probably influenced by the
murder in *Chuzzlewit,* had produced in 1866 a masterpiece on the theme at which Dickens is only just arriving
in 1869. Raskólnikov — *raskólnik* means dissenter — combines in his single person the two antisocial types of the
deliberate criminal and the rebel, which since Hugh in
Barnaby Rudge have always been kept distinct by Dickens. Dostoevsky, with the courage of his insight, has
studied the states of mind which are the results of a se-
cession from society: the contemptuous will to spurn and
to crush confused with the impulse toward human brotherhood, the desire to be loved twisted tragically with the
desire to destroy and to kill. But the English Dickens with
his middle-class audience would not be able to tell such a
story even if he dared to imagine it. In order to stage the
'war in the members,' he must contrive a whole machinery
of mystification: of drugs, of telepathic powers, of remote
oriental cults.

How far he has come and to how strange a goal we
recognize when we note that he has now returned to that

Rochester he so loved in his boyhood — the Rochester where he had made Mr. Pickwick put up at the Bull Inn and picnic on good wine and cold fowl out of the hampers of the Wardles' barouche. Gadshill was next door to Rochester, and the Cloisterham of the novel is Rochester; but what Dickens finds in Rochester today is the nightmare of John Jasper. There is plenty of brightness in *Edwin Drood* and something of the good things of life: Mrs. Crisparkle's jams, jellies and spices, Mr. Tartar's shipshape rooms; but this brightness has a quality new and queer. The vivid colors of *Edwin Drood* make upon us an impression more disturbing than the dustiness, the weariness, the dreariness, which set the tone for *Our Mutual Friend*. In this new novel, which is to be his last, Dickens has found a new intensity. The descriptions of Cloisterham are among the best written in all his fiction: they have a nervous concentration and economy — nervous in the old-fashioned sense — that produces a rather different effect from anything one remembers in the work of his previous phases. We are far from the prodigal improvisation of the poetical early Dickens: here every descriptive phrase is loaded with implication. It is as if Dickens' art, which in *Our Mutual Friend* had seemed to him so sorely fatigued, has now rested and found a revival. Dickens has at last here abandoned the task of analyzing society — British imperialism in the East is evidently to play some part in the story, but it is impossible to tell whether or not this is to have any moral significance. (A writer in the Princeton undergraduate publication *The Nassau Literary Magazine* of May, 1882, who complains of the little interest that has been shown in *Edwin Drood,* suggests that the opium traffic may provide the social issue here.) The novelist, as far as we can see, is at this point exclusively concerned with a psychological problem. The duality of high and low, rich and poor, has evidently here given place to the duality of good and evil.

The remarkable opening pages in which the Victorian choirmaster, with his side-whiskers and tall hat, mixes in his opium-vision the picture of the English cathedral with memories of the East and awakes in the squalid den to stagger out, short of breath, to his services, is, from the psychological point of view, for its time a complex piece of writing. But the characters that are healthy, pure and good — Rosa Budd, for example, with her baby name — seem almost as two-dimensional as colored paper dolls. We have got back to the fairy tale again. Yet this fairy tale contains no Pickwick: its most convincing figure is Jasper; and its most powerful artistic effect is procured by an instillation into the greenery, the cathedral, the winter sun, the sober and tranquil old town, of the suggestion of moral uncertainty, of evil. Even the English rooks, which in *The Old Curiosity Shop* had figured simply as a pleasant feature of the old English countryside in which Nell and her grandfather wandered, have here become the omens of a terror that comes from outside that English world. The Christmas season itself, of which Dickens had been the laureate, which he had celebrated so often with exuberant charity, hopeful prospects and hearty cheer, is now the appointed moment for the murder by an uncle of his nephew.

Mr. Jasper is, like Dickens, an artist: he is a musician, possesses an enchanting voice. He smokes opium, and so, like Dickens, leads a life of the imagination apart from that of common men. Like Dickens, he is a skilful magician, whose power over his fellows may be dangerous. Like Dickens, he is an alien from another world; yet, like Dickens he has made himself respected in the conventional English community. Is he a villain? From the point of view of the cathedral congregation of Cloisterham, who have admired his ability as an artist, he will be seen to have been playing a diabolic rôle. All that sentiment, all those edifying high spirits, which Dickens has been dispensing so long, which he is still making the effort to dispense – has all this now grown as false as those hymns to the glory of the Christian God which are performed by the worshiper of Kali? And yet in another land there exists another point of view from which Jasper is a good and faithful servant. It has been driven by his *alter ego* and acting in the name of his goddess that Jasper has committed his crime.

None the less, he is a damned soul here and now. All this bright and pious foreground of England is to open or fade away, and to show a man condemned to death. But it will not be the innocent Pickwick, the innocent Micawber, the innocent Dorrit, whom we are now to meet in jail: nor yet the wicked Fagin, the wicked Dennis, the wicked elder Rudge. It will here be a man who is both innocent and wicked. The protest against the age has turned into a protest against self. In this last moment, the old hierarchy of England does enjoy a sort of triumph over the weary and debilitated Dickens, for it has made him accept its ruling that he is a creature irretrievably tainted; and the mercantile middle-class England has had its triumph, too. For the Victorian hypocrite – developing from Pecksniff, through Murdstone, through Headstone, to his final incarnation in Jasper – has finally come to present an insoluble moral problem which is identified with Dickens' own. As Headstone makes his own knuckles bleed in striking them against the church and drowns himself in order to drown Riderhood, so Jasper is eventually to destroy himself. When he announces in the language of the Thugs that he 'devotes' himself to the 'destruction' of the murderer, he is preparing his own execution. (He is evidently quite sincere in making this entry in his diary, since he has now sobered up from the opium and resumed his official personality. It is exclusively of this personality that the diary is to be a record.) So Dickens, in putting his nerves to the torture by enacting the murder of Nancy, has actually invoked his own death.

In this last condemned cell of Dickens, the respectable half of the divided John Jasper was to be brought face to face with the other half. But this confrontation – 'difficult to work,' as Dickens had told Forster – was never, in fact, to take place. For Dickens in his moral confusion was never to dramatize himself completely, was not even in this final phase of his art to succeed in coming quite clear. He was to leave *Edwin Drood* half-finished, with the confession just around the corner.

He had put in a long day on *Drood* when (June 9, 1870) he had a stroke while he was eating dinner. He got up from the table in his stunned condition and said he must go to London; then he fell to the floor and never recovered consciousness. He died the next afternoon.

THE KIPLING THAT NOBODY READ

THE ECLIPSE of the reputation of Kipling, which began about 1910, twenty-five years before Kipling's death and when he was still only forty-five, has been of a peculiar kind. Through this period he has remained, from the point of view of sales, an immensely popular writer. The children still read his children's books; the college students still read his poetry; the men and women of his own generation still reread his early work. But he has in a sense been dropped out of modern literature. The more serious-minded young people do *not* read him; the critics do not take him into account. During the later years of his life and even at the time of his death, the logic of his artistic development attracted no intelligent attention. At a time when W. B. Yeats had outgrown his romantic youth and was receiving the reward of an augmented glory for his severer and more concentrated work, Rudyard Kipling, Yeats's coeval, who had also achieved a new concentration through the efforts of a more exacting discipline, saw the glory of his young-manhood fade away. And during the period when the late work of Henry James, who had passed into a similar eclipse, was being retrieved and appreciated, when the integrity and interest of his total achievement was finally being understood, no attempt was made, so far as I know, to take stock of Kipling's work as a whole.[1] The ordinary person said simply that Kipling

[1] Since this was written, Mr. Edward Shanks has published a book on Kipling. Mr. Shanks addresses himself to the task, but does not make very much progress with it.

was 'written out'; the reviewer rarely made any effort to trace the journey from the breeziness of the early short stories to the bitterness of the later ones. The thick, dark and surly little man who had dug himself into Bateman's, Burwash, Sussex, was left to his bristling privacy, and only occasionally evoked a rebuke for the intolerant and vindictive views which, emerging with the suddenness of a snapping turtle, he sometimes gave vent to in public.

But who *was* Kipling? What did he express? What was the history of that remarkable talent which gave him a place, as a craftsman of English prose, among the few genuine masters of his day? How was it that the art of his short stories became continually more skilful and intense, and yet that his career appears broken?

I

The publication of Kipling's posthumous memoirs — *Something of Myself for My Friends Known and Unknown* — has enabled us to see more clearly the causes for the anomalies of Kipling's career.

First of all, he was born in India, the son of an English artist and scholar, who had gone out to teach architectural sculpture at the Fine Arts School in Bombay and who afterwards became curator of the museum at Lahore. This fact is, of course, well known; but its importance must be specially emphasized. It appears that up to the age of six Kipling talked, thought and dreamed, as he says, in Hindustani, and could hardly speak English correctly. A drawing of him made by a schoolmate shows a swarthy boy with lank straight hair, who might almost pass for a Hindu.

The second important influence in Kipling's early life has not hitherto been generally known, though it figures in the first chapter of *The Light That Failed* and furnished the subject of *Baa, Baa, Black Sheep*, one of the most powerful things he ever wrote. This story had always

seemed rather unaccountably to stand apart from the rest
of Kipling's work by reason of its sympathy with the victims rather than with the inflictors of a severely repressive
discipline; and its animus is now explained by a chapter
in Kipling's autobiography and by a memoir recently published by his sister. When Rudyard Kipling was six and
his sister three and a half, they were farmed out for six
years in England with a relative of Kipling's father. John
Lockwood Kipling was the son of a Methodist minister,
and this woman was a religious domestic tyrant in the
worst English tradition of Dickens and Samuel Butler.
The boy, who had been petted and deferred to by the
native servants in India, was now beaten, bullied with the
Bible, pursued with constant suspicions and broken down
by cross-examinations. If one of the children spilled a drop
of gravy or wept over a letter from their parents in Bombay, they were forbidden to speak to one another for
twenty-four hours. Their guardian had a violent temper
and enjoyed making terrible scenes, and they had to learn
to propitiate her by fawning on her when they saw that
an outburst was imminent.

'Looking back,' says Mrs. Fleming, Kipling's sister, 'I
think the real tragedy of our early days, apart from Aunty's
bad temper and unkindness to my brother, sprang from
our inability to understand why our parents had deserted
us. We had had no preparation or explanation; it was like
a double death, or rather, like an avalanche that had swept
away everything happy and familiar. . . . We felt that
we had been deserted, "almost as much as on a doorstep,"
and what was the reason? Of course, Aunty used to say it
was because we were so tiresome, and she had taken us out
of pity, but in a desperate moment Ruddy appealed to
Uncle Harrison, and he said it was only Aunty's fun, and
Papa had left us to be taken care of, because India was too
hot for little people. But we knew better than that, because we had been to Nassick, so what was the real rea-

son? Mamma was not ill, like the seepy-weepy Ellen
Montgomery's mamma in *The Wide, Wide World*. Papa
had not had to go to war. They had not even lost their
money; if they had, we could have swept crossings or sold
flowers, and it would have been rather fun. But there was
no excuse; they had gone happily back to our own lovely
home, and had not taken us with them. They was no getting out of that, as we often said.

'Harry (Aunty's son), who had all a crow's quickness in
finding a wound to pick at, discovered our trouble and
teased us unmercifully. He assured us we had been taken
in out of charity, and must do exactly as he told us. . . .
We were just like workhouse brats, and none of our toys
really belonged to us.'

Rudyard had bad eyes, which began to give out altogether, so that he was unable to do his work at school.
One month he destroyed his report so that his guardians at
home shouldn't see it; and for punishment was made to
walk to school with a placard between his shoulders reading 'Liar.' He had finally a severe nervous breakdown, accompanied by partial blindness, and was punished by isolation from his sister. This breakdown, it is important to
note, was made horrible by hallucinations. As a mist,
which seemed to grow steadily thicker, shut him in from
the rest of the world, he would imagine that blowing curtains were specters or that a coat on a nail was an enormous black bird ready to swoop down upon him.

His mother came back at last, saw how bad things were
— when she went up to kiss him good-night, he instinc-
tively put up his hand to ward off the expected blow —
and took the children away. But the effects of those years
were lasting. Mrs. Fleming tells us that her revulsion
against Aunty's son Harry conditioned her reactions toward people who resembled him through all the rest of
her life, and says that when, thirty years later, she set out
in Southsea one day to see if the 'House of Desolation'

were still standing, her heart failed her, and she hurried back: 'I dared not face it.' Rudyard himself told her that he had had a similar experience. 'I think we both dreaded a kind of spiritual imprisonment that would affect our dreams. Less than four years ago [she is writing in 1939], I asked him whether he knew if the house still stood. "I don't know, but if so, I should like to burn it down and plough the place with salt." '

Kipling asserts that this ordeal had 'drained me of any capacity for real, personal hate for the rest of my days'; and his sister denies that it produced in him any permanent injurious effects: 'According to their gloomy theories [the theories of the psychoanalysts], my brother should have grown up morbid and misanthropic, narrow-minded, self-centered, shunning the world, and bearing it, and all men, a burning grudge; for certainly between the ages of six and eleven he was thwarted at every turn by Aunty and the odious Harry, and inhibitions were his daily bread.' Yet here is the conclusion of the story which Kipling made out of this experience: 'There! "Told you so," ' says the boy to his sister. 'It's all different now, and we see just as much of mother as if she had never gone.' But, Kipling adds: 'Not altogether, O Punch, for when young lips have drunk deep of the bitter water of Hate, Suspicion, and Despair, all the Love in the world will not wholly take away that knowledge; though it may turn darkened eyes for a while to the light, and teach Faith where no Faith was.'

And actually the whole work of Kipling's life is to be shot through with hatred.

He was next sent to a public school in England. This school, the United Services College, at a place called Westward Ho!, had been founded by Army and Navy officers who could not afford to send their sons to the more expensive schools. The four and a half years that Kipling spent there gave him *Stalky & Co.*; and the relation of the experience to the book provides an interesting psychological study. The book itself, of course, presents a hair-raising picture of the sadism of the English public-school system. The older boys have fags to wait on them, and they sometimes torment these younger boys till they have reduced them almost to imbecility; the masters are constantly caning the boys in scenes that seem almost as bloody as the floggings in old English sea stories; and the boys revenge themselves on the masters with practical jokes as catastrophic as the Whams and Zows of the comic strip.

The originals of two of Kipling's characters — Major-General L. C. Dunsterville and Mr. G. C. Beresford — have published in their later years (*Stalky's Reminiscences* and *Schooldays with Kipling*) accounts rather discrepant with one another of life at the United Services College. Mr. Beresford, who is a highbrow in *Stalky & Co.* and reads Ruskin in the midst of the mêlée, turns out to be a Nationalist Irishman, who is disgusted with his old friend's later imperialism. He insists that the fagging system did not exist at Westward Ho!; that the boys were never caned on their bare shoulders; and that Kipling, so far as he remembers, was never caned at all except by a single exceptional master. Dunsterville, on the other hand, reports that the younger boys were barbarously bullied by the older: held out of high windows by their ankles and dropped down a stair-well in 'hangings' which in one case broke the victim's leg; and that 'in addition to the blows and the kicks that inevitably accompanied the bullying,' he 'suffered a good deal from the canes of the masters, or the ground-ash sticks of the prefects. I must have been perpetually black and blue. That always sounds so dreadful. . . . But the truth of the matter is, any slight blow produces a bruise. . . . And with one or two savage exceptions, I am sure that the blows I received as a result of bullying or legitimate punishment were harmless enough.

. . .' 'Kicks and blows,' he goes on, 'I minded little, but
the moral effect was depressing. Like a hunted animal I
had to keep all my senses perpetually on the alert to escape
from the toils of the hunter — good training in a way, but
likely to injure permanently a not very robust temperament. I was robust enough, I am glad to say, and possibly
benefited by the treatment.'

Kipling was, of course, not robust; and the school evidently aggravated the injury which had been done him
during his captivity at Southsea. He admits, in *Something
of Myself*, that the fagging system was not compulsory;
but he asserts that the discipline was brutal, that the students were wretchedly fed, and that he himself, addicted
to books and too blind to participate in games, endured a
good deal of baiting. The important thing is that he suffered. If we compare the three accounts of Westward Ho!
— *Stalky & Co.* with the reminiscences of the two others —
the emphasis of Kipling's becomes plain. It is significant
that the single master whom Beresford mentions as perse-
cuting the boys should have been inquisitorial and morbidly suspicious — that is, that he should have treated Kipling in the same way that he had already been treated by
the *Baa, Baa, Black Sheep* people. And it is also significant
that this master does not figure in *Stalky & Co.*, but only
appears later in one of the more scrupulous stories which
Kipling afterward wrote about the school. The stimulus of
unjust suspicion, which did not leave any lasting bitterness with Beresford, had evidently the effect upon Kipling
of throwing him back into the state of mind which had
been created by the earlier relationship — just as the kick-
ings and canings that Dunsterville nonchalantly shook off
sunk deep into the spirit of Kipling. For a boy who has
been habitually beaten during the second six years of his
life, any subsequent physical punishment, however occa-
sional or light, may result in the reawakening of the terror
and hatred of childhood. It thrust him back into the night-

mare again, and eventually made a delirium of the memory of Westward Ho!. *Stalky & Co.* — from the artistic
point of view, certainly the worst of Kipling's books:
crude in writing, trashy in feeling, implausible in a series
of contrivances which resemble moving-picture 'gags' — is
in the nature of an hysterical outpouring of emotions kept
over from school-days, and it probably owes a part of its
popularity to the fact that it provides the young with
hilarious and violent fantasies on the theme of what they
would do to the school bully and their masters if the laws
of probability were suspended.

We shall deal presently with the social significance
which Kipling, at a later period, was to read back into
Westward Ho!. In the meantime, we must follow his adventures when he leaves it in July, 1882, not yet quite
seventeen, but remarkably mature for his age and with a
set of grown-up whiskers. He went back to his family in
India, and there he remained for seven years. The Hindu
child, who had lain dormant in England, came to life
when he reached Bombay, and he found himself reacting
to the old stimuli by beginning to talk Hindustani without understanding what he was saying. *Seven Years Hard*
is his heading for his chapter on this phase of his life. His
family — as we gather from his address on *Independence*
— were by no means well-to-do; and he started right in on
a newspaper in Lahore as sole assistant to the editor, and
worked his head off for a chief he detested. It was one of
the duties of the English journalist in India to play down
the periodical epidemics. Kipling himself survived dysen-
tery and fever, and kept on working through his severest
illnesses. One hot night in 1886, when he felt, as he says,
that he 'had come to the edge of all endurance' and had
gone home to his empty house with the sensation that
there was nothing left in him but 'the horror of a great
darkness, that I must have been fighting for some days,'
he read a novel by Walter Besant about a young man who

had wanted to be a writer and who had eventually succeeded in his aim. Kipling decided he would save some
money and get away to London. He wrote short stories
called *Plain Tales from the Hills,* which were run to fill
up space in the paper, and he brought out a book of verse.
His superiors disapproved of his flippancy, and when he
finally succeeded in leaving India, the managing director
of the paper, who had considered him overpaid, told the
young man that he could take it from him that he would
never be worth anything more than four hundred rupees
a month.

The Kipling of these early years is a lively and sympathetic figure. A newspaper man who has access to everything, the son of a scholar who has studied the natives, he
sees the community, like Asmodeus, with all the roofs removed. He is interested in the British of all classes and
ranks — the bored English ladies, the vagabond adventurers, the officers and the soldiers both. 'Having no position to consider,' he writes, 'and my trade enforcing it, I
could move at will in the fourth dimension. I came to
realize the bare horrors of the private's life, and the un-
necessary torments he endured. . . . Lord Roberts, at
that time Commander-in-chief of India, who knew my
people, was interested in the men, and — I had by then
written one or two stories about soldiers — the proudest
moment of my young life was when I rode up Simla Mall
beside him on his usual explosive red Arab, while he asked
me what the men thought about their accommodations,
entertainment-rooms, and the like. I told him, and he
thanked me as gravely as though I had been a full Colonel.' He is already tending to think about people in terms
of social and racial categories; but his interest in them at
this time is also personal: 'All the queer outside world
would drop into our workshop sooner or later ! say a Captain just cashiered for horrible drunkenness, who reported
his fall with a wry, appealing face, and then — disap-

peared. Or a man old enough to be my father, on the edge
of tears because he had been overpassed for Honors in the
Gazette. . . . One met men going up and down the lad-
der in every shape of misery and success.' And he gives us
in his soldier stories, along with the triumphs of discipline
and the exploits of the native wars, the hunger of Private
Ortheris for London when the horror of exile seizes him;
the vanities and vices of Mulvaney which prevent him
from rising in the service (*The Courting of Dinah Shadd*,
admired by Henry James, is one of the stories of Kipling
which sticks closest to unregenerate humanity); even the
lunatic obsessions and the crack-up of the rotter gentleman ranker in *Love-o'-Women*.

The natives Kipling probably understood as few Englishmen did in his time; certainly he presented them in
literature as nobody had ever done. That Hindu other self
of his childhood takes us through into its other world. The
voices of alien traditions — in the monologues of *In Black
and White* — talk an English which translates their own
idiom; and we hear of great lovers and revengers who live
by an alien code; young men who have been educated in
England and, half-dissociated from native life, find themselves impotent between two civilizations; fierce Afghan
tribesmen of the mountains, humble people who have
been broken to the mines; loyal Sikhs and untamed mu-
tineers. It is true that there is always the implication that
the British are bringing to India modern improvements
and sounder standards of behavior. But Kipling is obviously enjoying for its own sake the presentation of the
native point of view, and the whole Anglo-Indian situation is studied with a certain objectivity.

He is even able to handle without horror the mixture of
the black and the white. 'The "railway folk," ' says Mr.
E. Kay Robinson, who worked with him on the paper in
Lahore, 'that queer colony of white, half white and three-
quarters black, which remains an uncared-for and discred-

itable excrescence upon British rule in India, seemed to
have unburdened their souls to Kipling of all their grievances, their poor pride, and their hopes. Some of the best
of Kipling's work is drawn from the lives of these people;
although to the ordinary Anglo-Indian, whose social caste
restrictions are almost more inexorable than those of the
Hindu whom he affects to despise on that account, they
are as a sealed book.' And one of the most sympathetic of
these early stories — the once famous *Without Benefit of
Clergy* — is a picture of an Anglo-Indian union: an English official who lives with a Mahomedan girl. Though
Kipling deals rarely in fortunate lovers, these lovers enjoy
their happiness for a time. To their joy, the mother gives
birth to a son, who turns into a small gold-colored little
god,' and they like to sit on the roof and eat almonds and
watch the kites. But then the baby dies of the fever, and
the young wife dies of the cholera; and the husband is
called away to fight the famine and the epidemic. Even
the house where they have lived is destroyed, and the husband is glad that no one else will ever be able to live there.
This idyl, unhallowed and fleeting, is something that the
artist in Kipling has felt, and put down for its sweetness
and pathos.

Through all these years of school and of newspaper
work, with their warping and thwarting influences, Kipling worked staunchly at mastering his craft. For he had
been subjected to yet another influence which has not
been mentioned yet. His father was a painter and sculptor,
and two of his mother's sisters were married to artists —
one to Edward Poynter, the Academician, and the other
to the pre-Raphaelite, Burne-Jones. Besides India and the
United Services College, there had been the pre-Raphaelite movement. In England, Kipling's vacation had always
been spent in London with the Burne-Joneses. Mr. Beresford says that Kipling's attitude at school had been that of
the aesthete who disdains athletics and has no aptitude for

mechanical matters, that he was already preoccupied with writing, and that his literary proficiency and cultivation were amazingly developed for his age. He had had from his childhood the example of men who loved the arts for their own sake and who were particularly concerned about craftsmanship (it is also of interest that his father's family had distinguished themselves in the eighteenth century as founders of bronze bells). Kipling evidently owes his superiority as a craftsman to most of even the ablest English writers of fiction of the end of the century and the early nineteen hundreds, to this inspiration and training. Just as the ballad of *Danny Deever* derives directly from the ballad of *Sister Helen,* so the ideal of an artistic workmanship which shall revert to earlier standards of soundness has the stamp of William Morris and his circle. In 1878, when Rudyard was twelve years old, his father had taken him to the Paris Exhibition and insisted that he learn to read French. The boy had then conceived an admiration for the civilization of the French which evidently contributed later to his interest in perfecting the short story in English.

With all this, his earlier experience in the 'House of Desolation' had equipped him, he says, with a training not unsuitable for a writer of fiction, in that it had 'demanded constant wariness, the habit of observation, and attendance on moods and tempers; the noting of discrepancies between speech and action; a certain reserve of demeanor; and automatic suspicion of sudden favors.'

With such a combination of elements, what might one not expect? It is not surprising to learn that the young Kipling contemplated, after his return to England, writing a colonial *Comédie Humaine.* 'Bit by bit, my original notion,' he writes, 'grew into a vast, vague conspectus — Army and Navy List, if you like — of the whole sweep and meaning of things and efforts and origins throughout the Empire.' Henry James, who wrote an appreciative preface

for a collection of Kipling's early stories, said afterwards
that he had thought at that time that it might perhaps
be true that Kipling 'contained the seeds of an English
Balzac.'

II

What became of this English Balzac? Why did the author of the brilliant short stories never develop into an
important novelist?

Let us return to *Baa, Baa, Black Sheep* and the situation
with which it deals. Kipling says that his Burne-Jones
aunt was never able to understand why he had never told
anyone in the family about how badly he and his sister
were being treated, and he tries to explain this on the
principle that children tell little more than animals, for
what comes to them they accept as eternally established,'
and says that 'badly-treated children have a clear notion
of what they are likely to get if they betray the secrets of
a prison-house before they are clear of it.' But *is* this inevitably true? Even young children do sometimes run
away. And, in any case, Kipling's reaction to this experience seems an abnormally docile one. After all, Dickens
made David Copperfield bite Mr. Murdstone's hand and
escape; and he makes war on Mr. Murdstone through the
whole of his literary career. But though the anguish of
these years had given Kipling a certain sympathy with the
neglected and persecuted, and caused him to write this
one moving short story, it left him — whether as the result of the experience itself or because he was already
so conditioned — with a fundamental submissiveness to
authority.

Let us examine the two books in which Kipling deals,
respectively, with his schooldays and with his youth in
India: *Stalky & Co.* and *Kim*. These works are the products of the author's thirties, and *Kim*, at any rate, represents Kipling's most serious attempt to allow himself to

grow to the stature of a first-rate creative artist. Each of
these books begins with an antagonism which in the work
of a greater writer would have developed into a fundamental conflict; but in neither *Stalky* nor *Kim* is the conflict ever permitted to mount to a real crisis. Nor can it
even be said to be resolved: it simply ceases to figure as
a conflict. In *Stalky*, we are at first made to sympathize
with the baiting of the masters by the schoolboys as their
rebellion against a system which is an offense against human dignity; but then we are immediately shown that all
the ragging and flogging are justified by their usefulness
as a training for the military caste which is to govern the
British Empire. The boys are finally made to recognize
that their headmaster not only knows how to dish it out
but is also able to take it, and the book culminates in the
ridiculous scene — which may perhaps have its foundation
in fact but is certainly flushed by a hectic imagination —
in which the Head, in the inflexible justice, undertakes
personally to cane the whole school while the boys stand
by cheering him wildly.

There is a real subject in *Stalky & Co.*, but Kipling has
not had the intelligence to deal with it. He cannot see
around his characters and criticize them, he is not even
able properly to dramatize; he simply allows the emotions
of the weaker side, the side that is getting the worst of it,
to go over to the side of the stronger. You can watch the
process all too clearly in the episode in which Stalky and
his companions turn the tables on the cads from the
crammers' school. These cads have been maltreating a fag,
and a clergyman who is represented by Kipling as one of
the more sensible and decent of the masters suggests to
Stalky & Co. that they teach the bullies a lesson. The former proceed to clean up on the latter in a scene which
goes on for pages, to the reckless violation of proportion
and taste. The oppressors, true enough, are taught a lesson, but the cruelty with which we have already been

made disgusted has now passed over to the castigators' side, and there is a disagreeable implication that, though it is caddish for the cads to be cruel, it is all right for the sons of English gentlemen to be cruel to the cads.

Kim is more ambitious and much better. It is Kipling's only successful long story: an enchanting, almost a first-rate book, the work in which more perhaps than in any other he gave the sympathies of the imagination free rein to remember and to explore, and which has in consequence more complexity and density than any of his other works. Yet the conflict from which the interest arises, though it is very much better presented, here also comes to nothing: the two forces never really engage. Kim is the son of an Irish soldier and an Irish nursemaid, who has grown up as an orphan in India, immersed in and assimilated to the native life, so that he thinks, like the young Kipling, in Hindustani. The story deals with the gradual dawning of his consciousness that he is really a Sahib. As a child he has been in the habit of making a little money by carrying messages for a native agent of the British secret service, and the boy turns out to be so bright and so adept at acting the rôle of a native that the authorities decide to train him. He is sent to an English school but does not willingly submit to the English system. Every vacation he dresses as a native and disappears into the sea of native life. The Ideal of this side of his existence is represented by a Thibetan lama, a wandering Buddhist pilgrim, whom he accompanies in the character of a disciple.

Now what the reader tends to expect is that Kim will come eventually to realize that he is delivering into bondage to the British invaders those whom he has always considered his own people, and that a struggle between allegiances will result. Kipling has established for the reader — and established with considerable dramatic effect — the contrast between the East, with its mysticism and its sensuality, its extremes of saintliness and roguery, and the English, with their superior organization, their confidence in modern method, their instinct to brush away like cobwebs the native myths and beliefs. We have been shown two entirely different worlds existing side by side, with neither really understanding the other, and we have watched the oscillations of Kim, as he passes to and fro between them. But the parallel lines never meet; the alternating attractions felt by Kim never give rise to a genuine struggle. And the climax itself is double: the adventures of the Lama and of Kim simply arrive at different consummations, without any final victory or synthesis ever being allowed to take place. Instead, there are a pair of victories, which occur on separate planes and do not influence one another: the Lama attains to a condition of trance which releases him from what the Buddhists call the Wheel of Things at the same moment that the young Anglo-Indian achieves promotion in the British secret service.

The salvation of the Lama has been earned by penitence for a moment of passion: he had been tempted to kill a man who had torn his sacred chart and struck him, a Russian agent working against the British. But the pretenses of Kim to a spiritual vocation, whatever spell has been exerted over him by the Lama, are dispelled when the moment for action comes, when the Irishman is challenged to a fight: Kim knocks the Russian down and bangs his head against a boulder. 'I am Kim. I am Kim. And what is Kim?' his soul repeats again and again, in his exhaustion and collapse after this episode. He feels that his soul is 'out of gear with its surroundings — a cog-wheel unconnected with any machinery, just like the idle cogwheel of a cheap Beheea sugar-crusher laid by in a corner.' But he now gets this unattached soul to find a function in the working of the crusher — note the mechanical metaphor: dissociating himself from the hierarchy represented by the Abbot-Lama, he commits himself to a rôle in the hierarchy of a practical organization. (So the wolf-reared Mowgli of the *Jungle Books,* the prototype of Kim, ends up rather flatly as a ranger in the British Forestry Service.) Nor does Kipling allow himself to doubt that his hero has chosen the better part. Kim must now exploit his knowledge of native life for the purpose of preventing and putting down any native resistance to the British; but it never seems to occur to his creator that this constitutes a betrayal of the Lama. A sympathy with the weaker party in a relationship based on force has again given way without a qualm to a glorification of the stronger. As the bullying masters of *Stalky & Co.* turn into beneficent Chirons, so even the overbearing officer who figures on his first appearance in *Kim* as a symbol of British stupidity turns out to be none other than Strickland, the wily police superintendent, who has here been acting a part. (It should also be noted that the question of whether or not Kim shall allow himself to sleep with a native woman has here become very important, and that his final emergence as a Sahib is partly determined by his decision in the negative. This is no longer the Kipling of *Without Benefit of Clergy.*)

The Lama's victory is not of this world: the sacred river for which he has been seeking, and which he identifies in his final revelation with a brook near which his trance has occurred, has no objective existence, it is not on the British maps. Yet the anguish of the Lama's repentance — a scene, so far as I remember, elsewhere unmatched in Kipling — is one of the most effective things in the book; and we are to meet this Lama again in strange and unexpected forms still haunting that practical world which Kipling, like Kim, has chosen. The great eulogist of the builder and the man of action was no more able to leave the Lama behind than Kim had been able to reconcile himself to playing the game of English life without him.

III

The fiction of Kipling, then, does not dramatize any fundamental conflict because Kipling would never face one. This is probably one of the causes of his lack of success with long novels. You can make an effective short story, as Kipling so often does, about somebody's scoring off somebody else; but this is not enough for a great novelist, who must show us large social forces, or uncontrollable lines of destiny, or antagonistic impulses of the human spirit, struggling with one another. With Kipling, the right and the wrong of any opposition of forces is usually quite plain at the start; and there is not even the suspense which makes possible the excitement of melodrama. There is never any doubt as to the outcome. The Wrong is made a guy from the beginning, and the high point of the story comes when the Right gives it a kick in the pants. Where both sides are sympathetically presented, the battle is not allowed to occur.

But this only drives us back on another question: how was it that the early Kipling, with his sensitive understanding of the mixed population of India, became transformed into the later Kipling, who consolidated and codified his snobberies instead of progressively eliminating them as most good artists do, and who, like Kim, elected as his lifework the defense of the British Empire? The two books we have been discussing indicate the end of a period in the course of which Kipling had arrived at a decision. *Stalky* came out in 1899, and *Kim* in 1901. The decade of the nineties had been critical for Kipling; and in order to understand the new phase of his work which had begun by the beginning of the century, we must follow his adventures in the United States, which he visited in 1889, where he lived from 1892 to 1896, and to which he tried to return in 1899. Kipling's relations with America are certainly the most important factor in his experience during these years of his later twenties and early thirties; yet they are the link which has been dropped out of his story in most of the accounts of his life and which even his posthumous memoirs, revelatory in respect to his earlier years, markedly fail to supply.

The young man who arrived in London in the fall of 1889 was very far from being the truculent British patriot whom we knew in the nineteen hundreds. He had not even gone straight back to England, but had first taken a trip around the world, visiting Canada and the United States. Nor did he remain long in the mother-country when he got there. His whole attitude was that of the colonial who has sweated and suffered at the outposts of Empire, making the acquaintance of more creeds and customs than the philosophy of London dreamt of, and who feels a slight touch of scorn toward the smugness of the people at home, unaware of how big, varied and active the world around them is. His 'original notion,' he says, had been to try 'to tell the Empire something of the world outside England — not directly but by implication': 'What can they know of England who only England know?' He rounded out his knowledge of the colonies by traveling in New Zealand, Australia, South Africa and Southern India. In the January of 1892, he married an American wife.

Kipling's experience of the United States was in certain ways like that of Dickens. Neither of them fitted very well into the English system at home, and both seem to have been seeking in the new English-speaking nation a place where they could be more at ease. Both winced at the crudeness of the West; both were contemptuously shocked by the boasting — the Pacific Coast in Kipling's day was what the Mississippi had been in Dickens'. Both, escaping from the chilliness of England, resented the familiarity of the States. Yet Kipling, on the occasion of his first visit, which he records in *From Sea to Sea,* is obviously rejoiced by the naturalness of social relations in America. He tells of 'a very trim maiden' from New Hampshire, with 'a delightful mother and an equally delightful father, a heavy-eyed, slow-voiced man of finance,' whom he met in the Yellowstone. 'Now an English maiden who had stumbled on a dust-grimed, lime-washed, sun-peeled collarless wanderer come from and going to goodness knows where, would, her mother inciting her and her father brandishing his umbrella, have regarded him as a dissolute adventurer. Not so those delightful people from New Hampshire. They were good enough to treat me — it sounds almost incredible — as a human being, possibly respectable, probably not in immediate need of financial assistance. Papa talked pleasantly and to the point. The little maiden strove valiantly with the accent of her birth and that of her reading, and mamma smiled benignly in the background. Balance this with a story of a young English idiot I met knocking about inside his high collars, attended by a valet. He condescended to tell me that "you can't be too careful who you talk to in these parts," and stalked on, fearing, I suppose, every minute for his social chastity. Now that man was a barbarian (I took occasion to tell him so), for he comported himself after the manner of the headhunters of Assam, who are at perpetual feud one with another.'

He declares his faith in the Americans in a conversation with an Englishman 'who laughed at them.' ' "I admit everything," said I. "Their Government's provisional; their law's the notion of the moment; their railways are made of hairpins and matchsticks, and most of their good luck lives in their woods and mines and rivers and not in their brains; but, for all that, they be the biggest, finest, and best people on the surface of the globe! Just you wait a hundred years and see how they'll behave when they've had the screw put on them and have forgotten a few of the patriarchal teachings of the late Mr. George Washington. Wait till the Anglo-American-German-Jew — the Man of the Future — is properly equipped. He'll have just the least little kink in his hair now and again; he'll carry the English lungs above the Teuton feet that can walk forever; and he will wave long, thin, bony Yankee hands with the big blue veins on the wrist, from one end of the earth to the other. He'll be the finest writer, poet, and dramatist, 'specially dramatist, that the world as it recollects itself has ever seen. By virtue of his Jew blood — just a little, little drop — he'll be a musician and a painter, too. At present there is too much balcony and too little Romeo in the life-plays of his fellow-citizens. Later on, when the proportion is adjusted and he sees the possibilities of his land, he will produce things that will make the effete East stare. He will also be a complex and highly composite administrator. There is nothing known to man that he will not be, and his country will sway the world with one foot as a man tilts a see-saw plank!"

' "But this is worse than the Eagle at its worst. Do you seriously believe all that?" said the Englishman.

' "If I believe anything seriously, all this I most firmly believe. You wait and see. Sixty million people, chiefly of English instincts, who are trained from youth to believe that nothing is impossible, don't slink through the centuries like Russian peasantry. They are bound to leave their mark somewhere, and don't you forget it." '

'I love this People . . .' he wrote. 'My heart has gone out to them beyond all other peoples.' And he reiterated his faith, in the poem called *An American*, in which 'The American spirit speaks':

> Enslaved, illogical, elate,
>   He greets th' embarrassed Gods, nor fears
> To shake the iron hand of Fate
>   Or match with Destiny for beers.

So, imperturbable he rules,
  Unkempt, disreputable, vast —
And, in the teeth of all the schools,
  I — I shall save him at the last!

Kipling took his wife to America, and they lived for a time on the estate of her family in Brattleboro, Vermont; then Kipling built a large house: his books were already making him rich. They lived in the United States four years; two daughters were born to them there. Kipling was ready to embrace America, or those aspects of America which excited him; he began using American subjects for his stories: the railroads in .007, the Gloucester fishermen in *Captains Courageous.* He enormously admired Mark Twain, whose acquaintance he had made on his first visit. Yet the effect of contact with the United States was eventually to drive Kipling, as it had Dickens, back behind his British defenses. A disagreeable episode occurred which, undignified and even comic though it seems, is worth studying because it provided the real test of Kipling's fitness to flourish in America, and not merely the test of this, but, at a critical time in his life, of the basic courage and humanity of his character.

The story has been told since Kipling's death in a book called *Rudyard Kipling's Vermont Feud* by Mr. Frederick F. Van de Water. A brother of Mrs. Kipling's, Kipling's friend Wolcott Balestier, had been in the publishing business with Heinemann in London, and Mrs. Kipling had lived much in England and was by way of being an Anglophile. Thus the impulse on Kipling's part to assimilate himself to the Americans was neutralized in some degree by Mrs. Kipling's desire to be English. Kipling, who was accustomed to India, had his own instinctive rudeness. In Vermont, he and Mrs. Kipling tended to stick to the attitudes of the traditional governing-class English maintaining their caste in the colonies: they drove a tandem with a tophatted English coachman, dressed every night for dinner, kept their New England neighbors at a distance.

But Mrs. Kipling had a farmer brother who — the family were partly French — was as Americanized as possible. He was a drinker, a spendthrift and a great local card, famous alike for his ribaldry, his sleigh-racing and his gestures of generosity of a magnificence almost feudal. Mr. Van de Water tells us that, at the time he knew Beatty Balestier, he had the swagger of Cyrano de Bergerac and a leathery face like 'an ailing eagle.' His farm and family suffered. The Kiplings lent him money, and he is said to have paid it back; but they disapproved of his disorderly existence. They seem to have persisted in treating him with some lack of consideration or tact. Beatty was, in any case, the kind of man — unbalanced in character but independent in spirit — who is embittered by obligations and furiously resents interference. Kipling went to Beatty one day and offered to support his wife and child for a year if Beatty would leave town and get a job. He was surprised at the explosion he provoked. This was followed by a dispute about some land across the road from the Kiplings' house. The land belonged to Beatty and he sold it for a dollar to the Kiplings, who were afraid that someone would some day build on it — on the friendly understanding, as he claimed, that he could continue to use it for mowing. When the transfer had been effected, Mrs. Kipling set out to landscape-garden it. The result was that Beatty stopped speaking to them and refused to receive Kipling when he came to call.

This went on for about a year, at the end of which a crisis occurred. Kipling was indiscreet enough to remark to one of the neighbors that he had had 'to carry Beatty for the last year — to hold him up by the seat of his breeches.' This soon reached his brother-in-law's ears. One day Beatty, driving his team and drunk, met Kipling rid-

ing his bicycle. He blocked the road, making Kipling fall
off, and shouted angrily: 'See here! I want to talk to you!'
Kipling answered, 'If you have anything to say, say it to
my lawyers.' 'By Jesus, this is no case for lawyers!' retorted
Beatty, loosing a tirade of profanity and abuse. He threatened Kipling, according to Kipling, to kill him; according
to Beatty, merely to beat him up if he did not make a public retraction.

Kipling had always deplored the lawlessness of America; in his account of his first trip through the West, his
disgust and trepidation over the shootings of the frontier
are expressed in almost every chapter. And he now became seriously alarmed. He proceeded to have Beatty arrested on charges of 'assault with indecent and opprobri-
ous names and epithets and threatening to kill.' He did
not realize that that kind of thing was not done in the
United States, where such quarrels were settled man to
man, and he could not foresee the consequences. Beatty,
who loved scandal, was delighted. He allowed the case to
come into court and watched Kipling, who hated publicity, make himself ridiculous in public. The Kiplings at
last fled abroad – it was August, 1896 – before the case
could come before the Grand Jury.

'So far as I was concerned,' says Kipling of his relations
with Americans in general, 'I felt the atmosphere was to
some extent hostile.' It was a moment of antagonism to
ward England. In the summer of 1895, Venezuela had
appealed to the United States for protection against the
English in a dispute over the boundaries of British Gui-
ana, and President Cleveland had invoked the Monroe
Doctrine and demanded in strong language that England
submit the question to arbitration. The Jameson raid on
the Transvaal Republic early in 1896, an unauthorized
and defeated attempt by an agent of the British South
Africa Company to provoke a rising against the Boers,
had intensified the feeling against England. Kipling was

brought face to face with the issue by an encounter with another American who seemed almost as unrestrained as Beatty Balestier. When Kipling met Theodore Roosevelt, then Assistant Secretary of the Navy, the latter 'thanked God in a loud voice that he had not one drop of British blood in him,' that his ancestry was pure Dutch, and declared that American fear of the British would provide him with funds for a new navy. John Hay had told Kipling that it was hatred of the English that held the United States together.

But during the years that immediately followed the Kiplings' return to England, American relations with England improved. The United States took over the Philippines in 1898 as a result of the Spanish War, and annexed the Hawaiian Islands; and the imperialistic England of Joseph Chamberlain, in fear of Germany, which had favored the Spanish, became extremely sympathetic with the policy of the United States. At the beginning of 1899, then, Rudyard Kipling set forth on an attempt to retrieve his position in America, where he had abandoned the big Brattleboro house. He first composed the celebrated set of verses in which he exhorted the United States to collaborate with the British Empire in 'taking up the White Man's burden' of 'your new-caught, sullen peoples, half-devil and half-child,' who were to be benefited and disciplined in spite of themselves, though at a bitter expense to their captors; and had the poem published on both sides of the Atlantic early in February, at the moment of his sailing for America. But what confronted him on his landing was an announcement in the New York papers that Beatty Balestier was bringing a $50,000 countersuit against him for 'malicious persecution, false arrest and defamation of character'; and the report that Beatty himself either had arrived in New York or was just about to arrive. It was simply another of Beatty's gestures: no suit

was ever brought; but it prevented the Kiplings from returning to Vermont. Rudyard had caught cold on the
boat, and he now came down with double pneumonia and
seemed in danger of not pulling through. His two little
girls had pneumonia, too, and one of them died while he
was ill. When he recovered, he had to hear of her death.
He went back to England in June, as soon as he was able
to travel, and never tried to live in the United States
again.

'It will be long and long,' he wrote in a letter supposed
to date from 1900, 'before I could bring myself to look at
the land of which she [his daughter] was so much a part.'
And his cousin Angela Thirkell writes that, 'Much of the
beloved Cousin Ruddy of our childhood died with Jose-
phine and I feel that I have never seen him as a real person since that year.'

The fear and hatred awakened in Kipling by those fatal
six years of his childhood had been revived by the discipline of Westward Ho! The menaces of Beatty Balestier,
behind which must have loomed for Kipling all that was
wild, uncontrollable, brutal in the life of the United
States, seem to have prodded again the old inflammation.
The schoolboy, rendered helpless in a fight by his bad eyes
and his small stature, was up against the bully again, and
fear drove him to appeal to the authorities. How else can
we account for the fact that the relations of Kipling with
Beatty were ever allowed to get to this point? The truth
was, as Beatty himself later confessed to Mr. Van de
Water, that Rudyard had become involved in a family
quarrel between himself and his sister; and one's impulse
is to say that Kipling ought to have been able to find some
way of extricating himself and making contact with the
rather childlike friendliness that seems to have lurked behind the rodomontade of Beatty. But the terrible seriousness of the issue which the incident had raised for Kipling

is shown by his statement at the hearing that he 'would
not retract a word under threat of death from any living
man.'

It was the fight he had fought at school, and he would
not capitulate to Beatty Balestier. But he surrendered at
last to the 'Proosian Bates.' He invoked the protection of
the British system and at the same time prostrated himself
before the power of British conquest, which was feared in
the United States and which even at that moment in
South Africa — the Transvaal Republic declared war on
Great Britain in the October of the year of his return —
was chastising truculent farmers.

It is at the time of his first flight from America and
during the years before his attempt to return — 1897-99 —
that Kipling goes back to his school-days and depicts them
in the peculiar colors that we find in *Stalky & Co.* How
little inevitable these colors were we learn from Mr. Beresford's memoir. The head master of Westward Ho!, it appears, though really known as the 'Proosian Bates,' was by
no means the intent Spartan trainer for the bloody and
risky work of the Empire into which Kipling thought it
proper to transform him. The fact was that Mr. Cormell
Price had been literary rather than military, a friend of
Edward Burne-Jones and an earnest anti-Imperialist. He
and Burne-Jones had actually organized, at the time of the
Russo-Turkish War, a Workers' Neutrality Demonstration against British intervention. But Kipling must now
have a head master who will symbolize all the authority of
the British educational system, and a school that will represent all that he has heard or imagined — see his high-
lighting of the fagging system — about the older and more
official public schools. The colonial who has criticized the
motherland now sets out systematically to glorify her; and

it is the proof of his timidity and weakness that he should loudly overdo this glorification.

And now, having declared his allegiance, he is free to hate the enemies of England. His whole point of view has shifted. The bitter animus so deeply implanted by those six years of oppression of his childhood has now become almost entirely dissociated from the objects by which it was originally aroused. It has turned into a generalized hatred of those nations, groups and tendencies, precisely, which stand toward the dominating authority in the relationship of challengers or victims.

The ideal of the 'Anglo-American-German Jew,' which at the time of Kipling's first trip to America represented for him the future of civilization, now immediately goes by the board. His whole tone toward the Americans changes. In *An Error in the Fourth Dimension* – in *The Day's Work,* published in 1898 – he makes a rich Anglicized American, the son of a railroad king, deciding for no very good reason that he must immediately go to London, flag and stop an English express train. The railroad first brings charges against him, then decides that he must be insane. They cannot understand his temerity, and he cannot understand their consternation at having the British routine interrupted. Kipling no longer admires the boldness of Americans: this story is a hateful caricature, so one-sided that the real comedy is sacrificed. *The Captive* followed in 1902. Here a man from Ohio named Laughton O. Zigler sells to the Boers, during their war with the British, a new explosive and a new machine-gun he has invented. He is captured by the English, who grin at him and ask him why he 'wasn't in the Filipeens suppressing our war!' Later he runs into a man from Kentucky, who refuses to shake his hand and tells him that 'he's gone back on the White Man in six places at once – two hemispheres and four continents – America, England, Canada,

Australia, New Zealand, and South Africa. . . . Go on
and prosper . . . and you'll fetch up by fighting for nig-
gers, as the North did.' As a result of these taunts, and of
the respect which has been inspired in him by the spectacle of the splendid behavior of the British, Mr. Zigler
gives them the formula for his explosive, insists upon remaining their prisoner, and resolves to settle permanently
in South Africa. A still later story, *An Habitation En-
forced,* in a collection published in 1909, tells of the victory of the English countryside over an American business
man and his wife, who have been aimlessly traveling
about Europe. The American wife discovers that her own
ancestors came originally from the very locality where
they have settled, and they are finally — it is the climax of
the story — accepted by the English: 'That wretched San-
gres man has twice our money. Can you see Marm Conant
slapping him between the shoulders? Not by a jugful! The
poor beast doesn't exist!' The Americans succumb, deeply
gratified. The husband had had a breakdown from over-
work, but his equanimity is quite re-established. In short,
Kipling's attitude toward Americans has now been almost
reversed since the day of his first visit to the States when
he had written, 'I love this People.' He now approves of
them only when they are prepared to pay their tribute to
Mother England and to identify her interests with theirs.

Later still, during the first years of the World War
when Americans were figuring as neutrals, his bitterness
became absolutely murderous — as in *Sea Constables: A
Tale of '15.* And so had his feeling against the Germans
even before the war had begun. In *The Edge of the Evening* (1913), Laughton O. Zigler of Ohio turns up again,
this time in England, as occupant of a Georgian mansion
inherited by one of the British officers who captured him
in South Africa. 'Bein' rich suits me. So does your country, sir. My own country? You heard what that Detroit
man said at dinner. "A government of the alien, by the

alien, for the alien." Mother's right, too. Lincoln killed us.
From the highest motives – but he killed us.' What his
mother had said was that Lincoln had 'wasted the heritage
of his land by blood and fire, and had surrendered the
remnant to aliens': ' "My brother, suh," she said, "fell at
Gettysburg in order that Armenians should colonize New
England today." ' (*Something of Myself* confirms the assumption that these were Kipling's own views.) One
night a foreign plane makes a forced landing on the estate. Two men get out of the plane, and one of them
shoots at his lordship. Zigler lays him out with a golf-club
while another of the Englishmen present collars the other
man and breaks his neck (it is all right for an American
to be lawless, or even for the right sort of Englishman, if
he is merely laying low the alien who is the natural enemy of both). They put the dead German spies in the
plane and send it up and out over the Channel.

Kipling is now, in fact, implacably opposed to every
race and nation which has rebelled against or competed
with the Empire, and to every movement and individual
– such as the liberals and Fabians – in England who has
criticized the imperial policies. His attitude toward the
Irish, for example, illustrates the same simple-minded principle as his attitude toward the Americans. So long as the
Irish are loyal to England, Kipling shows the liveliest ap-
preciation of Irish recklessness and the Irish sense of mischief: Mulvaney is Irish, McTurk is Irish, Kim is Irish.
But the moment they display these same qualities in agitation against the English, they become infamous assassins
and traitors. Those peoples who have never given trouble
– the Canadians, the New Zealanders, the Australians –
though Kipling has never found them interesting enough
to write about on any considerable scale, he credits with
the most admirable virtues.

And as a basis for all these exclusions, he has laid down
a more fundamental principle for the hatred and fear of

his fellows: the anti-democratic principle. We are familiar with the case of the gifted man who has found himself at a disadvantage in relation to his social superiors and who makes himself the champion of all who have suffered in a similar way. What is not so familiar is the inverse of this: the case of the individual who at the period when he has most needed freedom to develop superior abilities has found himself cramped and tormented by the stupidity of social inferiors, and who has in consequence acquired a distrust of the whole idea of popular government. Rudyard Kipling was probably an example of this. The ferocious antagonism to democracy which finally overtakes him must have been fed by the fear of that household at Southsea which tried to choke his genius at its birth. His sister says that through all this period he was in the habit of keeping up their spirit by reminding himself and her that their guardian was 'of such low caste as not to matter . . . She was a *Kuch-nay*, a Nothing-at-all, and that secret name was a great comfort to us, and useful, too, when Harry practised his talent for eavesdropping.' Some very unyielding resistance was evidently built up at this time against the standards and opinions of people whom he regarded as lower-class.

The volume called *Traffics and Discoveries*, published in 1904, marks the complete metamorphosis of Kipling. The collection that preceded, *The Day's Work*, though these tendencies had already begun to appear in it, still preserves certain human values: the English officials in the Indian stories — *The Tomb of His Ancestors* and *William the Conqueror* — still display some sympathetic interest in the natives. But the Kipling of the South African stories is venomous, morbid, distorted.

When the Boer War finally breaks, Kipling is at once on the spot, with almost all the correct reactions. He is now at the zenith of his reputation, and he receives every official courtesy. And though he may criticize the handling of a campaign, he never questions the rightness of its object. He has the impulse to get close to the troops, edits a paper for the soldiers; but his attitude toward the Tommy has changed. He had already been entertained and enlightened by Lord Dufferin, the British Viceroy in India. Hitherto, he tells us in his memoirs, he 'had seen the administrative machinery from beneath, all stripped and overheated. This was the first time I had listened to one who had handled it from above.' Another passage from *Something of Myself* shows how his emphasis has altered: 'I happened to fall unreservedly, in darkness, over a man near the train, and filled my palms with gravel. He explained in an even voice that he was "fractured 'ip, sir. 'Ope you ain't 'urt yourself, sir?" I never got at this unknown Philip Sidney's name. They were wonderful even in the hour of death — these men and boys — lodgekeepers and ex-butlers of the Reserve and raw town-lads of twenty.' Here he is trying to pay a tribute; yet it is obvious that the Kipling who was proud to be questioned in India by Lord Roberts as if he were a colonel has triumphed over the Kipling who answered him as a spokesman for the unfortunate soldiers. Today he is becoming primarily a man whom a soldier addresses as 'sir,' as a soldier is becoming for Kipling a man whose capacity for heroism is indicated by remaining respectful with a fractured hip. The cockney Ortheris of *Soldiers Three* and the officer who had insulted him at drill had waived the Courts Martial manual and fought it out man to man; but by the time of the Boer War the virtue of Kipling's officers and soldiers consists primarily in knowing their stations.

Kipling had written at the beginning of the war, a poem called *The Absent-Minded Beggar,* which was an appeal for contributions to a fund for the families of the troops in South Africa; but this poem is essentially a money-raising poem: it had nothing like the spontaneous feeling of,

I went into a public-'ouse to get a pint o' beer;
The publican 'e up an' sez, 'We serve no red-coats here.'

The Barrack-Room Ballads were good in their kind: they gave the Tommy a voice, to which people stopped and listened. Kipling was interested in the soldier for his own sake, and made some effort to present his life as it seemed to the soldier himself. The poem called *Loot,* for example, which worries Mr. Edward Shanks because it appears to celebrate a reprehensible practice, is in reality perfectly legitimate because it simply describes one of the features of the soldier's experience in India. There is no moral one way or the other. The ballads of *The Five Nations,* on the other hand, the fruits of Kipling's experience in South Africa, are about ninety per cent mere rhymed journalism, decorating the readymade morality of a patriotic partisan. Compare one of the most successful of the earlier series with one of the most ambitious of the later.

> The Injian Ocean sets an' smiles
>   So sof', so bright, so bloomin' blue;
> There aren't a wave for miles an' miles
>   Excep' the jiggle from the screw:
> The ship is swep', the day is done,
>   The bugle's gone for smoke and play;
> An' black agin' the settin' sun
>   The Lascar sings, *'Hum deckty hai!'*
>
> *For to admire an' for to see,*
>   *For to be'old this world so wide —*
> *It never done no good to me,*
>   *But I can't drop it if I tried!*

Contrast this with *The Return* (from South Africa)

> Peace is declared, an' I return
>   To 'Ackneystadt, but not the same;

Things 'ave transpired which made me learn
   The size and meanin' of the game.
I did no more than others did,
   I don't know where the change began;
I started as an average kid,
   I finished as a thinkin' man.

If England was what England seems
   An' not the England of our dreams,
But only putty, brass an' paint,
   'Ow quick we'd drop 'er! But she ain't!

Before my gappin' mouth could speak
   I 'eard it in my comrade's tone;
I saw it on my neighbor's cheek
   Before I felt it flush my own.
An' last it come to me — not pride,
   Nor yet conceit, but on the 'ole
(If such a term may be applied),
   The makin's of a bloomin' soul.

This is hollow, synthetic, sickening. *'Having no position to consider and my trade enforcing it, I could move at will in the fourth dimension.'* He *has* a position to consider today, he eats at the captain's table, travels in special trains; and he is losing the freedom of that fourth dimension. There is a significant glimpse of the Kipling of the South African imperialist period in the diary of Arnold Bennett: 'I was responding to Pauline Smith's curiosity about the personalities of authors when Mrs. Smith began to talk about Kipling. She said he was greatly disliked in South Africa. Regarded as conceited and unapproachable. The officers of the Union Castle ships dreaded him, and prayed not to find themselves on the same ship as him. It seems that on one ship he had got all the information possible out of the officers, and had then, at the end of the voyage, reported them at headquarters for flirting with passengers — all except the chief engineer, an old Scotchman with whom he had been friendly. With this exception they were all called up to headquarters and reprimanded, and now they would have nothing to do with passengers.'

As for the Indians, they are now to be judged rigorously on the basis of their loyalty to the English in Africa. There are included in *Traffics and Discoveries* two jingoistic Sunday School stories which are certainly among the falsest and most foolish of Kipling's mature productions. In *The Comprehension of Private Copper,* he vents his contempt on an Anglicized Indian, the son of a settler in the Transvaal, who has sided with the Boers against the English; *A Sahibs' War,* on the other hand, presents an exemplary Sikh, who accompanies a British officer to South Africa, serves him with the devotion of a dog, and continues to practice after his leader's death the public-school principles of sportsmanship he has learned from him, in the face of the temptation to a cruel revenge against the treachery of the Boers. As for the Boers themselves, Kipling adopts toward them a systematic sneer. The assumption appears to be that to ambush the British is not cricket. Though the Dutch are unquestionably white men, Kipling manages somehow to imply that they have proved renegades to white solidarity by allying themselves with the black natives.

One is surprised to learn from *Something of Myself* that over a period of seven years after the war (1900-07), Kipling spent almost half his time in South Africa, going there for five or six months of every year. He seems to have so little to show for it: a few short stories, and most of these far from his best. He had made the acquaintance of Cecil Rhodes, and must simply have sat at his feet. The Kiplings lived in a house just off the Rhodes estate; and Kipling devotes long pages to the animals in Rhodes's private zoo and to architectural details of Rhodes's houses.

Even writing in 1935, he sounds like nothing so much as a high-paid publicity agent. It turns out that the Polonius-precepts in the celebrated verses called *If* —— were inspired by Kipling's conception of the character of Dr. Jameson, the leader of the Jameson raid.

It may be worth mentioning here in connection with Kipling's submission to official authority that he has been described by a close friend, Viscount Castlerosse, as having abdicated his authority also in other important relations. 'They [the Kiplings],' he says, 'were among the few happy pairs I have ever met; but as far as Kipling was concerned, his married life was one of complete surrender. To him Carrie, as he called her, was more than a wife. She was a mistress in the literal sense, a governess and a matron. In a lesser woman I should have used the term "nurse." Kipling handed himself over bodily, financially and spiritually to his spouse. He had no banking account. All the money which he earned was handed over to her, and she, in turn, would dole him out so much pocket money. He could not call his time or even his stomach his own. . . .

'Sometimes in the evening, enlivened by wine and company, he would take a glass more than he was accustomed to, and then those great big eyes of his would shine brightly behind his strong spectacles, and Rud would take to talking faster and his views would become even more emphatic. If Mrs. Kipling was with him, she would quickly note the change and, sure enough, in a decisive voice she would issue the word of command: "Rud, it is time you went to bed," and Rud always discovered that it was about time he went to bed.

'I myself during the long years never once saw any signs of murmuring or of even incipient mutiny.'

In any case, Kipling has committed one of the most serious sins against his calling which are possible for an imaginative writer. He has resisted his own sense of life and discarded his own moral intelligence in favor of the point of view of a dominant political party. To Lord Roberts and Joseph Chamberlain he has sacrificed the living world of his own earlier artistic creations and of the heterogeneous human beings for whom they were offered as symbols. Here the constraint of making the correct pro-imperialist point is squeezing out all the kind of interest which is proper to a work of fiction. Compare a story of the middle Kipling with a story of Stephen Crane or Joseph Conrad, who were dealing with somewhat similar subjects. Both Conrad and Crane are pursuing their independent researches into the moral life of man. Where the spy who is the hero of *Under Western Eyes* is a tormented and touching figure, confused in his allegiances by the circumstances of his birth, a secret agent in Kipling must invariably be either a stout fellow, because his ruses are to the advantage of the British, or a sinister lying dog, because he is serving the enemy. Where the killing of *The Blue Hotel* is made to implicate everybody connected with it in a common human guilt, a killing in a story by Kipling must absolutely be shown to be either a dastardly or a virtuous act.

To contrast Kipling with Conrad or Crane is to enable us to get down at last to what is probably the basic explanation of the failure of Kipling's nerve. He lacked faith in the artist's vocation. We have heard a good deal in modern literature about the artist in conflict with the bourgeois world. Flaubert made war on the bourgeois; Rimbaud abandoned poetry as piffling in order to realize the adventure of commerce; Thomas Mann took as his theme the emotions of weakness and defeat of the artist overshadowed by the business man. But Kipling neither faced the fight like Flaubert, nor faced the problem in his life like Rimbaud, nor faced the problem in his art like Mann. Something in him, something vulgar in the middle-class British way, something perhaps connected with the Methodist ministers who were his grandfathers on both sides, a tradition which understood preaching and could understand craftsmanship, but had a good deal of respect for the powers that governed the material world and never thought of putting the artist on a par with them — something of this sort at a given point prevented Kipling from playing through his part, and betrayed him into dedicating his talents to the praise of the practical man. Instead of *becoming* a man of action like Rimbaud, a course which shows a boldness of logic, he fell into the ignominious rôle of the artist who prostrates his art before the achievements of soldiers and merchants, and who is always declaring the supremacy of the 'doer' over the man of ideas.

The results of this are very curious and well worth studying from the artistic point of view — because Kipling, it must always be remembered, was a man of really remarkable abilities. Certain of the symptoms of his case have been indicated by George Moore and Dixon Scott, whose discussions of him in *Avowals* and *Men of Letters* are among the few first-rate pieces of criticism that I remember to have seen on the subject. George Moore quotes a passage from *Kim*, a description of evening in India, and praises it for 'the perfection of the writing, of the strong masculine rhythm of every sentence, and of the accuracy of every observation'; but then goes on to point out that 'Mr. Kipling has seen much more than he has felt,' that 'when we come to analyze the lines we find a touch of local color not only in every sentence, but in each part between each semicolon.' So Scott diagnoses admirably the mechanical ingenuity of plot that distinguishes the middle Kipling. 'Switch,' he says, 'this imperatively map-making, pattern-making method upon . . . the element of human nature, and what is the inevitable result? Inevitably, there is the same sudden stiffening and formulation. The characters spring to attention like soldiers on parade; they respond briskly to a sudden description; they wear a fixed set of idiosyncrasies like a uniform. A mind like this *must* use types and set counters; it feels dissatisfied, ineffective, unsafe, unless it can reduce the fluid waverings of character, its flitting caprices and twilit desires, to some tangible system. The characters of such a man will not only be definite; they will be definitions.' And he goes on to show how Kipling's use of dialect makes a screen for his relinquishment of his grip on the real organism of human personality: 'For dialect, in spite of all its air of ragged lawlessness, is wholly impersonal, typical, fixed, the code of a caste, not the voice of an individual. It is when the novelist sets his characters talking the King's English that he really puts his capacity for reproducing the unconventional and capricious on its trial. Mr. Kipling's plain conversations are markedly unreal. But honest craftsmanship and an ear for strong rhythms have provided him with many suits of dialects. And with these he dresses the talk till it seems to surge with character.'

The packed detail, the automatic plot, the surfaces lacquered with dialect, the ever-tightening tension of form, are all a part of Kipling's effort to impose his scheme by main force. The strangest result of this effort is to. be seen in a change in the subject matter itself. Kipling actually tends at this time to abandon human beings altogether. In that letter of Henry James in which he speaks of his former hope that Kipling might grow into an English Balzac, he goes on: 'But I have given that up in proportion as he has come steadily from the less simple in subject to the more simple — from the Anglo-Indians to the natives, from the natives to the Tommies, from the Tommies to the quadrupeds, from the quadrupeds to the fish, and from the fish to the engines and screws.' This increasing addiction of Kipling to animals, insects and machines is evidently to be explained by his need to find characters which will yield themselves unresistingly to being presented as parts of a system. In the *Jungle Books,* the animal characters are each one all of a piece, though in their ensemble they still provide a variety, and they are dominated by a 'Law of the Jungle,' which lays down their duties and rights. The animals have organized the Jungle, and the Jungle is presided over by Mowgli in his function of forest ranger, so that it falls into its subsidiary place in the larger organization of the Empire.

Yet the *Jungle Books* (written in Vermont) are not artistically off the track; the element of obvious allegory is not out of place in such fairy tales. It is when Kipling takes to contriving these animal allegories for grown-ups that he brings up the reader's gorge. What is proved in regard to human beings by the fable called *A Walking Delegate,* in which a pastureful of self-respecting horses turn and rend a yellow loafer from Kansas, who is attempting to incite them to rebellion against their master, Man? A labor leader and the men he is trying to organize are after all, not horses but men. Does Kipling mean to imply that the ordinary workingman stands in the same relation to the employing and governing classes as that in which the horse stands to its owner? And what is proved by *The Mother Hive,* in which an invasion of wax-moths that ruin the stock of the swarm represents the infiltration of socialism? (Compare these with that more humane fable of 1893, *The Children of the Zodiac,* which deals with gods become men.) And, though the discipline of a military unit or of the crew of a ship or a plane may provide a certain human interest, it makes us a little uncomfortable to find Kipling taking up locomotives and representing '.007' instead of the engineer who drives it as the hero of the American railroad; and descending even to the mechanical parts, the rivets and planks of a ship, whose drama consists solely of being knocked into place by the elements so that it may function as a co-ordinated whole.

We may lose interest, like Henry James, in the animal or mechanical characters of Kipling's middle period; but we must admit that these novel productions have their own peculiar merit. It is the paradox of Kipling's career that he should have extended the conquests of his craftsmanship in proportion to the shrinking of the range of his dramatic imagination. As his responses to human beings became duller, his sensitivity to his medium increased.

In both tendencies he was, of course, quite faithful to certain aspects of the life of his age. It was a period, those early nineteen hundreds, of brilliant technological improvement and of generally stunted intelligence. And Kipling now appeared as the poet both of the new mechanical methods and of the ideals of the people who spread them. To re-read these stories today is to feel again a little of the thrill of the plushy transcontinental Pullmans and the spic-and-span transatlantic liners that carried us around in our youth, and to meet again the bright and bustling people, talking about the polo field and the stock market, smart Paris and lovely California, the latest musical comedy and Kipling, in the smoking-rooms or among the steamer-chairs.

Kipling reflected this mechanical progress by evolving a new prose technique. We have often since Kipling's day been harangued by the Futurists and others about the need for artistic innovations appropriate to the life of the machine age; but it is doubtful whether any rhapsodist of motor-cars or photographer of dynamos and valves has been so successful at this as Kipling was at the time he wrote *The Day's Work*. These stories of his get their effects with the energy and accuracy of engines, by means of words that, hard, short and close-fitting, give the impression of ball-bearings and cogs. Beside them, the spout-

ings of the machine fans look like the old-fashioned rhetoric they are. For these latter could merely whoop and
roar in a manner essentially romantic over the bigness, the
power, the speed of the machines, whereas Kipling ex-
emplified in his form itself the mechanical efficiency and
discipline, and he managed to convey with precision both
the grimness and the exhilaration which characterized the
triumph of the machine.

He also brought to perfection the literary use of the
language of the specialized industrial world. He must
have been the principal artisan in the creation of that peculiar modern *genre* in which we are made to see some
comedy or tragedy through the cheapening or obscuring
medium of technical vocabulary or professional slang. He
did not, of course, invent the dialect monologue; but it is
improbable that we should have had, for example, either
the baseball stories of Ring Lardner or the Cyclops episode in *Ulysses* if Kipling had never written.

This is partly no doubt pure virtuosity. Mr. Beresford
says that Kipling was by nature as unmechanical as possible, could do nothing with his hands except write; and
I have heard an amusing story of his astonishment and
admiration at the mechanical proficiency of an American
friend who had simply put a castor back on a chair. He
had never worked at any of the processes he described,
had had to get them all up through the methods of the
attentive reporter. But it is virtuosity on a much higher
level than that of the imitation literature so often admired
in that era. Where Stevenson turns out paler *pastiches* of
veins which have already been exploited, Kipling really
finds new rhythms, new colors and textures of words, for
things that have not yet been brought into literature. For
the most part a second-rate writer of verse, because though
he can imitate the language of poetry as he can imitate all
the other languages, he cannot compensate for the falsity
of his feeling by his sharp observation and his expert

technique, he is extraordinary as a worker in prose. It is impossible still for a prose writer to read, for example, the first part of *The Bridge-Builders* without marveling at the author's mastery. How he has caught the very look and feel of the materials that go to make bridges and of the various aspects of the waters they have to dominate! And the maneuvers of modern armies against the dusty South African landscapes, and the tempo of American trains, and the relation of the Scotch engineer to the patched-up machines of his ship. The Kipling who put on record all these things was an original and accomplished artist.

For the rest, he writes stories for children. One is surprised in going back over Kipling's work to find that, dating from the time of his settling with his family in Vermont, he published no less than nine children's books: the two *Jungle Books, Captains Courageous, Just So Stories, Stalky & Co., Puck of Pook's Hill, Rewards and Fairies, A History of England, Land and Sea Tales for Scouts and Scouts Masters.* It is as if the natural human feelings progressively forced out of his work by the rigors of organization for its own sake were seeking relief in a reversion to childhood, when one has not yet become responsible for the way that the world is run, where it is enough to enjoy and to wonder at what we do not yet understand. And, on the other hand, the simplified morality to which Kipling has now committed himself is easier to make acceptable to one's readers and oneself if one approaches it from the point of view of the child. (The truth is that much of his work of this period which aims at the intelligence of grown people might almost equally well be subtitled *For Scouts and Scouts Masters.*) These stories, excellent at their best, are most successful when they are *most* irresponsible — as in the *Just So Stories;*

least so, as in *Captains Courageous,* when they lean most heavily on the schoolboy morality.

The most ambitious of them — the two series about Puck of Pook's Hill (1906 and 1910) — have, I know, been much admired by certain critics, including the sensitive Dixon Scott; but my own taste rejects them on re-reading them as it did when I read them first at the age for which they were presumably intended. Kipling tells us that the stories in *Rewards and Fairies* were designed to carry a meaning for adults as well as to interest children. But their technical sophistication puts them slightly above the heads of children at the same time that their sugared exploitation of Kipling's Anglo-Spartan code of conduct makes them slightly repugnant to grown-ups.

They are, to be sure, the most embroidered productions of Kipling's most elaborate period. The recovery of obsolete arts and crafts, the re-creation of obsolete idioms, are new pretexts for virtuosity. Kipling's genius for words has been stimulated by the discovery of the English earth and sea; he spreads on the rich grassiness of the English country, the dense fogginess of the English coast, the layers upon layers of tradition that cause the English character to seem to him deep-rooted, deep-colored, deep-meaning. He has applied all his delicacy and strength to this effort to get the mother-country into prose; but his England is never so real as was his India; and the effect, for all the sinewy writing, is somehow fundamentally decadent. The Normans and the Saxons and the Elizabethans, the great cathedral-builders and sailors and divines, perpetrating impossible 'gags,' striking postures that verge on the 'ham,' seem almost to anticipate Hollywood. The theme of the rôle and the ordeal of the artist which figures in *Rewards and Fairies* suffers from being treated in the vein of *Stalky & Co.* In the story called *The Wrong Thing,* he embarks on a promising subject: the discrepancy between the aim of the artist who is straining to top the standards of his craft, and the quite irrelevant kinds of interest that the powers that employ him may take in him; but he turns it into a farce and ruins it.

Kipling's England is perhaps the most synthetic of all his creations of this period, when he depends so much on tools and materials as distinguished from sympathy and insight. Scott says that these stories are opalescent; and this is true, but they show the defects of opals that have been artificially made and whose variegated glimmerings and shiftings do not seem to convey anything mysterious.

v

Yet, in locating the Ideal in the Empire, Kipling was not without his moments of uneasiness. If the Empire is really founded on self-discipline, the fear of God, the code of *noblesse oblige,* if it really involves a moral system, then we are justified in identifying it with 'the Law'; but suppose that it is not really so dedicated.

> If England was what England seems,
> An' not the England of our dreams,
> But only putty, brass an' paint,
> 'Ow quick we'd drop 'er! *But she ain't!*

Yet *Recessional,* perhaps the best set of verses that Kipling ever wrote, is a warning that springs from a doubt; and the story called *The Man Who Would Be King* is surely a parable of what might happen to the English if they should forfeit their moral authority. Two low-class English adventurers put themselves over on the natives of a remote region beyond Afghanistan, organize under a single rule a whole set of mountain tribes; but the man who has made himself king is destroyed by the natives that have adored him the instant they come to realize that he is not a god, as they had supposed, but a man. The Wesleyan preacher in Kipling knows that the valiant dust of man can build only on dust if it builds not in the name of God; and he is prepared to pound the pulpit and call down the Almighty's anger when parliamentarians or ministers or generals debauch their office or hold it light. Kipling always refused official honors in order to keep himself free; and his truculence had its valuable aspect in that it aided him to resist the briberies of his period of glory and fortune. In the volume of his collected addresses, which he calls *A Book of Words,* there are some sincere and inspiriting sermons. 'Now I do not ask you not to be carried away by the first rush of the great game of life. That is expecting you to be more than human,' he told the students at McGill University in the fall of 1907, when the height of his popularity was past. 'But I *do* ask you, after the first heat of the game, that you draw breath and watch your fellows for a while. Sooner or later, you will see some man to whom the idea of wealth as mere wealth does not appeal, whom the methods of amassing that wealth do not interest, and who will not accept money if you offer it to him at a certain price. At first you will be inclined to laugh at this man and to think that he is not "smart" in his ideas. I suggest that you watch him closely, for he will presently demonstrate to you that money dominates everybody except the man who does not want money. You may meet that man on your farm, in your village, or in your legislature. But be sure that, whenever or wherever you meet him, as soon as it comes to a direct issue between you, his little finger will be thicker than your loins. You will go in fear of him: he will not go in fear of you. You will do what he wants: he will not do what you want. You will find that you have no weapon in your armoury with which you can attack him; no argument with which you can appeal to him. Whatever you gain, he will gain more.'

If Kipling *had* taken a bribe, it was not that of reputation or cash; it was rather the big moral bribe that a political system can offer: the promise of mental security. And even here a peculiar integrity — as it were, an integrity of *temperament* that came to exist in dissociation from the intellect — survived the collapse of the system and saved Kipling in the end from his pretenses. How this happened is the last chapter of his story.

There was, as I say, a Wesleyan preacher in Kipling. The Old Testament served him as an armory of grim instances and menacing visions to drive home the imperial code; or, on occasions when the imperial masters failed to live up to this code, of scorching rhetorical language (though with more of malignancy than of grandeur) for the chastisement of a generation of vipers. But Kipling had no real religion. He exploited, in his poems and his fiction, the mythology of a number of religions.

We may be inclined to feel, in reading Kipling — and to some extent we shall be right — that the various symbols and gods which figure in his stories and poems are mere properties which the writer finds useful for his purposes of rhetoric or romance. Yet we cannot but suspect in *Kim* and in the stories of metempsychosis that Kipling has been seriously influenced by the Buddhism which he had imbibed with his first language in his boyhood. Mr. Beresford corroborates this: he says that the Kipling of Westward Ho! talked Buddhism and reincarnation. And it is certainly with Buddhism that we first find associated a mystical side of Kipling's mind which, in this last phase, is to emerge into the foreground.

We left the Lama of *Kim* attaining the Buddhist ecstasy and escaping from the Wheel of Things at the same moment that Kim gets promotion and finally becomes a spoke in the wheel of British administration. But the world-beyond of the Lama is to seep back into Kipling's work in queer and incongruous forms. Among the strained political fables of the collection called *Traffics and Discoveries*, which is the beginning of the more somber later Kipling, there is a story of a wireless operator who is possessed by the soul of Keats. It may be that Kipling's Southsea experience, in driving him back into his imagination for defense against the horror of reality, had had the effect both of intensifying his fancies and of dissociating them from ordinary life — so that the ascent out of the Wheel of Things and the visitations of an alien soul became ways of representing this. The effort of the grown-up Kipling to embrace by the imagination, to master by a disciplined art, what he regarded as the practical realities is to be subject to sudden recoils. In the Kipling of the middle period, there is a suppressed but vital element which thrusts periodically a lunatic head out of a window of the well-bricked façade.

This element is connected with the Lama, but it is also connected with something else more familiar to the Western world: the visitations and alienations of what is now known as neurotic personality. Here again Kipling was true to his age. While the locomotives and airplanes and steamers were beating records and binding continents, the human engine was going wrong. The age of mechanical technique was also the age of the nerve sanitarium. In the stories of the early Kipling, the intervention of the supernatural has, as a rule, within the frame of the story itself, very little psychological interest; but already in 'They' and *The Brushwood Boy* the dream and the hallucination are taking on a more emphatic significance. With *The House Surgeon* and *In the Same Boat*, they are in process of emerging from the fairy tale: they become recognizable as psychiatric symptoms. The depression described in *The House Surgeon* has been transferred, by the artifice of the story, to persons unconcerned in the tragedy through the influence from a distance of someone else; but the woman with whom the terror originates is suffering morbidly from feelings of guilt, and the sensations are evidently based on the first-hand experience of the author.

'And it was just then that I was aware of a little gray shadow, as it might have been a snowflake seen against the light, floating at an immense distance in the background of my brain. It annoyed me, and I shook my head to get rid of it. Then my brain telegraphed that it was the forerunner of a swift-striding gloom which there was yet time to escape if I would force my thoughts away from it, as a man leaping for life forces his body forward and away from the fall of a wall. But the gloom overtook me before I could take in the meaning of the message. I moved toward the bed, every nerve already aching with the foreknowledge of the pain that was to be dealt it, and sat down, while my amazed and angry soul dropped, gulf by gulf, into that horror of great darkness which is spoken of in the Bible, and which, as the auctioneers say, must be experienced to be appreciated.

'Despair upon despair, misery upon misery, fear after fear, each causing their distinct and separate woe, packed in upon me for an unrecorded length of time, until at last they blurred together, and I heard a click in my brain like the click in the ear when one descends in a diving bell, and I knew that the pressures were equalized within and without, and that, for the moment, the worst was at an end. But I knew also that at any moment the darkness might come down anew; and while I dwelt on this speculation precisely as a man torments a raging tooth with his tongue, it ebbed away into the little gray shadow on the brain of its first coming, and once more I heard my brain, which knew what would recur, telegraph to every quarter for help, release or diversion.'

And although the periodical irrational panics of the couple of *In the Same Boat* are explained as the result of pre-natal shocks, the description of the man and woman themselves, with their 'nerve doctors,' their desperate drug-taking, their shaky and futile journeys in flight from their neurotic fears, their peculiar neurotic relationship, constitutes an accurate account of a phenomenon of contemporary life which, at the time that Kipling was writing, had hardly been described in fiction.

Observe that in both these stories, as in the stories of war neurosis that will follow, the people who suffer thus are quite innocent, their agony is entirely unearned. I believe that the only cases in which the obsessive horror is connected with any kind of guilt are those in which a man is hounded to death by the vision of a woman he has wronged. This theme recurs regularly with Kipling from the time of *The Phantom Rickshaw,* one of the very first of his short stories, through the remarkable *Mrs. Bathurst* of his middle period, and up to the strange and poisoned *Dayspring Mishandled,* which was one of the last things he wrote. We cannot speculate with very much assurance on the relation of this theme of betrayal to the other recurring themes of Kipling's work. We do not know enough about his life to be able to assign it to an assumption on the part of the six-year-old Kipling that he must somehow have sinned against the mother who had abandoned him so inexplicably at Southsea; or to relate it to the strange situation of Dick Heldar in *The Light That Failed,* who vainly adores, and goes blind in adoring, the inexplicably obdurate Maisie. All we can say is that the theme of the anguish which is suffered without being deserved has the appearance of having been derived from a morbid permanent feeling of injury inflicted by his experience at Southsea.

Certainly the fear of darkness passing into the fear of blindness which runs all through his work from *The Light That Failed to 'They'* is traceable directly to his breakdown and to the frightening failure of his eyes. This was a pattern he seems to have repeated. Illnesses were critical for Kipling. It was after his illness in India that he set out to contend with a society which must have seemed to him indifferent and brutal by making himself a writer; and it was after his illness in New York that he decided to turn his back on America and to accept all the values that that retreat implied. It was after the breakdown in which Kim had brooded on his true identity that he emerged as a fullblown British agent. From the darkness and the physical weakness, the Kipling of the middle period has come forth with tightened nerves, resolved to meet a state of things in which horses are always being whipped or having their heads blown off, in which schoolboys are bullied and flogged, in which soldiers are imprisoned in barracks and fed to the bayonets and guns, by identifying himself with horses — as in the story called *A Walking Delegate* — that gang together to kick and maul another horse, with schoolboys — as in *The Moral Reformers* of *Stalky* — that gloat in torturing other schoolboys, with soldiers that get the sharpest satisfaction from stabbing and pot-shotting other soldiers. He has set himself with all the stiff ribs of a metal-armatured art to stand up to this world outside that gets its authority from its power to crush and kill: the world of the Southsea house that has turned into the world of the Empire; to compete with it on its own terms. And yet the darkness and the illness return. It is a key to the whole work of Kipling that the great celebrant of physical courage should prove in the long run to convey his most moving and convincing effects in describing moral panic. Kipling's bullyings and killings are contemptible: they are the fantasies of the physically helpless. The only authentic heroism to be found in the fiction of Kipling is the heroism of moral fortitude on the edge of a nervous collapse.

And in the later decades of Kipling's life the blackness and the panic close down; the abyss becomes more menacing. It is the Crab, both devil and destiny, which in the story called *The Children of the Zodiac* lies always in wait for the poet and finally comes to devour him. The nurse-like watchfulness of Mrs. Kipling and Kipling's fear of stepping out of her régime, which appeared to his friend an impediment to the development of his genius, were no doubt, on the contrary, in his extreme instability, a condition of his being able to function at all — just as the violence of his determination to find the answer to the problems of society and a defense against the forces that plagued him in the program of an imperialist government was evidently directly related to the violence of desperation of his need.

But now both of these shelters he had built himself — the roof of his family life, the confidence of his political idealism — were suddenly to be broken down.

In 1914-18, the British Empire collided with a competitor. All England went to war, including Kipling's only son. The boy, not yet out of his teens, was killed in an attack before Loos in September, 1915, and his body was never found. John Kipling had at first been reported missing, and his father waited for months in the hope of getting a letter from Germany announcing that he had been taken prisoner.

These war years left Kipling defenseless. It had been easy to be grimly romantic on the subject of the warfare in India when Kipling had never seen fighting; it had even been possible, as a reporter at the front, to Meissonier the campaign in South Africa in the bright colors of the new nineteenth centry. But the long systematic waste of the trench warfare of the struggle against Germany discouraged the artistic exploitation of the cruelties and gallantries of battle. The strain of the suspense and the horror taxed intolerably those attitudes of Kipling's which had been in the first instance provoked by a strain and which had only at the cost of a strain been kept up.

From even before the war, the conduct of British policy

had been far from pleasing to Kipling. He saw clearly the careerism and the venality of the modern politician; and he was bitterly opposed on principle to the proposals of the radicals and liberals. In May, 1914, when civil war with Ulster was threatening, he delivered at Tunbridge Wells and allowed to be circulated as a penny leaflet a speech against the Home Rule Bill of a virulence almost hysterical. The attempt to free Ireland he excoriates as on a level with the Marconi scandals. 'The Home Rule Bill,' he declares, 'broke the pledged faith of generations; it officially recognized sedition, privy conspiracy and rebellion; it subsidized the secret forces of boycott, intimidation and murder; and it created an independent stronghold in which all these forces could work together, as they have always and openly boasted that they would, for the destruction of Great Britain.'

This was to remain Kipling's temper in public questions. The victory of the Bolsheviks in Russia of course made the picture blacker: one sixth of the area of the globe, he said, had 'passed bodily out of civilization.'

> Our world has passed away,
> In wantonness o'erthrown.
> There is nothing left to-day
> But steel and fire and stone!

he wrote when the war began. And when Kipling was sickened and broken with steel and fire and stone, there was little for his spirit to lean on.

Little but the practice of his craft, which now reflects only the twisted fragments of Kipling's exploded cosmos.

These latest stories of Kipling's have attracted meager attention for reasons that are easily comprehensible. The disappearance in the middle Kipling of the interest in human beings for their own sake and the deliberate cul-

tivation of the excommunicatory imperialist hatreds had
already had the effect of discouraging the appetite of the
general public; and when the human element reappeared
in a new tormented form in Kipling's later stories, the
elliptical and complex technique which the writer had by
that time developed put the general reader off. On the
other hand, the highbrows ignored him, because, in the
era of Lawrence and Joyce, when the world was disgusted
with soldiering and when the imperialisms were apparently deflated, they could take no interest in the point of
view. In their conviction that Kipling could never hold
water, they had not even enough curiosity to wonder
what had happened to an author who must have enchanted them in their childhood. And in a sense they
were, of course, correct. Kipling *had* terribly shrunk; he
seemed a man who had had a stroke and was only half
himself — whereas Yeats was playing out superbly the last
act of a personal drama which he had sustained unembarrassed by public events, and Henry James was now
seen in retrospect to have accomplished, in his long career,
a prodigy of disinterested devotion to an art and a criticism
of life. Where there was so much wreckage around, political, social and moral, the figure of the disinterested
artist commanded especial respect.

Yet the Kipling who limped out of the wreckage,
shrunken and wry though he looks, has in a sense had his
development as an artist. Some of these stories are the
most intense in feeling as they are among the most concentrated in form that Kipling ever wrote; to a writer, they
are perhaps the most interesting. The subjects are sometimes hard to swallow, and the stories themselves —
through a tasteless device which unfortunately grew on
Kipling as he got older — are each preceded and followed
by poems which elaborate or elucidate their themes in the
author's synthetic verse and which dull the effect of
the excellent prose. But here Kipling's peculiar method,

trained with deadly intention, scores some of its cleanest hits.

Let us, however, first consider the subjects of these final collections of stories (A Diversity of Creatures, Debits and Credits, and Limits and Renewals). The fragments of the disintegrated Kipling fall roughly into five classes: tales of hatred, farces based on practical jokes, studies of neurotic cases, tales of fellowship in religion, and tales of personal bereavement.

The tales of hatred — hatred of Americans and the Germans: Sea Constables and Mary Postgate — become murderous at the time of the war (though they give place to other kinds of themes later). The hatred of democracy — in the satire called As Easy as A.B.C. (which appeared in 1912) — is carried to lengths that would be Swiftian if Kipling had subjected the whole human race to the death ray of his abstract contempt, but which — as Edward Shanks points out — is rendered rather suspect by the exemption from the annihilating irony of a group of disciplined officials. The morals of these stories are odious and the plots mostly contrived and preposterous; yet they acquire a certain dignity from the desperation of bitterness that animates them.

Then there are the practical jokes — a category which includes the comic accidents: practical jokes engineered by the author. These have always been a feature of Kipling. His addiction to this form of humor seems to have derived originally from the boobytraps and baitings of Westward Ho!; later, changing sides, he identified them rather with the lickings-into-shape inflicted by regimental raggings. The victims of these pulverizing hoaxes fall into two classes: petty tyrants, who humilate and bully, and who always have to be cads; and political idealists and godless intellectuals, who have to be nincompoops. Kipling likes nothing better than to hurl one of these latter into a hive of bees or, as in one of his early stories, to silence his opinions by a sunstroke. A first principle of Kipling's world is revenge: the humiliated must become the humiliator. One might expect this kind of thing to disappear in the work of the latest Kipling; but the formula becomes instead much more frequent, and it comes to play a special rôle. The practical joke with its extravagant laughter is a violent if hollow explosion for the relief of nervous strain; and the severity of this strain may be gauged by the prodigious dimensions of the hoaxes in which Kipling now labors to concentrate the complex calculation of an Ibsen and the methodical ferocity of a Chinese executioner.

In some of these stories, the comic disaster is exploited as a therapeutic device. There are six stories of war neurosis in Kipling's last two collections. The situation of the shattered veteran provided him with an opportunity for studying further a subject which had haunted him all his life: the condition of people who seem to themselves on the borderline of madness. Here the sufferers are still perfectly guiltless. In one case, an appearance of guilt, in another, a conviction of guilt, turn out to be actually unjustified. But the picture is now more realistically filled out than it was by the pre-natal occurrences which were the best Kipling could do for motivation for the neurotics of *In the Same Boat*. The war supplies real causes for derangement; and Kipling sees that such short-circuits may be mended by going back to the occasion that gave rise to the obsession and disentangling the crossed wires. But his principal prescriptions for saving people from the effects of the horror and the strain of the war are such apropos comic accidents and well-aimed benevolent frauds as, in reality, are rarely possible and which would be of doubtful efficacy if they were. In one story, the fantasy of the sick man turns out to be based on a reading in hospital of a novel by Mrs. Ewing (as the soldiers in *The Janeites* find solace in the novels of Jane Austen) —

which also gives the veteran, when he recovers, a beneficent interest in life: that of planting wayside gardens.
Another ex-soldier is saved by a dog.

Kipling's homeless religious sense resorts to strange fel-
lowships and faiths to bolster up his broken men. He had
been made a Freemason in India, and Freemasonry had
figured in *Kim* and had seemed to crop up in the guise of
Mithraism in the Roman stories of *Puck of Pook's Hill*.
Now he invents, for a new series of stories, a circle of
philanthropic Masons who meet in the back room of a
tobacconist's and who try to help men that have been
wrecked by the war. A new ideal — but a new ideal conceived by a tired and humbled man — of a brotherhood
which shall not be delimited by the exclusions of a fighting unit or caste begins to appear in these stories. Mithraism figures again in *The Church That Was at Antioch*:
the young Roman officer turned Mithraist says of his
mother, 'She follows the old school, of course — the home-
worships and the strict Latin Trinity. . . . But one wants
more than that'; and he ends by getting murdered by the
Jews in revenge for his protection of the Apostle Paul. In
another story, *The Manner of Men*, Saint Paul appears
again and rescues a neurotic sea-captain: 'Serve Caesar,'
says Paul. 'You are not canvas I can cut to advantage at
present. But if you serve Caesar you will be obeying at
least some sort of law. . . . If you take refuge under
Caesar at sea, you may have time to think. Then I may
meet you again, and we can go on with our talks. But that
is as the God wills. What concerns you *now*,' he concludes, in a tone that recalls at the same time the Buch-
manite and the psychoanalyst, 'is that, by taking service,
you will be free from the fear that has ridden you all your
life.'

The Paul of these final stories, so different from his
early heroes, may evidently tell us something about Kipling's changed conception of himself. Paul had preached

the Word to the Gentiles as Kipling had preached the
Law to the colonials and the Americans; Paul, like Kipling, is ill-favored and undersized, 'a little shrimp of a
man,' who has 'the woman's trick of taking the tone and
color of whoever he talked to' and who is scarred from
old floggings and from his encounters with the beasts of
the arena. Paul, like Kipling, is brash and tense; he is
dedicated to a mission which has saved him from fear. But
observe that, though he advises the shaky captain to take
service with Caesar for a time, he has himself gone on to
something higher.

This, then, is quite another Kipling. His prophets have
an altered message: Kipling is losing his hatred. His captains have been afraid all their lives. His soldiers are no
longer so cocky, so keen to kill inferior peoples, so intent
on the purposes of the Empire. And officers and soldiers
are now closer, as they were in the earliest stories: they
are now simply civilians back in mufti, between whom
the bond of having been in the war is stronger than the
class differences of peace-time. And they are the remnants
of a colossal disaster. I shall quote one of the pieces in
verse with which Kipling supplements these stories, because, indifferent though it is as poetry, it strikingly illustrates this change:

> I have a dream — a dreadful dream —
>   A dream that is never done,
> I watch a man go out of his mind,
>   And he is My Mother's Son.
>
> They pushed him into a Mental Home,
>   And that is like the grave:
> For they do not let you sleep upstairs,
>   And you're not allowed to shave.
>
> And it was *not* disease or crime
>   Which got him landed there,

But because they laid on My Mother's Son
     More than a man could bear.

What with noise, and fear of death,
     Waking, and wounds and cold,
They filled the Cup for My Mother's Son
     Fuller than it could hold.

They broke his body and his mind
     And yet they made him live,
And they asked more of My Mother's Son
     Than any man could give.

For, just because he had not died
     Nor been discharged nor sick:
They dragged it out with My Mother's Son
     Longer than he could stick. . . .

And no one knows when he'll get well —
     So, there he'll have to be:
And, 'spite of the beard in the looking-glass,
     I know that man is me!

The theme of inescapable illness dominates the whole
later Kipling. In some cases, the diseases are physical, but
there is always the implication of a psychological aspect.
In *A Madonna of the Trenches* and *The Wish House* —
gruesome ghost stories of love and death that make *The
End of the Passage* and *The Mark of the Beast* look like
harmless bogey tales for children — cancer serves as a
symbol for rejected or frustrated love. And it is not clear
in *Dayspring Mishandled* whether the detestable literary
man Castorley is being poisoned by his wife and the doctor or by the consciousness of the wrong he has committed. The strangest of all these stories is *Unprofessional*,
in which cancer, spasms of insanity, the aftermath of the

war, and the influence of the something beyond human life combine in a clinical fantasy on the beneficent possibilities of science. Here the white mice and the London woman convulsed with suicidal seizures, sets toward death periodically imparted by mysterious cosmic tides, are Kipling's uncanniest image for the workings of nervous disorders.

The old great man is back again in the 'House of Desolation' at Southsea, tormented unjustly, ill, deserted by those he loves, and with the haunted darkness descending on that world which his determined effort had once enabled him to see so distinctly. In one of the latest of his stories, *Proofs of Holy Writ*, he makes Shakespeare speak to Ben Jonson of a man whom Shakespeare describes as 'going down darkling to his tomb 'twixt cliffs of ice and iron' — phrases hardly characteristic of Shakespeare but extremely appropriate to Kipling.

It is striking that some of the most authentic of Kipling's early stories should deal with children forsaken by their parents and the most poignant of his later ones with parents bereaved of their children. The theme of the abandoned parent seems to reflect in reversal the theme of the abandoned child. The former theme has already appeared in *'They'* (written after the death of Kipling's daughter), associated with the themes of blindness and the deprivation of love; and even before that, in *Without Benefit of Clergy*.

Certainly two of these last stories of Kipling's are among the most moving he wrote. There is a passage in *Mary Postgate* like the plucking of a tightened string that is just about to break. The plain and dull English female 'companion' is to burn up the belongings of a young soldier — like most of Kipling's children, an orphan — to whom she has stood in a maternal rôle and who has just been killed in a plane. Kipling tells in one of his typical inventories of the items, mainly relics of boyhood sports, that Mary has to destroy; and then: 'The shrubbery was filling with twilight by the time she had completed her arrangements and sprinkled the sacrificial oil. As she lit the match that would burn her heart to ashes, she heard a groan or a grunt behind the dense Portugal laurels.' *The match that would burn her heart to ashes*: they are the first words that we have yet encountered, the only words that we shall have encountered, that are not matter-of-fact; and here the observation of Kipling, of which George Moore complained that it was too systematic and too technical, making it *Portugal laurels* where another writer would have simply written *shrubbery* — here this hardness of concrete detail is suddenly given new value by a phrase on another plane.

So in that other remarkable story, *The Gardener*, Kipling's method of preparing a finale by concealing essential information in an apparently casual narrative produces an effect of tremendous power. This method, which Kipling has developed with so much ingenuity and precision, serves in some of his stories to spring surprises that are merely mechanical; but it has always had its special appropriateness to those aspects of the English character with which Kipling has been particularly concerned in that it masks emotion and purpose under a pretense of coldness and indifference; and here it is handled in a masterly fashion to dramatize another example of the impassive Englishwoman. The implications of *Mary Postgate* prevent us from accepting it fully: we know too well that the revengeful cruelty which impels the heroine of the story to let the shattered German aviator die is shared by the author himself. But *The Gardener* may conquer us completely. I am not sure that it is not really the best story that Kipling ever wrote. Like the rest of even the best of Kipling, it is not quite on the highest level. He must still have his fairy-tale properties; and we may be disposed to protest at his taste when we find that the Puck of Pook's Hill element is supplied by the apparition of Jesus. But if we have been following Kipling's development, we recognize that this fact is significant. The rôle that Christ has formerly played in Kipling — as in the poem called *Cold Iron* — has been that of a *pukka Sahib* who knows how to take his punishment. This is the first time, so far as I remember, that Kipling's Christ has shown pity — as Kipling pities now rather than boasts about the self-disciplined and much-enduring British. And the symbol at once bares the secret and liberates the locked-up emotion with a sudden and shocking force. The self-repression and the hopeless grief of the unmarried mother in *The Gardener* speak for the real Kipling. Here he has found for them intense expression in the concentrated forms of his art.

The big talk of the work of the world, of the mission to command of the British, even the hatefulness of fear and disappointment, have largely faded away for Kipling. He composes as a memorial to his son and to the system in devotion to which the half-American boy has died a history of the Irish Guards in the war, in which Lieutenant John Kipling is hardly mentioned. But, meticulously assembling, by the method by which he once seemed to build so solidly, the scattered memories of his son's battalion, he seems merely to be striving, by wisps and scraps, to re-create the terrible days that preceded the death of his child. Even the victory over the Germans can never make that right.

UNCOMFORTABLE CASANOVA

WHY has Jacques Casanova attracted so little attention in English? So far as I know there is nothing very serious except Havelock Ellis's essay, and that does not go far into the subject. Mr. S. Guy Endore's book, though a good piece of work in its way, is only a popular biography. Yet the Chevalier de Seingalt was a most remarkable man, who had some of the qualities of greatness. The Prince de Ligne listed his name with those of Louis XV, Frederick the Great, Beaumarchais, d'Alembert and Hume as among the most interesting men he had known, and the great sharper really belongs in that company.

When we begin reading Casanova's *Memoirs*, we think him amusing but cheap. Yet we end by being genuinely impressed by him.

He was a type who was very familiar in the America of the boom of the twenties. In our time he might have had the career of a Rothstein or a Nicky Arnstein or a Dapper Don Tourbillon, but he would have far transcended the sphere of such men and he would have felt for them the uneasy scorn that he felt for St. Germain and Cagliostro. For Casanova was only half of the underworld – he lived half in darkness, half in light. But the sound and superior part of him was always insecure because it was based on knavery: hence his succession of misadventures and the final unsatisfactoriness of his life. Casanova was an uncomfortable man – he could never make his life come right. And it makes us uncomfortable to read about him.

There is a sound kind of coarseness, which is not incompatible with the finest work or the most scrupulously ordered life: the coarseness of animality or of the hand-to-hand struggle with existence, which may nourish such work and such a life. And there is a bad kind of coarseness which spoils everything, even where a man is equipped with genuinely superior gifts. The coarseness of Casanova was the bad kind. He came out of the Venetian actors' world, and was never sure whether his mother, a shoemaker's daughter, had had him by a down-at-heels nobleman who had gone on the stage and married her or by the manager of the theater where she acted. From some heritage of moral squalor Casanova could never emerge, and he was ravaged by it all his life more vitally than by any of the diseases that were his mere superficial exasperations.

But the superior qualities of such a man have continually to keep themselves sharp against the dangers that always confront him, the dangers that he can never get away from because they are part of himself. The drama of Casanova's career creates a tension which is both exciting and trying because his highly developed intelligence, his genius as an actor on the stage of life, are always poised on the brink of a pit where taste, morals, the social order, the order of the world of the intellect, may all be lost in the slime. Yet even when he has slipped to the bottom, he keeps his faculties clear; and so he commands our respect.

We have had an immense amount of controversy as to whether Casanova told the truth in connection with this or that incident, and a good many inaccuracies have been proved on him. But whether he falsified the facts unconsciously or deliberately makes very little difference. In his own way Casanova was truthful; it may even be said that one of his most admirable traits — not as a man but as a writer — was precisely a fidelity to truth. He may have invented some of the adventures in the *Memoirs*, but his story follows reality for all that. Someone has said that if the *Memoirs* is a novel, Casanova is the greatest novelist who ever lived. Though he was personally extremely vain, he certainly spares himself as little as any autobiographer on record. It is not true, as the popular legend seems to have it, that he represents himself as triumphing easily over innumerable complacent women. On the contrary, he will sometimes devote the better part of a volume to a detailed description of some siege in which he ignominiously failed. The ultimate aim of Casanova is not so much to glorify himself as to tell us an astonishing story that illustrates how people behave, the way in which life works out.

When other writers borrow from Casanova, they are likely to sentimentalize or romanticize him where Casanova's great virtue is his mercilessness with romantic and sentimental conventions. I remember an attempt at a popular play based on the Henriette episode. Henriette in the *Memoirs* is a young French girl who has run away from home in men's clothes and whom the youthful Casanova meets in his travels. She is the first French girl he has known, the first *jeune fille spirituelle*; and his love affair with her has a freshness and seriousness, almost a kind of ecstasy, that none has ever had for him before and that none is ever to have again. He happens to have money at the time and is able to buy her a whole wardrobe of pretty clothes. They go to Parma together, and there they live in style. Casanova gets a box at the opera; they take the air in the public gardens with the royalties — till she is recognized by one of the courtiers and is compelled to go back to her family. Casanova's account of this episode is one of the most attractive love affairs in literature. When he and Henriette have finally had to part, at Geneva, he finds that she has written with her diamond on the window of their room at the inn: 'You will forget Henriette, too.' Now the contemporary play I speak of exploited this charming story and then followed it with a conventional sequel made up out of the whole cloth, in which Casanova many years later was made to come back to the inn to find Henriette grown old and with a son who turns out to be his.

But what happens in the *Memoirs* is quite different. Casanova does come back to the inn, middle-aged, down on his luck and with a depressing venereal disease. He *has* forgotten about staying there with Henriette, and he does not even recognize their room till he notices the writing on the window: 'Remembering in a flash the moment when Henriette had written those words thirteen years before, I felt the hair stand up on my head. . . . Overcome, I dropped into a chair. . . . Comparing the self I was now with the self I had been then, I had to recognize that I was less worthy to possess her. I still knew how to love, but I realized I had no longer the delicacy that I had had in those earlier days, nor the feelings which really justify the transports of the senses, nor the same tender ways, nor finally a certain probity which extends itself even to one's weaknesses; but what frightened me was to have to acknowledge that I no longer possessed the same vigor.'

Years afterwards, while he is traveling in Provence, his coach breaks down in the middle of the night and some people who live near the road take him in. The mistress of the house hides her face in the hood she has worn out-of-doors — then as soon as they have got into the house, she announces that she has sprained her ankle and is obliged to take to her bed, so that Casanova is only permitted to wait upon her in her room and talk to her through the bed-curtains. He does not find out till after he has left that the countess is Henriette, who has by this time grown so fat that she cannot bear to have him see her. But he has been traveling with a tough little Venetian

girl of bisexual capabilities, and the countess carries on a
flirtation with her and finally makes her sleep with her.
This is all life has left of their romance.

The real theme of Casanova is the many things a life
may hold – the many rôles a man may play and the
changes brought by time. I have never read a book –
either autobiography or fiction – which seems to give
you a life so completely. I know of no book which shows
so strikingly the rhythmic recurrences which character
produces in personal destiny. Casanova's adventures are
always different but always the same thing. He arrives in
some new place, he puts himself over, he achieves brilliant social successes or performs dashing deeds, his best
qualities and gifts have full scope, then he overplays his
hand or misses his step or something discreditable is discovered about him, and he has to make his getaway. There
was something about him, one supposes, that in the long
run made people find him intolerable. And his love affairs
have their pattern, too: when the responsibilities involved
in them become onerous, he marries the ladies off if he
can; if not, he gently lets the affair lapse.

The first part of the story is funny and gay – it has a
Venetian carnival liveliness; the last part, although it is
told with the eighteenth-century rapidity and dryness, is
almost unbearably sad. It is probable that Casanova was
never able to bring himself to finish it. The manuscript as
we have it does not cover the whole of the period indicated by Casanova in his title: it stops just as he is returning to Venice, but gets him no farther than Trieste. He
had been banished by the Inquisition and was allowed to
return to his native city only at the price of acting as a
spy for them. It was the most humiliating episode in his
life; and he has remarked by the way several times that he
is not sure he will have the courage to go through with
his original project of writing his life up to the year 1797.
He may also have been guilty of a Freudian oversight in

dropping out two chapters near the end. They were missing in the Brockhaus manuscript, but were found later by Arthur Symons at Dux; and they turn out to contain the dismal climax of Casanova's adventure with two girls upon whom he had been trying to work by an old and well-tried technique of his. He had discovered that you could go a long way with girls if you took them to masquerades in pairs; but on this occasion the girls did not fall, and Casanova before the evening was over got mercilessly razzed by the masqueraders.

Yet in his final asylum at Dux, where his patron left him alone for long periods and where he was constantly bedeviled by the servants, where he sometimes contemplated suicide, he did get down most of the story; and it is one of the most remarkable presentations in literature of a man's individual life as it seems to him in the living. All the appetites are there — fine dinners, attractive women, amusements; and the exhilaration of travel, of fighting for one's personal pride, of the winning of wealth and consideration, of winning one's personal liberty. There is in Casanova's account of his escape from the Leads prison in Venice, whether he fabricated the story or not, something more than a mere tale of adventure: he has made of it a thrilling expression of the hatred of the human spirit for jails, of the will to be free that breaks away in contempt of the remonstrances of reason (in the person of the appalled old count who refuses to join the others and keeps telling them why they cannot succeed).

There is even the appetite of the intellect. the great raconteur loved the conversation of men like d'Alembert and Voltaire; and the master gambler was an amateur mathematician. And when one can have no more brilliant dinners and make love to no more women, when one has no longer appreciative companions to listen to one's stories and can no longer travel and try one's luck — one can at least summon one's intellectual resources, work at problems, write one's memoirs; one can still test one's nerve and strength by setting down an account of life as one has found it, with all its anticlimax and scandal, one's own impossible character and all. The writing of the *Memoirs* represented a real victory of the mind and the spirit. Scoundrels like Casanova do not usually put themselves on record, and when they do they are usually at pains to profess the morality of respectable people. There is a certain amount of this, as we shall see in a moment, in Casanova's autobiography, too; but when all Casanova's obeisances to the established authorities have been made, life itself in his story turns out to be an outlaw like him. He confesses in his preface that he considers it a creditable deed to fleece a fool; and in reading him, we get to a point where we ourselves almost feel impatience when Casanova's prospective victims fail to succumb to his confidence games. He said that he feared the *Memoirs* were *'par trop cynique'* ever to be published. And he was apparently partly right: the original manuscript still lies locked up in Brockhaus's vaults in Leipzig, and no one knows what the editors may have omitted.

The *Memoirs*, then, required the courage of an individual point of view — and they required a capacity for feeling. Has any novelist or poet ever rendered better than Casanova the passing glory of the personal life? — the gaiety, the spontaneity, the generosity of youth: the ups and downs of middle age when our character begins to get us and we are forced to come to terms with it; the dreadful blanks of later years, when what is gone is gone. All that a life of this kind can contain Casanova put into his story. And how much of the world! — the eighteenth century as you get it in no other book; society from top to bottom; Europe from England to Russia; a more brilliant variety of characters than you can find in any eighteenth-century novel.

But the interests of such a man are limited. Casanova knew better than anyone how the world and how one's personal vicissitudes went. But he had very little imagination for the larger life of society. He saw the corruption of the old régime in France and commented on it after the Revolution, but he had never been among those who wanted to see the old régime go. On the contrary — like a Rothstein — he was content with the world as he found it. Though the Inquisition had nearly done for him, he never ceased to treat it with respect and was willing in his last bad days to turn informer and report to these censors — though rather inefficiently, it appears — on naked models in the Venetian art-schools and indecent and ungodly books in the libraries. Though he had at other times called himself a 'philosopher' and in his speculative writings had vaguely foreshadowed Darwinism, he had never criticized Church or State. He accepted all the current worldly values — the hierarchies, institutions, dominations. He never questioned, never protested, defended his honor according to the code, but never brought up in connection with anything the principle of a larger issue. Casanova's originality was largely confined to a sort of personal effrontery which, having persisted all through his life in spite of his repeated attempts to reform it, had ended by acquiring in his *Memoirs* a certain intellectual dignity when he had found finally that all his struggles to make himself a place in society were vain and that this was the only companion that was left him in his solitude at Dux.

A man of superior intelligence as he knew himself to be, he had always aimed at the good things of the world as the rich and powerful judged good things. What he really wanted, to be sure, was something different from what they wanted. He does not seem to have cared about social position or financial security for their own sakes: what he enjoyed was the adventure of playing a rôle, creating a situation; whereas the powerful and the rich only wanted to follow their routine. But his drama was usually conceived in terms of their values. It was the cheap side of him, the lackey in him, which did not look beyond the habits of his masters.

And this is a part of the explanation of the fact that Casanova has attracted comparatively so little serious attention. In English of course it is his scandalous reputation which has made him practically taboo — so that he has remained largely unknown to the English-reading public save for volumes of erotic excerpts in libraries of classic pornography. But in general it may be said that what is good in Casanova makes serious readers too uneasy and what is inferior disgusts them too much for him to become an accepted classic. There are a whole host of people on the Continent studying Casanova; but Casanovists seem almost in the category of stamp and coin collectors and people who devote their lives to looking for buried Spanish treasure. They are mostly preoccupied with verifying dates and tracking down identities. Casanova, fascinating though he is, does not lead to anything bigger than himself.

Compare him with Rousseau, for example. Rousseau was a much less attractive man, and his *Confessions* are infinitely less readable than Casanova's *Memoirs*. At his best, to my taste at any rate, he is still pretty flavorless and Swiss. Yet the Geneva clockmaker's son in a situation not unlike Casanova's — he, too, had been a vagabond, a thief, a hanger-on of the great, had suffered as a battered-about apprentice and a servant in rich men's houses — made an issue of his maladjustment. Casanova could show considerable strength of character in compelling the great to treat him as an equal — as when he forced Count Branicki to fight a duel and afterwards became his friend; but it never seems to have occurred to the actor's son to say, after he had come one of his croppers masquerading as a man of quality: 'I am better at being a great lord than you people are yourselves – for I have the personality and the imagination and the brains to create such a gorgeous great lord as your silly conventional society never dreamed of – hence I am superior to you and hence do not need to compete with you!' Whereas Rousseau finally came to the conclusion that the times must be out of joint when Rousseau found himself out of place. From the moment of his sudden revelation, on the way to see Diderot at Vincennes, that man was by nature good and that it was institutions alone which had corrupted him, that all his own miseries had been due, not to his aberrations and shortcomings, but to the sins of the society that had bred him – from this moment he stuck to his point at the price of resigning from society, of exiling himself even from those circles in which the other eighteenth-century philosophers had found so agreeable a welcome and so sympathetic a hearing.

You may say that it was Rousseau's neurotic character which prevented him from getting on with people and that he took it out in scolding society; and you may say that Casanova was at least as near to an accurate account of the situation when he attributed his own misfortunes to his faults. But the fact was that Rousseau had been led to a general truth by his individual case and, in spite of his ignominious adventures, had the courage and dignity of one who knew it. He belonged to the class of thinkers who, in opposing the prevalent philosophy of their time, find that they have behind them a great pressure of unformulated general feeling and who themselves prevail as the spokesmen of the age that follows theirs.

Casanova once came with a lady of quality to pay a visit to Rousseau in his retirement. The callers found him lacking in affability and failed to get very much out of him though Casanova admitted that Rousseau had talked intelligently. Madame d'Urfé thought him boorish, and they laughed about him after they had left.

Casanova, ignoring his many humiliations, was still trying to crash the gate at a time when Rousseau, for all his clumsiness, had got hold of the lever of the Revolution.

JUSTICE TO EDITH WHARTON

BEFORE Edith Wharton died, the more commonplace work of her later years had had the effect of dulling the reputation of her earlier and more serious work. It seemed to me that the notices elicited by her death did her, in general, something less than justice; and I want to try to throw into relief the achievements which did make her important during a period — say, 1905-1917 — when there were few American writers worth reading. This essay is therefore no very complete study, but rather in the nature of an impression by a reader who was growing up at that time.

Mrs. Wharton's earliest fiction I never found particularly attractive. The influences of Paul Bourget and Henry James seem to have presided at the birth of her talent; and I remember these books as dealing with the artificial moral problems of Bourget and developing them with the tenuity of analysis which is what is least satisfactory in James. The stories tended to take place either in a social void or against a background of Italy or France which had somewhat the character of expensive upholstery. It was only with *The House of Mirth,* published in 1905, that Edith Wharton emerged as an historian of the American society of her time. For a period of fifteen years or more, she produced works of considerable interest both for its realism and its intensity.

One has heard various accounts of her literary beginnings. She tells us in her autobiography that a novel which she had composed at eleven and which began, 'Oh, how do you do, Mrs. Brown? . . . If only I had known you were going to call, I should have tidied up the drawing room' — had been returned by her mother with the chilling comment, 'Drawing-rooms are always tidy.' And it is said that a book of verse which she had written and had had secretly printed was discovered and destroyed by her parents, well-to-do New Yorkers of merchant stock, who thought it unladylike for a young woman to write. It seems to be an authentic fact, though Mrs. Wharton does not mention it in her memoirs, that she first seriously began to write fiction after her marriage during the period of a nervous breakdown, at the suggestion of Dr. S. Weir Mitchell, who himself combined the practice of literature with his pioneer work in the field of female neuroses. Thereafter she seems to have depended on her writing to get her through some difficult years, a situation that became more and more painful. Her husband, as she tells us, had some mental disease which was steadily growing worse from the very first years of their marriage, and he inhabited a social world of the rich which was sealed tight to intellectual interests. Through her writing, she came gradually into relation with the international literary world and made herself a partially independent career.

Her work was, then, the desperate product of a pressure of maladjustments; and it very soon took a direction totally different from that of Henry James, as a lesser disciple of whom she is sometimes pointlessly listed. James's interests were predominantly esthetic: he is never a passionate social prophet; and only rarely — as in *The Ivory Tower*, which seems in turn to have derived from Mrs. Wharton — does he satirize plutocratic America. But a passionate social prophet is precisely what Edith Wharton became. At her strongest and most characteristic, she is a brilliant example of the writer who relieves an emotional strain by denouncing his generation.

It is true that she combines with indignation against a

specific phase of American society a general sense of inexorable doom for human beings. She was much haunted by the myth of the Eumenides; and she had developed her own deadly version of the working of the Aeschylean necessity — a version as automatic and rapid, as decisive and as undimmed by sentiment, as the mechanical and financial processes which during her lifetime were transforming New York. In these books, she was as pessimistic as Hardy or Maupassant. You find the pure expression of her hopelessness in her volume of poems, *Artemis to Actaeon*, published in 1909, which, for all its hard accent and its ponderous tone, its 'impenetrables' and 'incommunicables' and 'incommensurables,' its 'immemorial altitudes august,' was not entirely without interest or merit. 'Death, can it be the years shall naught avail?' she asks in one of the sonnets called *Experience:* ' "Not so," Death answered. "They shall purchase sleep." ' But in the poem called *Moonrise over Tyringham*, she seems to be emerging from a period of strain into a relatively tranquil stoicism. She is apostrophizing the first hour of night:

> Be thou the image of a thought that fares
> Forth from itself, and flings its ray ahead,
> Leaping the barriers of ephemeral cares,
> To where our lives are but the ages' tread,
>
> And let this year be, not the last of youth,
> But first — like thee! — of some new train of hours,
> If more remote from hope, yet nearer truth,
> And kin to the unpetitionable powers.

But the catastrophe in Edith Wharton's novels is almost invariably the upshot of a conflict between the individual and the social group. Her tragic heroines and heroes are the victims of the group pressure of convention; they are passionate or imaginative spirits, hungry for emotional and intellectual experience, who find themselves locked into a small closed system, and either destroy themselves by beating their heads against their prison or suffer a living death in resigning themselves to it. Out of these themes she got a sharp pathos all her own. The language and some of the machinery of *The House of Mirth* seem old-fashioned and rather melodramatic today; but the book had some originality and power, with its chronicle of a social parasite on the fringes of the very rich, dragging out a stupefying routine of week-ends, yachting trips and dinners, and finding a window open only twice, at the beginning and at the end of the book, on a world where all the values are not money values.

The Fruit of the Tree, which followed it in 1907, although its characters are concerned with larger issues, is less successful than *The House of Mirth,* because it is confused between two different kinds of themes. There is a more or less trumped-up moral problem *à la* Bourget about a 'mercy killing' by a high-minded trained nurse, who happened to have an 'affinity,' as they used to say at that period, with the husband of the patient. But there is also the story of an industrial reformer, which is on the whole quite ably handled — especially in the opening scenes, in which the hero, assistant manager of a textile mill, is aroused by an industrial accident to try to remove the conditions which have caused it and finds himself up against one of those tight family groups that often dominate American factory towns, sitting ensconced in their red-satin drawing-rooms on massively upholstered sofas, amid heavy bronze chandeliers and mantels surrounded by obelisk clocks; and in its picture of his marriage with the mill-owning widow and the gradual drugging of his purpose under the influence of a house on Long Island of a quality more gracious and engaging but on an equally overpowering scale.

Edith Wharton had come to have a great hand with all kinds of American furnishings and with their concomitant landscape-gardening. Her first book had been a work on interior decorating; and now in her novels she adopts the practice of inventorying the contents of her characters' homes. Only Clyde Fitch, I think, in those early nineteen-hundreds made play to the same degree with the miscellaneous material objects with which Americans were surrounding themselves, articles which had just been manufactured and which people were being induced to buy. I suppose that no other writer of comedies of any other place or time has depended so much on stage sets and, especially, on stage properties: the radiators that bang in *Girls,* the artificial orange in *The Truth,* the things that are dropped under the table by the ladies in the second act of *The Climbers.* But in the case of Edith Wharton, the *décors* become the agents of tragedy. The characters of Clyde Fitch are embarrassed or tripped up by these articles; but the people of Edith Wharton are pursued by them as by spirits of doom and ultimately crushed by their accumulation. These pieces have not been always made newly: sometimes they are *objets d'art,* which have been expensively imported from Europe. But the effect is very much the same: they are something extraneous to the people and, no matter how old they may be, they seem to glitter and clank with the coin that has gone to buy them. A great many of Mrs. Wharton's descriptions are, of course, satiric or caustic; but when she wants to produce an impression of real magnificence, and even when she is writing about Europe, the thing still seems rather inorganic. She was not only one of the great pioneers, but also the poet, of interior decoration.

In *The Custom of the Country* (1913), Mrs. Wharton's next novel about the rich — *The Reef* is a relapse into 'psychological problems' — she piles up the new luxury of the era to an altitude of ironic grandeur, like the glass mountain in the *Arabian Nights,* which the current of her imagination manages to make incandescent. The first scene sets the key for the whole book: 'Mrs. Spragg and her visitor were enthroned in two heavy gilt armchairs in one of the private drawing-rooms of the Hotel Stentorian. The Spragg rooms were known as one of the Looey suites, and the drawing-room walls, above their wainscoting of highly varnished mahogany, were hung with salmon-pink damask and adorned with oval portraits of Marie Antoinette and the Princess de Lamballe. In the center of the florid carpet a gilt table with a top of Mexican onyx sustained a palm in a gilt basket tied with a pink bow. But for this ornament, and a copy of *The Hound of the Baskervilles* which lay beside it, the room showed no traces of human use, and Mrs. Spragg herself wore as complete an air of detachment as if she had been a wax figure in a show-window.' In the last pages — it is an admirable passage — Undine Spragg's little boy is seen wandering alone amid the splendors of the Paris *hôtel* which has crowned his mother's progress from the Stentorian: 'the white fur rugs and brocade chairs' which 'seemed maliciously on the watch for smears and ink-spots,' 'his mother's wonderful lacy bedroom, all pale silks and velvets, artful mirrors and veiled lamps, and the boudoir as big as a drawing-room, with pictures he would have liked to know about, and tables and cabinets holding things he was afraid to touch,' the library, with its 'rows and rows of books, bound in dim browns and golds, and old faded reds as rich as velvet: they all looked as if they might have had stories in them as splendid as their bindings. But the bookcases were closed with gilt trellising, and when Paul reached up to open one, a servant told him that Mr. Moffatt's secretary kept them locked because the books were too valuable to be taken down.'

It is a vein which Sinclair Lewis has worked since — as in the opening pages of *Babbitt*, where Babbitt is shown entangled with his gadgets; and in other respects *The Custom of the Country* opens up the way for Lewis, who dedicated *Main Street* to Edith Wharton. Mrs. Wharton has already arrived at a method of doing crude and harsh people with a draftsmanship crude and harsh. Undine Spragg, the social-climbing divorcée, though a good deal less humanly credible than Lily Bart of *The House of Mirth*, is quite a successful caricature of a type who was to go even farther. She is the prototype in fiction of the 'gold-digger,' of the international cocktail bitch. Here the pathos has been largely subordinated to an implacable animosity toward the heroine; but there is one episode both bitter and poignant, in which a discarded husband of Undine's, who has been driven by her demands to work in Wall Street and left by her up to his neck in debt, goes home to Washington Square through 'the heat, the noise, the smells of disheveled midsummer' New York, climbs to the room at the top of the house where he has kept his books and other things from college, and shoots himself there.

The other side of this world of wealth, which annihilates every impulse toward excellence, is a poverty which also annihilates. The writer of one of the notices on Mrs. Wharton's death was mistaken in assuming that *Ethan Frome* was a single uncharacteristic excursion outside the top social strata. It is true that she knew the top strata better than she knew anything else; but both in *The House of Mirth* and *The Fruit of the Tree*, she is always aware of the pit of misery which is implied by the wastefulness of the plutocracy, and the horror or the fear of this pit is one of the forces that determine the action. There is a Puritan in Edith Wharton, and this Puritan is always insisting that we must face the unpleasant and the ugly. Not to do so is one of the worst sins in her morality; sybarites like Mr. Langhope in *The Fruit of the Tree*, amusing himself with a dilettante archaeology on his income from a badly-managed factory, like the fatuous mother of *Twilight Sleep,* who feels so safe with her facial massage and her Yogi, while her family goes to pieces under her nose, are among the characters whom she treats with most scorn. And the three novels I have touched on above were paralleled by another series — *Ethan Frome, Bunner Sisters* and *Summer* — which dealt with *milieux* of a different kind.

Ethan Frome is still much read and well-known; but *Bunner Sisters* has been undeservedly neglected. It is the last piece in the volume called *Xingu* (1916), a short novel about the length of *Ethan Frome.* This story of two small shopkeepers on Stuyvesant Square and a drug-addict clockmaker from Hoboken, involved in a relationship like a triple noose which will gradually choke them all, is one of the most terrible things that Edith Wharton ever wrote; and the last page, in which the surviving sister, her lifelong companion gone and her poor little business lost, sets out to look for a job, seems to mark the grimmest moment of Edith Wharton's darkest years. Here is not even the grandeur of the heroic New England hills: ' "Ain't you going to leave the *ad*-dress?" the young woman called out after her. Ann Eliza went out into the thronged street. The great city, under the fair spring sky, seemed to throb with the air of innumerable beginnings. She walked on, looking for another shop window with a sign in it.'

Summer (1917), however, returns to the Massachusetts of *Ethan Frome,* and, though neither so harrowing nor so vivid, is by no means an inferior work. Making hats in a millinery shop was the abyss from which Lily Bart recoiled; the heroine of *Summer* recoils from the nethermost American social stratum, the degenerate 'mountain people. Let down by the refined young man who works in the public library and wants to become an architect, in a way that anticipates the situation in Dreiser's *American Tragedy,* she finds that she cannot go back to her own people and allows herself to be made an honest woman by the rather admirable old failure of a lawyer who had brought her down from the mountain in her childhood. It is the first sign on Mrs. Wharton's part of a relenting in the cruelty of her endings. 'Come to my age,' says Charity Royall's protector, 'a man knows the things that matter and the things that don't; that's about the only good turn life does us.' Her blinding bitterness is already subsiding.

But in the meantime, before *Summer* was written, she had escaped from the hopeless situation created by her husband's insanity. The doctors had told her he was hopeless; but she had had difficulty in inducing his family to allow her to leave him with an attendant. The tragedy of *Bunner Sisters* is probably a transposition of this; and the relief of the tension in *Summer* is evidently the result of her new freedom. She was at last finally detached from her marriage; and she took up her permanent residence in France. The war came, and she threw herself into its activities.

And now the intensity dies from her work as the American background fades. One can see this already in *Summer*, and *The Age of Innocence* (1930) is really Edith Wharton's valedictory. The theme is closely related to those of *The House of Mirth* and *Ethan Frome*: the frustration of a potential pair of lovers by social or domestic obstructions. But setting it back in the generation of her parents, she is able to contemplate it now without quite the same rancor, to soften it with a poetic mist of distance. And yet even here the old impulse of protest still makes itself felt as the main motive. If we compare *The Age of Innocence* with Henry James's *Europeans*, whose central situation it reproduces, the pupil's divergence from the master is seen in the most striking way. In both cases, a Europeanized American woman — Baroness Münster, Countess Olenska — returns to the United States to intrude upon and disturb the existence of a conservative

provincial society; in both cases, she attracts and almost
captivates an intelligent man of the community who turns
out, in the long run, to be unable to muster the courage
to take her, and who allows her to go back to Europe.
Henry James makes of this a balanced comedy of the conflict between the Bostonian and the cosmopolitan points
of view (so he reproached her with not having developed
the theme of Undine Spragg's marriage with a French
nobleman in terms of French and American manners, as
he had done with a similar one in *The Reverberator*); but
in Edith Wharton's version one still feels an active resentment against the pusillanimity of the provincial group and
also, as in other of her books, a special complaint against
the timid American male who has let the lady down.

Up through *The Age of Innocence*, and recurring at all
points of her range from *The House of Mirth* to *Ethan
Frome*, the typical masculine figure in Edith Wharton's
fiction is a man set apart from his neighbors by education,
intellect and feeling, but lacking the force or the courage
either to impose himself or to get away. She generalizes
about this type in the form in which she knew it best in
her autobiographical volume: 'They combined a cultivated taste with marked social gifts,' she says; but 'their
weakness was that, save in a few cases, they made so little
use of their ability': they were content to 'live in dilet-
tanish leisure,' rendering none of 'the public services that
a more enlightened social system would have exacted of
them.' But she had described a very common phenomenon
of the America of after the Civil War. Lawrence Selden,
the city lawyer, who sits comfortably in his bachelor apart-
ment with his flowerbox of mignonette and his first edition of La Bruyere and allows Lily Bart to drown, is the
same person as Lawyer Royall of *Summer*, with his lofty
orations and his drunken lapses. One could have found
him during the big-business era in almost any American
city or town: the man of superior abilities who had the

impulse toward self-improvement and independence, but
who had been more or less rendered helpless by the surf
of headlong money-making and spending which carried
him along with its breakers or left him stranded on the
New England hills — in either case thwarted and stunted
by the mediocre level of the community. In Edith Wharton's novels these men are usually captured and dominated by women of conventional morals and middle-class
ideals; when an exceptional woman comes along who is
thirsting for something different and better, the man is
unable to give it to her. This special situation Mrs. Wharton, with some conscious historical criticism but chiefly
impelled by a feminine animus, has dramatized with much
vividness and intelligence. There are no first-rate men in
these novels.

The Age of Innocence is already rather faded. But now
a surprising lapse occurs. (It is true that she is nearly
sixty.)

When we look back on Mrs. Wharton's career, it seems
that everything that is valuable in her work lies within a
quite sharply delimited area — between *The House of
Mirth* and *The Age of Innocence*. It is sometimes true of
women writers — less often, I believe, of men — that a
manifestation of something like genius may be stimulated
by some exceptional emotional strain, but will disappear
when the stimulus has passed. With a man, his professional, his artisan's life is likely to persist and evolve as a
partially independent organism through the vicissitudes
of his emotional experience. Henry James in a virtual
vacuum continued to possess and develop his *métier* up to
his very last years. But Mrs. Wharton had no *métier* in
this sense. With her emergence from her life in the
United States, her settling down in the congenial society
of Paris, she seems at last to become comfortably adjusted;
and with her adjustment, the real intellectual force which

she has exerted through a decade and a half evaporates almost completely. She no longer maims or massacres her characters. Her grimness melts rapidly into benignity. She takes an interest in young people's problems, in the solicitude of parents for children; she smooths over the misunderstandings of lovers; she sees how things may work out very well. She even loses the style she has mastered. Beginning with a language rather ponderous and stiff, the worst features of the style of Henry James and a stream of clichés from old novels and plays, she finally — about the time of *Ethan Frome* — worked out a prose of flexible steel, bright as electric light and striking out sparks of wit and color, which has the quality and pace of New York and is one of its distinctive artistic products. But now not merely does she cease to be brilliant, she becomes almost commonplace.

The Glimpses of the Moon, which followed *The Age of Innocence,* is, as someone has said, scarcely distinguishable from the ordinary serial in a women's magazine; and indeed it is in the women's magazines that Mrs. Wharton's novels now begin first to appear. *A Son at the Front* is a little better, because it had been begun in 1918 and had her war experience in it, with some of her characteristic cutting satire at the expense of the belligerents behind the lines. It is not bad as a picture of the emotions of a middle-aged civilian during the war — though not so good as Arnold Bennett's *The Pretty Lady.*

Old New York was a much feebler second boiling from the tea-leaves of *The Age of Innocence.* I have read only one of Mrs. Wharton's novels written since *Old New York: Twilight Sleep* is not so bad as her worst, but suffers seriously as a picture of New York during the middle nineteen-twenties from the author's long absence abroad. Mrs. Wharton is no longer up on her American interior-decorating — though there are some characteristic passages of landscape-gardening: ' "Seventy-five thousand bulbs

this year!" she thought as the motor swept by the sculp-
tured gateway, just giving and withdrawing a flash of turf
sheeted with amber and lilac, in a setting of twisted and
scalloped evergreens.'

The two other books that I have read since then — *The
Writing of Fiction* (which does, however, contain an excellent essay on Proust) and the volume of memoirs called
A Backward Glance — I found rather disappointing. The
backward glance is an exceedingly fleeting one which
dwells very little on anything except the figure of Henry
James, of whom Mrs. Wharton has left a portrait enter-
taining but slightly catty and curiously superficial. About
herself she tells us nothing much of interest; and she
makes amends to her New York antecedents for her satire
of *The Age of Innocence* by presenting them in tinted
miniatures, prettily remote and unreal. It is the last irony
of *The Age of Innocence* that Newland Archer should
become reconciled to 'old New York.' 'After all,' he eventually came to tell himself, 'there was good in the old
ways.' Something like this seems to have happened to
Edith Wharton. Even in *A Backward Glance,* she confesses that 'the weakness of the social structure' of her
parents' generation had been 'a blind dread of innovation';
but her later works show a dismay and a shrinking before
what seemed to her the social and moral chaos of an age
which was battering down the old edifice that she herself
had once depicted as a prison. Perhaps, after all, the old
mismated couples who had stayed married in deference to
the decencies were better than the new divorced who were
not aware of any duties at all.

The only thing that does survive in *A Backward Glance*
is some trace of the tremendous blue-stocking that Mrs.
Wharton was in her prime. The deep reverence for the
heroes of art and thought — though she always believed
that Paul Bourget was one of them — of the woman who
in earlier days had written a long blank-verse poem about

Vesalius, still makes itself felt in these memoirs. Her culture was rather heavy and grand — a preponderance of Goethe and Schiller, Racine and La Bruyère — but it was remarkably solid for an American woman and intimately related to her life. And she was one of the few Americans of her day who cared enough about serious literature to take the risks of trying to make some contribution to it. Professor Charles Eliot Norton — who had, as she dryly remarks, so admirably translated Dante — once warned her that 'no great work of the imagination' had 'ever been based on illicit passion.' Though she herself in her later years was reduced to contemptuous complaints that the writers of the new generations had 'abandoned creative art for pathology,' she did have the right to insist that she had 'fought hard' in her earlier days 'to turn the wooden dolls' of conventional fiction 'into struggling, suffering human beings.' She had been one of the few such human beings in the America of the early nineteen hundreds who found an articulate voice and set down a durable record.

The above was written in 1937. An unfinished novel by Edith Wharton was published in 1938. This story, *The Buccaneers,* deserves a word of postscript. The latter part of it, even allowing for the fact that it was never carried beyond a first draft, seems banal and a little trashy. Here as elsewhere the mellowness of Mrs. Wharton's last years has dulled the sharp outlines of her fiction: there are passages in *The Buccaneers* which read like an old-fashioned story for girls. But the first section has a certain brilliance. The figures of the children of the *nouveaux riches* at Saratoga during the seventies, when the post-Civil-War fortunes were rolling up, come back rather diminished in memory but in lively and charming colors, like the slides of those old magic lanterns that are mentioned as one of their forms of entertainment. And we learn from Mrs. Wharton's scenario for the unfinished part of the tale that it was to have had rather an interesting development. She has here more or less reversed the values of the embittered *Custom of the Country*: instead of playing off the culture and tradition of Europe against the vulgar Americans who are insensible to them, she dramatizes the climbing young ladies as an air-clearing and revivifying force. In the last pages she lived to write she made it plain that the hard-boiled commercial elements on the rise in both civilizations were to come to understand one another perfectly. But there is also an Anglo-Italian woman, the child of Italian revolutionaries and a cousin of Dante Gabriel Rossetti, who has been reduced to working as a governess and who has helped to engineer the success of the American girls in London. The best of these girls has been married to a dreary English duke, who represents everything least human in the English aristocratic system. Laura Testvalley was to forfeit her own hopes of capturing an amateur esthete of the older generation of the nobility in order to allow the young American to elope with an enterprising young Englishman; and thus to have let herself in for the fate of spending the rest of her days in the poverty and dulness of her home, where the old revolution had died. As the light of Edith Wharton's art grows dim and at last goes out, she leaves us, to linger on our retina, the large dark eyes of the clever spinster, the serious and attentive governess, who trades in worldly values but manages to rebuff these values; who, in following a destiny of solitude and discipline, contends for the rights of the heart; and who, child of a political movement played out, yet passes on something of its impetus to the emergence of the society of the future.

ERNEST HEMINGWAY's *In Our Time* was an odd and original book. It had the appearance of a miscellany of stories and fragments; but actually the parts hung together and produced a definite effect. There were two distinct series of pieces which alternated with one another: one a set of brief and brutal sketches of police shootings, bullfight crises, hangings of criminals, and incidents of the war; and the other a set of short stories dealing in its principal sequence with the growing-up of an American boy against a landscape of idyllic Michigan, but interspersed also with glimpses of American soldiers returning home. It seems to have been Hemingway's intention — *'In Our Time'* — that the war should set the key for the whole. The cold-bloodedness of the battles and executions strikes a discord with the sensitiveness and candor of the boy at home in the States; and presently the boy turns up in Europe in one of the intermediate vignettes as a soldier in the Italian army, hit in the spine by machine-gun fire and trying to talk to a dying Italian: *'Senta,* Rinaldi. *Senta,'* he says, 'you and me, we've made a separate peace.'

But there is a more fundamental relationship between the pieces of the two series. The shooting of Nick in the war does not really connect two different worlds: has he not found in the butchery abroad the same world that he knew back in Michigan? Was not life in the Michigan woods equally destructive and cruel? He had gone once with his father, the doctor, when he had performed a

Caesarean operation on an Indian squaw with a jackknife and no anaesthetic and had sewed her up with fishing leaders, while the Indian hadn't been able to bear it and had cut his throat in his bunk. Another time, when the doctor had saved the life of a squaw, her Indian had picked a quarrel with him rather than pay him in work. And Nick himself had sent his girl about her business when he had found out how terrible her mother was. Even fishing in Big Two-Hearted River — away and free in the woods — he had been conscious in a curious way of the cruelty inflicted on the fish, even of the silent agonies endured by the live bait, the grasshoppers kicking on the hook.

Not that life isn't enjoyable. Talking and drinking with one's friends is great fun; fishing in Big Two-Hearted River is a tranquil exhilaration. But the brutality of life is always there, and it is somehow bound up with the enjoyment. Bullfights are especially enjoyable. It is even exhilarating to build a simply priceless barricade and pot the enemy as they are trying to get over it. The condition of life is pain; and the joys of the most innocent surface are somehow tied to its stifled pangs.

The resolution of this dissonance in art made the beauty of Hemingway's stories. He had in the process tuned a marvelous prose. Out of the colloquial American speech, with its simple declarative sentences and its strings of Nordic monosyllables, he got effects of the utmost subtlety. F. M. Ford has found the perfect simile for the impression produced by this writing: 'Hemingway's words strike you, each one, as if they were pebbles fetched fresh from a brook. They live and shine, each in its place. So one of his pages has the effect of a brook-bottom into which you look down through the flowing water. The words form a tesellation, each in order beside the other.'

Looking back, we can see how this style was already being refined and developed at a time — fifty years before

—when it was regarded in most literary quarters as hope-
lessly non-literary and vulgar. Had there not been the
nineteenth chapter of *Huckleberry Finn?* — 'Two or three
nights went by; I reckon I might say they swum by; they
slid along so quick and smooth and lovely. Here is the way
we put in the time. It was a monstrous big river down
there — sometimes a mile and a half wide,' and so forth.
These pages, when we happen to meet them in Carl Van
Doren's anthology of world literature, stand up in a striking way beside a passage of description from Turgenev;
and the pages which Hemingway was later to write about
American wood and water are equivalents to the tran-
scriptions by Turgenev — the *Sportsman's Notebook* is
much admired by Hemingway — of Russian forests and
fields. Each has brought to an immense and wild country
the freshness of a new speech and a sensibility not yet
conventionalized by literary associations. Yet it *is* the
European sensibility which has come to Big Two-Hearted
River, where the Indians are now obsolescent; in those
solitudes it feels for the first time the cold current, the hot
morning sun, sees the pine stumps, smells the sweet fern.
And along with the mottled trout, with its 'clear water-
over-gravel color,' the boy from the American Middle
West fishes up a nice little masterpiece.

In the meantime there had been also Ring Lardner,
Sherwood Anderson, Gertrude Stein, using this American
language for irony, lyric poetry or psychological insight.
Hemingway seems to have learned from them all. But he
is now able to charge this naïve accent with a new complexity of emotion, a new shade of emotion: a malaise.
The wholesale shattering of human beings in which he
has taken part has given the boy a touch of panic.

II

The next fishing trip is strikingly different. Perhaps the
first had been an idealization. Is it possible to attain to

such sensuous bliss merely through going alone into the woods: smoking, fishing, and eating, with no thought about anyone else or about anything one has ever done or will ever be obliged to do? At any rate, today, in *The Sun Also Rises,* all the things that are wrong with human life are there on the holiday, too — though one tries to keep them back out of the foreground and to occupy one's mind with the trout, caught now in a stream of the Pyrenees, and with the kidding of the friend from the States. The feeling of insecurity has deepened. The young American now appears in a seriously damaged condition: he has somehow been incapacitated sexually through wounds received in the war. He is in love with one of those international sirens who flourished in the cafés of the post-war period and whose ruthless and uncontrollable infidelities, in such a circle as that depicted by Hemingway, have made any sort of security impossible for the relations between women and men. The lovers of such a woman turn upon and rend one another because they are powerless to make themselves felt by *her.*

The casualties of the bullfight at Pamplona, to which these young people have gone for the *fiesta,* only reflect the blows and betrayals of demoralized human beings out of hand. What is the tiresome lover with whom the lady has just been off on a casual escapade, and who is unable to understand that he has been discarded, but the man who, on his way to the bull ring, has been accidentally gored by the bull? The young American who tells the story is the only character who keeps up standards of conduct, and he is prevented by his disability from dominating and directing the woman, who otherwise, it is intimated, might love him. Here the membrane of the style has been stretched taut to convey the vibrations of these qualms. The dry sunlight and the green summer landscapes have been invested with a sinister quality which must be new in literature. One enjoys the sun and the green as one enjoys suckling pigs and Spanish wine, but the uneasiness and apprehension are undruggable.

Yet one can catch hold of a code in all the drunkenness and the social chaos. 'Perhaps as you went along you did learn something,' Jake, the hero, reflects at one point. 'I did not care what it was all about. All I wanted to know was how to live in it. Maybe if you found out how to live in it you learned from that what it was all about.' 'Everybody behaves badly. Give them the proper chance,' he says later to Lady Brett.

' "You wouldn't behave badly." Brett looked at me.' In the end, she sends for Jake, who finds her alone in a hotel. She has left her regular lover for a young bullfighter, and this boy has for the first time inspired her with a respect which has restrained her from 'ruining' him: 'You know it makes one feel rather good deciding not to be a bitch.' We suffer and we make suffer, and everybody loses out in the long run; but in the meantime we can lose with honor.

This code still markedly figures, still supplies a dependable moral backbone, in Hemingway's next book of short stories, *Men Without Women*. Here Hemingway has mastered his method of economy in apparent casualness and relevance in apparent indirection, and has turned his sense of what happens and the way in which it happens into something as hard and clear as a crystal but as disturbing as a great lyric. Yet it is usually some principle of courage, of honor, of pity — that is, some principle of sportsmanship in its largest human sense — upon which the drama hinges. The old bullfighter in *The Undefeated* is defeated in everything except the spirit which will not accept defeat. You get the bull or he gets you: if you die, you can die game; there are certain things you cannot do. The burlesque show manager in *A Pursuit Race* refrains from waking his advance publicity agent when he overtakes him and realizes that the man has just lost a long struggle against whatever anguish it is that has driven him to drink and dope. 'They got a cure for that,' the manager had said to him before he went to sleep; ' "No," William Campbell said, "they haven't got a cure for anything.' " The burned major in *A Simple Enquiry* — that strange picture of the bedrock stoicism compatible with the abasement of war — has the decency not to dismiss the orderly who has rejected his proposition. The brutalized Alpine peasant who has been in the habit of hanging a lantern in the jaws of the stiffened corpse of his wife, stood in the corner of the woodshed till the spring will make it possible to bury her, is ashamed to drink with the sexton after the latter has found out what he has done. And there is a little sketch of Roman soldiers just after the Crucifixion: 'You see me slip the old spear into him? — You'll get into trouble doing that some day. — It was the least I could do for him. I'll tell you he looked pretty good to me in there today.'

This Hemingway of the middle twenties — *The Sun Also Rises* came out in '26 — expressed the romantic disillusion and set the favorite pose for the period. It was the moment of gallantry in heartbreak, grim and nonchalant banter, and heroic dissipation. The great watchword was 'Have a drink'; and in the bars of New York and Paris the young people were getting to talk like Hemingway.

III

The novel, *A Farewell to Arms*, which followed *Men Without Women*, is in a sense not so serious an affair. Beautifully written and quite moving of course it is. Probably no other book has caught so well the strangeness of life in the army for an American in Europe during the war. The new places to which one was sent of which one had never heard, and the things that turned out to be in them; the ordinary people of foreign countries as one saw them when one was quartered among them or obliged to perform some common work with them; the pleasures of which one managed to cheat the war, intensified by the uncertainty and horror — and the uncertainty, nevertheless, almost become a constant, the horror almost taken for granted; the love affairs, always subject to being suddenly broken up and yet carried on while they lasted in a spirit of irresponsible freedom which derived from one's having forfeited control of all one's other actions — this Hemingway got into his book, written long enough after the events for them to present themselves under an aspect fully idyllic.

But *A Farewell to Arms* is a tragedy, and the lovers are shown as innocent victims with no relation to the forces that torment them. They themselves are not tormented within by that dissonance between personal satisfaction and the suffering one shares with others which it has been Hemingway's triumph to handle. *A Farewell to Arms,* as the author once said, is a *Romeo and Juliet.* And when Catherine and her lover emerge from the stream of action — the account of the Caporetto retreat is Hemingway's best sustained piece of narrative — when they escape from the alien necessities of which their romance has been merely an accident, which have been writing their story for them, then we see that they are not in themselves convincing as human personalities. And we are confronted with the paradox that Hemingway, who possesses so remarkable a mimetic gift in getting the tone of social and national types and in making his people talk appropriately, has not shown any very solid sense of character, or, indeed, any real interest in it. The people in his short stories are satisfactory because he has only to hit them off: the point of the story does not lie in personalities, but in the emotion to which a situation gives rise. This is true even in *The Sun Also Rises,* where the characters are sketched with wonderful cleverness. But in *A Farewell to Arms,* as soon as we are brought into real intimacy with the lovers, as

soon as the author is obliged to see them through a searching personal experience, we find merely an idealized relationship, the abstractions of a lyric emotion.

With *Death in the Afternoon*, three years later, a new
development for Hemingway commences. He writes a
book not merely in the first person, but in the first person
in his own character as Hemingway, and the results are
unexpected and disconcerting. *Death in the Afternoon* has
its value as an exposition of bullfighting; and Hemingway
is able to use the subject as a text for an explicit statement
of his conception of man eternally pitting himself — he
thinks the bullfight a ritual of this — against animal force
and the odds of death. But the book is partly infected by
a queer kind of maudlin emotion, which sounds at once
neurotic and drunken. He overdoes his glorification of the
bravery and martyrdom of the bullfighter. No doubt the
professional expert at risking his life single-handed is impressive in contrast to the flatness and unreality of much
of the business of the modern world; but this admirable
miniaturist in prose has already made the point perhaps
more tellingly in the little prose poem called *Banal Story*.
Now he offsets the virility of the bullfighters by anecdotes
of the male homosexuals that frequent the Paris cafés, at
the same time that he puts his chief celebration of the
voluptuous excitement of the spectacle into the mouth of
an imaginary old lady. The whole thing becomes a little
hysterical.

The master of that precise and clean style now indulges
in purple patches which go on spreading for pages. I am
not one of those who admire the last chapter of *Death in
the Afternoon*, with its rich, all too rich, unrollings of
memories of good times in Spain, and with its what seem
to me irrelevant reminiscences of the soliloquy of Mrs.
Bloom in *Ulysses*. Also, there are interludes of kidding of
a kind which Hemingway handles with skill when he
assigns them to characters in his stories, but in connection

with which he seems to become incapable of exercising good sense or good taste as soon as he undertakes them in his own person (the burlesque *Torrents of Spring* was an early omen of this). In short, we are compelled to recognize that, as soon as Hemingway drops the burning-glass of the disciplined and objective art with which he has learned to concentrate in a story the light of the emotions that flood in on him, he straightway becomes befuddled, slops over.

This befuddlement is later to go further, but in the meantime he publishes another volume of stories — *Winner Take Nothing* — which is almost up to its predecessor. In this collection he deals much more effectively than in *Death in the Afternoon* with that theme of contemporary decadence which is implied in his panegyric of the bullfighter. The first of these stories, *After the Storm*, is another of his variations — and one of the finest — on the theme of keeping up a code of decency among the hazards and pains of life. A fisherman goes out to plunder a wreck: he dives down to break in through a porthole, but inside he sees a woman with rings on her hands and her hair floating loose in the water, and he thinks about the passengers and crew being suddenly plunged to their deaths (he has almost been killed himself in a drunken fight the night before). He sees the cloud of sea birds screaming around, and he finds that he is unable to break the glass with his wrench and that he loses the anchor grapple with which he next tries to attack it. So he finally goes away and leaves the job to the Greeks, who blow the boat open and clean her out.

But in general the emotions of insecurity here obtrude themselves and dominate the book. Two of the stories deal with the hysteria of soldiers falling off the brink of their nerves under the strain of the experiences of the war, which here no longer presents an idyllic aspect; another deals with a group of patients in a hospital, at the same

time crippled and hopeless; still another (a five-page masterpiece) with a waiter, who, both on his own and on his
customers' account, is reluctant to go home at night, because he feels the importance of a 'clean well-lighted cafe'
as a refuge from the 'nothing' that people fear. *God Rest
You Merry, Gentlemen* repeats the theme of castration of
The Sun Also Rises; and four of the stories are concerned
more or less with male or female homosexuality. In the
last story, *Fathers and Sons,* Hemingway reverts to the
Michigan woods, as if to take the curse off the rest: young
Nick had once enjoyed a nice Indian girl with plump legs
and hard little breasts on the needles of the hemlock
woods.

These stories and the interludes in *Death in the Afternoon* must have been written during the years that followed the stock-market crash. They are full of the apprehension of losing control of oneself which is aroused by
the getting out of hand of a social-economic system, as
well as of the fear of impotence which seems to accom-
pany the loss of social mastery. And there is in such a story
as *A Clean Well-Lighted Place* the feeling of having got
to the end of everything, of having given up heroic attitudes and wanting only the illusion of peace.

IV

And now, in proportion as the characters in his stories
run out of fortitude and bravado, he passes into a phase
where he is occupied with building up his public personality. He has already now become a legend, as Mencken
was in the twenties; he is the Hemingway of the hand-
some photographs with the sportsmen's tan and the out-
door grin, with the ominous resemblance to Clark Gable,
who poses with giant marlin which he has just hauled in
off Key West. And unluckily — but for an American inevitably — the opportunity soon presents itself to exploit
this personality for profit: he turns up delivering Hem-

ingway monologues in well-paying and trashy magazines; and the Hemingway of these loose disquisitions, arrogant, belligerent and boastful, is certainly the worst-invented character to be found in the author's work. If he is obnoxious, the effect is somewhat mitigated by the fact that he is intrinsically incredible.

There would be no point in mentioning this journalism at all, if it did not seem somewhat to have contributed to the writing of certain unsatisfactory books. *Green Hills of Africa* (1935) owes its failure to falling between the two *genres* of personal exhibitionism and fiction. 'The writer has attempted,' says Hemingway, 'to write an absolutely true book to see whether the shape of a country and the pattern of a month's action can, if truly presented, compete with a work of the imagination.' He does try to present his own rôle objectively, and there is a genuine Hemingway theme — the connection between success at big-game hunting and sexual self-respect — involved in his adventures as he presents them. But the sophisticated technique of the fiction writer comes to look artificial when it is applied to a series of real happenings; and the necessity of sticking to what really happened makes impossible the typical characters and incidents which give point to a work of fiction. The monologues by the false, the publicity, Hemingway with which the narrative is interspersed are almost as bad as the ones that he has been writing for the magazines. He inveighs with much scorn against the literary life and against the professional literary man of the cities; and then manages to give the impression that he himself is a professional literary man of the touchiest and most self-conscious kind. He delivers a self-confident lecture on the high possibilities of prose writing; and then produces such a sentence as the following: 'Going downhill steeply made these Spanish shooting boots too short in the toe and there was an old argument, about this length of boot and whether the bootmaker, whose part I had taken, unwittingly first, only as interpreter, and finally embraced his theory patriotically as a whole and, I believed, by logic, had overcome it by adding onto the heel.' As soon as Hemingway begins speaking in the first person, he seems to lose his bearings, not merely as a critic of life, but even as a craftsman.

In another and significant way, *Green Hills of Africa* is disappointing. *Death in the Afternoon* did provide a lot of data on bullfighting and build up for us the bull-fighting world; but its successor tells us little about Africa. Hemingway keeps affirming — as if in accents of defiance against those who would engage his attention for social problems — his passionate enthusiasm for the African country and his perfect satisfaction with the hunter's life; but he has produced what must be one of the only books ever written which make Africa and its animals seem dull. Almost the only thing we learn about the animals is that Hemingway wants to kill them. And as for the natives, though there is one fine description of a tribe of marvelous trained runners, the principal impression we get of them is that they were simple and inferior people who enormously admired Hemingway.

It is not only that, as his critics of the Left had been complaining, he shows no interest in political issues, but that his interest in his fellow beings seems actually to be drying up. It is as if he were throwing himself on African hunting as something to live for and believe in, as something through which to realize himself; and as if, expecting of it too much, he had got out of it abnormally little, less than he is willing to admit. The disquiet of the Hemingway of the twenties had been, as I have said, undruggable — that is, in his books themselves, he had tried to express it, not drug it, had given it an appeasement in art; but now there sets in, in the Hemingway of the thirties, what seems to be a deliberate self-drugging. The situation is indicated objectively in *The Gambler, the Nun and the*

Radio, one of the short stories of 1933, in which everything from daily bread to 'a belief in any new form of government' is characterized as 'the opium of the people' by
an empty-hearted patient in a hospital.

But at last there did rush into this vacuum the blast of
the social issue, which had been roaring in the wind like
a forest fire.

Out of a series of short stories that Hemingway had
written about a Florida waterside character he decided to
make a little epic. The result was *To Have and Have
Not,* which seems to me the poorest of all his stories. Certainly some deep agitation is working upon Hemingway
the artist. Craftsmanship and style, taste and sense, have
all alike gone by the board. The negative attitude toward
human beings has here become definitely malignant: the
hero is like a wooden-headed Punch, always knocking
people on the head (inferiors — Chinamen or Cubans);
or, rather, he combines the characteristics of Punch with
those of Popeye the Sailor in the animated cartoon in the
movies. As the climax to a series of prodigies, this stu-
pendous pirate-smuggler named Harry Morgan succeeds,
alone, unarmed, and with only a hook for one hand —
though at the cost of a mortal wound — in outwitting and
destroying with their own weapons four men carrying re-
volvers and a machine gun, by whom he has been shang-
haied in a launch. The only way in which Hemingway's
outlaw suffers by comparison with Popeye is that his creator has not tried to make him plausible by explaining that
he does it all on spinach.

The impotence of a decadent society has here been exploited deliberately, but less successfully than in the earlier short stories. Against a background of homosexuality,
impotence and masturbation among the wealthy holiday-
makers in Florida, Popeye-Morgan is shown gratifying his
wife with the same indefatigable dexterity which he has

displayed in his other feats; and there is a choral refrain of praise of his *cojones,* which wells up in the last pages of the book when the abandoned Mrs. Popeye regurgitates Molly Bloom's soliloquy.

To be a man in such a world of maggots is noble, but it is not enough. Besides the maggots, there are double-crossing rats, who will get you if they are given the slightest chance. What is most valid in *To Have and Have Not* is the idea — conveyed better, perhaps, in the first of the series of episodes than in the final scenes of massacre and agony — that in an atmosphere (here revolutionary Cuba) in which man has been set against man, in which it is always a question whether your companion is not preparing to cut your throat, the most sturdy and straightforward American will turn suspicious and cruel. Harry Morgan is made to realize as he dies that to fight this bad world alone is hopeless. Again Hemingway, with his barometric accuracy, has rendered a moral atmosphere that was prevalent at the moment he was writing — a moment when social relations were subjected to severe tensions, when they seemed sometimes already disintegrating. But the heroic Hemingway legend has at this point invaded his fiction and, inflaming and inflating his symbols, has produced an implausible hybrid, half Hemingway character, half nature myth.

Hemingway had not himself particularly labored this moral of individualism *versus* solidarity, but the critics of the Left labored it for him and received his least creditable piece of fiction as the delivery of a new revelation. The progress of the Communist faith among our writers since the beginning of the depression has followed a peculiar course. That the aims and beliefs of Marx and Lenin should have come through to the minds of intellectuals who had been educated in the bourgeois tradition as great awakeners of conscience, a great light, was quite natural and entirely desirable. But the conception of the dynamic

Marxist will, the exaltation of the Marxist religion, seized
the members of the professional classes like a capricious
contagion or hurricane, which shakes one and leaves his
neighbor standing, then returns to lay hold on the second
after the first has become quiet again. In the moment of
seizure, each one of them saw a scroll unrolled from the
heavens, on which Marx and Lenin and Stalin, the Bolsheviks of 1917, the Soviets of the Five-Year Plan, and the
GPU of the Moscow trials were all a part of the same
great purpose. Later the convert, if he were capable of it,
would get over his first phase of snow blindness and learn
to see real people and conditions, would study the development of Marxism in terms of nations, periods, personalities, instead of logical deductions from abstract proposi-
tions or — as in the case of the more naïve or dishonest —
of simple incantatory slogans. But for many there was at
least a moment when the key to all the mysteries of human
history seemed suddenly to have been placed in their
hands, when an infallible guide to thought and behavior
seemed to have been given them in a few easy formulas.

Hemingway was hit pretty late. He was still in *Death in
the Afternoon* telling the 'world-savers,' sensibly enough,
that they should 'get to see' the world 'clear and as a
whole. Then any part you make will represent the whole,
if it's made truly. The thing to do is work and learn to
make it.' Later he jibed at the literary radicals, who talked
but couldn't take it; and one finds even in *To Have and
Have Not* a crack about a 'highly paid Hollywood director, whose brain is in the process of outlasting his liver so
that he will end up calling himself a Communist, to save
his soul.' Then the challenge of the fight itself — Hemingway never could resist a physical challenge — the natural
impulse to dedicate oneself to something bigger than big-
game hunting and bullfighting, and the fact that the class
war had broken out in a country to which he was roman-

tically attached, seem to have combined to make him align himself with the Communists as well as the Spanish Loyalists at a time when the Marxist philosophy had been pretty completely shelved by the Kremlin, now reactionary as well as corrupt, and when the Russians were lending the Loyalists only help enough to preserve, as they imagined would be possible, the balance of power against Fascism while they acted at the same time as a police force to beat down the real social revolution.

Hemingway raised money for the Loyalists, reported the battle fronts. He even went so far as to make a speech at a congress of the League of American Writers, an organization rigged by the supporters of the Stalinist régime in Russia and full of precisely the type of literary revolutionists that he had been ridiculing a little while before. Soon the Stalinists had taken him in tow, and he was feverishly denouncing as Fascists other writers who criticized the Kremlin. It has been one of the expedients of the Stalin administration in maintaining its power and covering up its crimes to condemn on trumped-up charges of Fascist conspiracy, and even to kidnap and murder, its political opponents of the Left; and, along with the food and munitions, the Russians had brought to the war in Spain what the Austrian journalist Willi Schlamm called that diversion of doubtful value for the working class: 'Herr Vyshinsky's Grand Guignol.'

The result of this was a play, *The Fifth Column*, which, though it is good reading for the way the characters talk, is an exceedingly silly production. The hero, though an Anglo-American, is an agent of the Communist secret police, engaged in catching Fascist spies in Spain; and his principal exploit in the course of the play is clearning out, with the aid of a single Communist, an artillery post manned by seven Fascists. The scene is like a pushover and getaway from one of the cruder Hollywood Westerns.

It is in the nature of a small boy's fantasy, and would probably be considered extravagant by most writers of books for boys.

The tendency on Hemingway's part to indulge himself in these boyish day-dreams seems to begin to get the better of his realism at the end of *A Farewell to Arms,* where the hero, after many adventures of fighting, escaping, love-making and drinking, rows his lady thirty-five kilometers on a cold and rainy night; and we have seen what it could do for Harry Morgan. Now, as if with the conviction that the cause and the efficiency of the GPU have added several cubits to his stature, he has let this tendency loose; and he has also found in the GPU's grim duty a pretext to give rein to the appetite for describing scenes of killing which has always been a feature of his work. He has progressed from grasshoppers and trout through bulls and lions and kudus to Chinamen and Cubans, and now to Fascists. Hitherto the act of destruction has given rise for him to complex emotions: he has identified himself not merely with the injurer but also with the injured; there has been a masochistic complement to the sadism. But now this paradox which splits our natures, and which has instigated some of Hemingway's best stories, need no longer present perplexities to his mind. The Fascists are dirty bastards, and to kill them is a righteous act. He who had made a separate peace, who had said farewell to arms, has found a reason for taking them up again in a spirit of rabietic fury unpleasantly reminiscent of the spy mania and the sacred anti-German rage which took possession of so many civilians and staff officers under the stimulus of the last war.

Not that the compensatory trauma of the typical Hemingway protagonist is totally absent even here. The main episode is the hero's brief love affair and voluntary breaking off with a beautiful and adoring girl whose acquaintance he has made in Spain. As a member of the Junior

League and a graduate of Vassar, she represents for him —
it seems a little hard on her — that leisure-class playworld
from which he is trying to get away. But in view of the
fact that from the very first scenes he treats her with more
or less open contempt, the action is rather lacking in suspense as the sacrifice is rather feeble in moral value. One
takes no stock at all in the intimation that Mr. Philip may
later be sent to mortify himself in a camp for training
Young Pioneers. And in the meantime he has fun killing
Fascists.

In *The Fifth Column*, the drugging process has been
carried further still: the hero, who has become finally in-
distinguishable from the false or publicity Hemingway,
has here dosed himself not only with whiskey, but with a
seductive and desirous woman, for whom he has the most
admirable reasons for not taking any responsibility, with
sacred rage, with the excitement of a bombardment, and
with indulgence in that headiest of sports, for which he
has now the same excellent reasons: the bagging of human beings.

v

You may fear, after reading *The Fifth Column*, that
Hemingway will never sober up; but as you go on to his
short stories of this period, you find that your apprehen-
sions were unfounded. Three of these stories have a great
deal more body — they are longer and more complex —
than the comparatively meager anecdotes collected in
Winner Take Nothing. And here are his real artistic successes with the material of his adventures in Africa, which
make up for the miscarried *Green Hills: The Short Happy
Life of Francis Macomber* and *The Snows of Kilimanjaro*,
which disengage, by dramatizing them objectively, the
themes he had attempted in the earlier book but that had
never really got themselves presented. And here is at least
a beginning of a real artistic utilization of Hemingway's

experience in Spain: an incident of the war in two pages which outweighs the whole of *The Fifth Column* and all his Spanish dispatches, a glimpse of an old man, 'without politics,' who has so far occupied his life in taking care of eight pigeons, two goats and a cat, but who has now been dislodged and separated from his pets by the advance of the Fascist armies. It is a story which takes its place among the war prints of Callot and Goya, artists whose union of elegance with sharpness has already been recalled by Hemingway in his earlier battle pieces: a story which might have been written about almost any war.

And here — what is very remarkable — is a story, *The Capital of the World*, which finds an objective symbol for, precisely, what is wrong with *The Fifth Column*. A young boy who has come up from the country and waits on table in a pension in Madrid gets accidentally stabbed with a meat knife while playing at bullfighting with the dishwasher. This is the simple anecdote, but Hemingway has built in behind it all the life of the pension and the city: the priesthood, the working-class movement, the grown-up bullfighters who have broken down or missed out. 'The boy Paco,' Hemingway concludes, 'had never known about any of this nor about what all these people would be doing on the next day and on other days to come. He had no idea how they really lived nor how they ended. He did not realize they ended. He died, as the Spanish phrase has it, full of illusions. He had not had time in his life to lose any of them, or even, at the end, to complete an act of contrition.' So he registers in this very fine piece the discrepancy between the fantasies of boyhood and the realities of the grown-up world. Hemingway the artist, who feels things truly and cannot help recording what he feels, has actually said good-bye to these fantasies at a time when the war correspondent is making himself ridiculous by attempting to hang on to them still.

The emotion which principally comes through in *Fran-*

cis *Macomber* and *The Snows of Kilimanjaro* — as it figures also in *The Fifth Column* — is a growing antagonism
to women. Looking back, one can see at this point that the
tendency has been there all along. In *The Doctor and the
Doctor's Wife,* the boy Nick goes out squirrel-hunting
with his father instead of obeying the summons of his
mother; in *Cross Country Snow,* he regretfully says farewell to male companionship on a skiing expedition in
Switzerland, when he is obliged to go back to the States
so that his wife can have her baby. The young man in
Hills Like White Elephants compels his girl to have an
abortion contrary to her wish; another story, *A Canary for
One,* bites almost unbearably but exquisitely on the lone-
liness to be endured by a wife after she and her husband
shall have separated; the peasant of *An Alpine Idyll*
abuses the corpse of his wife (these last three appear under the general title *Men Without Women*). Brett in *The
Sun Also Rises* is an exclusively destructive force: she
might be a better woman if she were mated with Jake,
the American; but actually he is protected against her and
is in a sense revenging his own sex through being unable
to do anything for her sexually. Even the hero of *A Farewell to Arms* eventually destroys Catherine — after enjoying her abject devotion — by giving her a baby, itself born
dead. The only women with whom Nick Adams' relations
are perfectly satisfactory are the little Indian girls of his
boyhood who are in a position of hopeless social disadvantage and have no power over the behavior of the white
male — so that he can get rid of them the moment he has
done with them. Thus in *The Fifth Column* Mr. Philip
brutally breaks off with Dorothy — he has been rescued
from her demoralizing influence by his enlistment in the
Communist crusade, just as the hero of *The Sun Also
Rises* has been saved by his physical disability — to revert
to a little Moorish whore. Even Harry Morgan, who is
represented as satisfying his wife on the scale of a Paul

Bunyan, deserts her in the end by dying and leaves her racked by the cruelest desire.[1]

And now this instinct to get the woman down presents itself frankly as a fear that the woman will get the man down. The men in both these African stories are married to American bitches of the most soul-destroying sort. The hero of *The Snows of Kilimanjaro* loses his soul and dies of futility on a hunting expedition in Africa, out of which he has failed to get what he had hoped. The story is not quite stripped clean of the trashy moral attitudes which have been coming to disfigure the author's work: the hero, a seriously intentioned and apparently promising writer, goes on a little sloppily over the dear early days in Paris when he was earnest, happy and poor, and blames a little hysterically the rich woman whom he has married and who has debased him. Yet it is one of Hemingway's remarkable stories. There is a wonderful piece of writing at the end when the reader is made to realize that what has seemed to be an escape by plane, with the sick man looking down on Africa, is only the dream of a dying man. The other story, *Francis Macomber*, perfectly realizes its purpose. Here the male saves his soul at the last minute,

[1] There would probably be a chapter to write on the relation between Hemingway and Kipling, and certain assumptions about society which they share. They have much the same split attitude toward women. Kipling anticipates Hemingway in his beliefs that 'he travels the fastest that travels alone' and that 'the female of the species is more deadly than the male; and Hemingway seems to reflect Kipling in the submissive infra-Anglo-Saxon women that make his heroes such perfect mistresses. The most striking example of this is the amoeba-like little Spanish girl, Maria, in *For Whom the Bell Tolls*. Like the docile native 'wives' of English officials in the early stories of Kipling, she lives only to serve her lord and to merge her identity with him; and this love affair with a woman in a sleeping-bag, lacking completely the kind of give and take that goes on between real men and women, has the all-too-perfect felicity of a youthful erotic dream. One suspects that *Without Benefit of Clergy* was read very early by Hemingway and that it made on him a lasting impression. The pathetic conclusion of this story of Kipling's seems unmistakably to be echoed at the end of *A Farewell to Arms*.

and then is actually shot down by his woman, who does not want him to have a soul. Here Hemingway has at last got what Thurber calls the war between men and women right out into the open and has written a terrific fable of the impossible civilized woman who despises the civilized man for his failure in initiative and nerve and then jealously tries to break him down as soon as he begins to exhibit any. (It ought to be noted, also, that whereas in *Green Hills of Africa* the descriptions tended to weigh down the narrative with their excessive circumstantiality, the landscapes and animals of *Francis Macomber* are alive and unfalteringly proportioned.)

Going back over Hemingway's books today, we can see clearly what an error of the politicos it was to accuse him of an indifference to society. His whole work is a criticism of society: he has responded to every pressure of the moral atmosphere of the time, as it is felt at the roots of human relations, with a sensitivity almost unrivaled. Even his preoccupation with licking the gang in the next block and being known as the best basketball player in high school has its meaning in the present epoch. After all, whatever is done in the world, political as well as athletic, depends on personal courage and strength. With Hemingway, courage and strength are always thought of in physical terms, so that he tends to give the impression that the bullfighter who can take it and dish it out is more of a man than any other kind of man, and that the sole duty of the revolutionary socialist is to get the counter-revolutionary gang before they get him.

But ideas, however correct, will never prevail by themselves: there must be people who are prepared to stand or fall with them, and the ability to act on principle is still subject to the same competitive laws which operate in sporting contests and sexual relations. Hemingway has expressed with genius the terrors of the modern man at the danger of losing control of his world, and he has also, within his scope, provided his own kind of antidote. This antidote, paradoxically, is almost entirely moral. Despite Hemingway's preoccupation with physical contests, his heroes are almost always defeated physically, nervously, practically: their victories are moral ones. He himself, when he trained himself stubbornly in his unconventional unmarketable art in a Paris which had other fashions, gave the prime example of such a victory; and if he has sometimes, under the menace of the general panic, seemed on the point of going to pieces as an artist, he has always pulled himself together the next moment. The principle of the Bourdon gauge, which is used to measure the pressure of liquids, is that a tube which has been curved into a coil will tend to straighten out in proportion as the liquid inside it is subjected to an increasing pressure.

The appearance of *For Whom the Bell Tolls* since this essay was written in 1939 carries the straightening process further. Here Hemingway has largely sloughed off his Stalinism and has reverted to seeing events in terms of individuals pitted against specific odds. His hero, an American teacher of Spanish who has enlisted on the side of the Loyalists, gives his life to what he regards as the cause of human liberation; but he is frustrated in the task that has been assigned him by the confusion of forces at cross-purposes that are throttling the Loyalist campaign. By the time that he comes to die, he has little to sustain him but the memory of his grandfather's record as a soldier in the American Civil War. The psychology of this young man is presented with a certain sobriety and detachment in comparison with Hemingway's other full-length heroes; and the author has here succeeded as in none of his earlier books in externalizing in plausible characters the elements of his own complex personality. With all this, there is an historical point of view which he has learned from his political adventures: he has aimed to reflect in this episode the whole course of the Spanish War and the tangle of tendencies involved in it.

The weaknesses of the book are its diffuseness — a shape that lacks the concision of his short stories, that sometimes sags and sometimes bulges; and a sort of exploitation of the material, an infusion of the operatic, that lends itself all too readily to the movies.

THE DREAM OF H. C. EARWICKER

JAMES JOYCE's *Ulysses* was an attempt to present directly the thoughts and feelings of a group of Dubliners through the whole course of a summer day. *Finnegans Wake* is a complementary attempt to render the dream fantasies and the half-unconscious sensations experienced by a single person in the course of a night's sleep.

This presents a more difficult problem to the reader as well as to the writer. In *Ulysses,* the reader was allowed to perceive the real objective world in which the Blooms and Dedalus lived, and their situation and relationships in that world, so that its distortions or liquefactions under the stress of special psychological states still usually remained intelligible. But in *Finnegans Wake* we are not supplied with any objective data until the next to the last chapter, when the hero — and then only rather dimly — wakes up for a short time toward morning; and we are dealing with states of consciousness which, though they sometimes have something in common with the drunken imaginations of the Night Town scene in *Ulysses* or the free associations of Mrs. Bloom's insomniac reveries, are even more confused and fluid than these; so that it becomes on a first reading the reader's prime preoccupation to puzzle out who the dreamer is and what has been happening to him. And since Joyce has spent seventeen years elaborating and complicating this puzzle, it is hardly to be expected that one reading will suffice to unravel it completely.

Let me try to establish, however, some of the most important facts which provide the realistic foundation for this immense poem of sleep. The hero of *Finnegans Wake* is a man of Scandinavian blood, with what is apparently an adapted Scandinavian name: Humphrey Chimpden Earwicker, who keeps a pub called The Bristol in Dublin. He is somewhere between fifty and sixty, blond and ruddy, with a walrus mustache, very strong but of late years pretty fat. When embarrassed, he has a tendency to stutter. He has tried his hand at a number of occupations; has run for office and has gone through a bankruptcy. He is married to a woman named Ann, a former salesgirl, who is more or less illiterate and whose maiden name seems to have begun with Mac. They are both Protestants in a community of Catholics, he an Episcopalian and she a Presbyterian; and by reason both of his religion and of his queer-sounding foreign name, he feels himself, like Bloom in *Ulysses,* something of an alien among his neighbors. The Earwickers have three children — a girl named Isobel, who has evidently passed adolescence, and two younger boys, twins: Kevin and Jerry. There are also a maid-of-all-work called Kate and a man about the place called Tom.

It is a Saturday night in summer, after a disorderly evening in the pub. Somebody — probably Earwicker himself — has been prevailed upon to sing a song: later, when it was closing time, he had to put a man outside, who abused him and threw stones at the window. There has also been a thunderstorm. Earwicker has been drinking off and on all day and has perhaps gone to bed a little drunk. At any rate, his night is troubled. At first he dreams about the day before, with a bad conscience and a sense of humiliation: then, as the night darkens and he sinks more deeply into sleep, he has to labor through a nightmare oppression.

He and his wife are sleeping together; but he has no longer any interest in her as a woman. He is preoccupied now with his children. His wife is apparently much younger than he, was only a girl when he married her; so that it is easy for him to confuse his first feelings for her with something like an erotic emotion which is now being aroused by his daughter. And his affection for his favorite son is even acquiring homosexual associations. Little Kevin is relatively sedate: named after the ascetic St. Kevin, he may be destined for the Catholic priesthood. Jerry (Shem) is more volatile and has given evidences of a taste for writing; and it is Jerry rather than Kevin (Shaun) with whom the father has tended to identify himself.

To tell the story in this way, however, is to present it the wrong way around. It depends for its dramatic effect on our not finding out till almost the end — pages 555-590, in which Earwicker partially wakes up — that the flights of erotic fantasy and the horrors of guilt of his dream have been inspired by his feelings for his children. The pub is on the edge of the Phoenix Park, between it and the River Liffey and not far from the suburb of Chapelizod, which is said to have been the birthplace of Iseult. At the very beginning of the dream, we find Earwicker figuring as Tristram; and through the whole night he is wooing Iseult; he carries her off, he marries her. The Freudian censor has intervened to change *Isobel* into *Iseult la Belle* — as well as to turn the ana (upper)-Liffey, which figures in the dream as a woman, into *Anna Livia Plurabelle*. The idea of incest between father and daughter is developed on page 115; the transition from Isobel to Iseult is indicated in the 'Icy-la-Belle' of page 246; and the sister of the twins is designated by her family nickname 'Izzy' on page 431. But, though the boys have been given their real names and planted pretty clearly — on pages 26-27 — it is not until almost the end — on page 556 — that a definite identification of Earwicker's daughter with Iseult is made. In the same way, it is not until the passage on pages 564-565 that we are led to connect with Earwicker's son the homosexual motif which has first broken into his dream with the ominous incident of the father's accosting a soldier in the park and subsequently being razzed by the police, and which works free toward morning — page 474 — to the idea, not related to actuality, of 'some chubby boy-bold love of an angel.'

In the meantime, the incest taboo and the homosexuality taboo have together — as in the development of Greek tragedy out of the old myths of cannibalism and incest — given rise, during Earwicker's effortful night, to a whole mythology, a whole morality. He is Tristram stealing Iseult, yes; but — at the suggestion of an Adam's mantelpiece in the bedroom where he is sleeping — he is also Adam, who has forfeited by his sin the Paradise of the Phoenix Park; at the suggestion of a copy of Raphael's picture of Michael subduing Satan which hangs on the bedroom wall, he is an archangel wrestling with the Devil. And he has fallen not merely as Adam but also as Humpty Dumpty (he is fat and his first name is Humphrey); as the hero of the ballad of *Finnegan's Wake*, who fell off a scaffold while building a house (but came to life again at the sound of the word 'Whisky'); and as Napoleon (an obelisk dedicated to Wellington is a feature of the Phoenix Park, though there is apparently no Wellington Museum). Since the landmarks of the life of Swift still keep their prestige in Dublin, he is Swift, who loved Stella and Vanessa with the obstructed love of a father and whose mind was finally blotted by madness: Swift's cryptic name for Stella, 'Ppt,' punctuates the whole book.

And Earwicker is also making up in sleep for an habitual feeling of helplessness due to his belonging to a racial and religious minority. He is sometimes the first Danish conqueror of Ireland, who sailed up that very Liffey; sometimes Oliver Cromwell, that other hated heathen invader.

But it is Joyce's further aim to create, through Earwicker's mythopœic dream, a set of symbols even more general and basic. He has had the idea of making Earwicker, resolved into his elemental components, include the whole of humanity. The river, with its feminine personality, Anna Livia Plurabelle, comes to represent the feminine principle itself. At one time or another all the women who figure in Earwicker's fantasy are merged into this stream of life which, always renewed, never pausing, flows through the world built by men. The daughter, still a little girl, is early identified with a cloud, which will come down to earth as rain and turn into the rapid young river; the Anna Livia Plurabelle chapter describes a lively woman's coming-of-age; in the end, the mature river, broader and slower now, will move toward her father, the sea. The corresponding masculine principle is symbolized by the Hill of Howth, which rises at the mouth of the Liffey; and the idea of the hill as a citadel and the idea of the city as a male construction associate themselves with this: the man is a hill that stands firm while the river runs away at his feet; he is a fortress, he is Dublin, he is all the cities of the world.

And if Earwicker is animated in sleep by the principles of both the sexes, he has also a double existence in the rôles of both Youth and Old Age. Canalizing his youthful impulses in a vision of himself as his favorite son, he dreams himself endowed with a resilience to go out and try life again; exalted by a purity of idealism which has not yet been tainted by experience, and yet bubbling with roguish drolleries, blithely beloved by the girls. On the other hand, foreshadowing his own decline, he sees the vision of a chorus of old men, who, drivelingly reminiscent, at the same time gloat and scold at the thought of the vigorous young Tristram kissing Iseult on the other side of the bushes, and exclaim in admiration — an expansion of Earwicker's feelings at the sight of his own sleeping son — over the form of the sleeping Earwicker (Shaun-Jerry). The old men are named Matthew Gregory, Marcus Lyons, Luke Tarpey and Johnny MacDougall; and they are iden-

tified variously with the four apostles, the Four Masters
(early sages of Irish legend), the Four Waves of Irish
mythology, the four courts of Dublin, and the four prov-
inces of Ireland (Johnny MacDougall is evidently Ulster:
he always follows at some distance behind the others).
These fathers are always associated with a gray ass and
sycamore trees, and have perhaps been suggested to Earwicker by four sycamore trees on the Liffey, among which
a neighbor's donkey has been grazing. All of these major
motifs are woven in and out from beginning to end of the
book, and each at a given point receives a complete development: the woman-river in pages 196-216 — the well-
known Anna Livia Plurabelle chapter; the male city-
fortress-hill in pages 532-554 (already published separately
as *Haveth Childers Everywhere*); the Young Man in the
chapters about Shaun, pages 403-473; and the Old Men,
providing a contrast, just before, in 383-399.

There are also a stone and an elm on opposite sides of
the Liffey, which represent the death principle and the
life principle (Ygdrasil). The tree has several graciously
rustling solos (a notable one at the end, beginning on
page 619), and in the Anna Livia Plurabelle chapter she
has a long conversation with the stone, which blends with
the gossip of two old washerwomen drying clothes on the
riverbank. This dialogue is only one of many dialogues
which are really always the same disputation, and in
which one of the parties, like the stone, is always hard-
boiled, immobile and prosaic, while the other is sensitive,
alive, rather light-mindedly chattering or chirping. The
tougher of the two parties in these interchanges is always
browbeating or bullying the other. Sometimes they are
Satan and Saint Michael; sometimes they are transmogrified antitheses derived from Aesop's fables: the Mookse
and the Gripes (the Fox and the Grapes), the Ondt and
the Gracehoper (the Ant and the Grasshopper); but all
these dualisms are evidently connected with the diverse

temperaments of Earwicker's twins (who sometimes appear as Cain and Abel), and represent the diverse elements in the character of Earwicker himself, as these struggle within his own consciousness, the aggressive side sometimes reflecting certain powers in the external world — the force of hostile opinion or the police — which he now fears, now feels he can stand up to. The various pairs, however, shift their balance and melt into one another so readily that it is impossible to give any account of them which will cover all the cases in the book.

Besides all this, just as Joyce in *Ulysses* laid the *Odyssey* under requisition to help provide a structure for his material — material which, once it had begun to gush from the rock of Joyce's sealed personality at the blow of the Aaron's rod of free association, threatened to rise and submerge the artist like the flood which the sorcerer's apprentice let loose by his bedeviled broom; so in the face of an even more formidable danger, he has here brought in the historical theory of the eighteenth-century philosopher, Giambattista Vico, to help him to organize *Finnegans Wake*. It was Vico's idea that civilizations always pass through three definite phases: a phase when people imagine gods, a phase when they make up myths about heroes, and a phase when they see things in terms of real men. It will be noted that the figures mentioned above divide themselves among these three categories of beings. Vico further believed that history moved in cycles and that it was always repeating itself, which — to the frequent exasperation of the reader — *Finnegans Wake* is also made to do. And there is also a good deal more out of Vico, which you can find out about in *Our Exagmination*[1] but which

[1] *Our Exagmination Round His Factification for Incamination of Work in Progress,* published by New Directions at Norfolk, Connecticut. This is a collection of papers from *Transition,* the Paris magazine in which *Finnegans Wake* first appeared. The writers have taken their cues from Joyce himself, and he seems to have

seems even more idle and forced than the most forced and idle aspects of the Odysseyan parallel in *Ulysses*. The fact that there is a Vico Road in the Dublin suburb Dalkey — 'The Vico Road goes round and round to meet where terms begin' — gives Joyce a peg in actuality on which to hang all this theory.

There is one important respect in which Joyce may seem to depart from Vico. Vico, so far as is known, did not believe in progress: his cycles did not spiral toward an earthly goal; his hope for salvation was in heaven. But the cycles of *Finnegans Wake* do result in a definite progression. As Earwicker lives through from darkness to light, he does slough off his feeling of guilt. By morning the Devil has been vanquished by Michael; Youth has bounded free of Age; the Phoenix of Vico and the Phoenix Park has risen from its ashes to new flight; Tristram has built a castle (Howth Castle) for his bride; and Iseult, once the object of an outlawed love, now married and growing older, turns naturally and comfortably at last into the lawful wife in the bed beside him, whom Earwicker is making an effort not to jab with his knees; the tumult and turbidity of Saturday night run clear in the peace of Sunday morning; the soul, which has been buried in sleep, is resurrected, refreshed, to life.

Yet if one looks at the book as a whole, one finds that the larger cycle does return upon itself. This will be seen when I discuss the last pages. In the meantime, let me merely point out that we do not find in *Finnegans Wake* any climax of exaltation comparable either to the scene where Stephen Dedalus realizes his artist's vocation or to Molly Bloom's great affirmative. The later book represents an aging phase in the constant human subject with which

chosen this way of providing the public with a key. It is, in fact, rather doubtful whether without the work done by *Transition* it would be possible to get the hang of the book at all. See also Mr. Max Eastman's account of an interview with Joyce on the subject in Part III, Chapter III, of *The Literary Mind*.

the series of Joyce's books has dealt. This subject — which must never be lost sight of, though in this case it is easy to do so — is the nexus of intimate relationships involved in a family situation. We find it first in the *Portrait of an Artist* in the attitude of Dedalus toward his family, and in the delicate but vital displacement in the relations of the young married couple who figure in the short story called *The Dead.* In *Exiles,* another young married couple come back from abroad with a son, and a more serious displacement takes place when the wife meets an old lover. In *Ulysses,* the relations of man and wife, by this time almost middle-aged, have been affected by more serious readjustments, and they are related in a complex way to the relations of the Blooms to their children, of Dedalus to his parents, and of both the Blooms to Dedalus. Now, in *Finnegans Wake,* the husband and wife have reached an age at which, from the emotional point of view, they seem hardly important to one another, and at which the chief source of interest is the attitude of the father toward the children — 'the child we all love to place our hope in,' as Earwicker thinks in the last moments before the rising sun wakes him up. (We have already had intimations of this relationship in the adoptively paternal instincts of Bloom toward the spiritually parentless Dedalus; in Joyce's little lyric poems, poignant to the point of anguish, that deal with his own children; and in the poem called *Ecce Puer,* in which the family cycle appears.)

Here this family situation has been explored more profoundly by Joyce than in any of his previous books. In sleep, the conventions and institutions with which we discipline and give shape to our lives are allowed partly to dissolve and evaporate, so as partly to set free the impulses of the common human plasm out of which human creatures are made; and then the sexual instincts of the man and the woman, the child's instinct and the parent's instinct, the masculine and feminine principles themselves, come into play in confusing ways, shadow forth disturbing relationships, which yet spring from the prime processes of life. *Finnegans Wake* carries even farther the kind of insight into such human relations which was already carried far in *Ulysses;* and it advances with an astounding stride the attempt to find the universally human in ordinary specialized experience which was implied in the earlier book by the Odysseyan parallel. Joyce will now try to build up inductively the whole of human history and myth from the impulses, conscious and dormant, the unrealized potentialities, of a single human being, who is to be a man even more obscure and even less well-endowed, even less civilized and aspiring, than was Leopold Bloom in *Ulysses.*

Finnegans Wake, in conception as well as in execution, is one of the boldest books ever written.

II

In order to get anything out of *Finnegans Wake,* you must grasp a queer literary convention. It has been said by T. S. Eliot that Joyce is the greatest master of language in English since Milton. Eliot has also pointed out that Milton is mainly a writer for the *ear.* Now Joyce through a large part of his adult life has been almost as blind as Milton; and he has ended, just as Milton did, by dealing principally in auditory sensations. There is as little visualization in *Finnegans Wake* as in *Samson Agonistes.* Our first criticism, therefore, is likely to be that nothing is *seen* in Earwicker's dream. It is, after all, not uncommon in dreams to have the illusion of seeing people and places as clearly as when we are awake; and in the dream literature with which we are already familiar — *Alice in Wonderland, The Temptation of Saint Anthony* — the dreamers are visited by plain apparitions, not merely by invisible voices. But we must assume with *Finnegans Wake* that Earwicker's imagination, like Joyce's is almost entirely auditory and verbal. We have been partly prepared by *Ulysses,* in which we listen to the thoughts of the characters but do not see them very distinctly.

But there is another and more serious difficulty to be got over. We are continually being distracted from identifying and following Earwicker, the humble proprietor of a public house, who is to encompass the whole microcosm of the dream, by the intrusion of all sorts of elements — foreign languages, literary allusions, historical information — which could not possibly have been in Earwicker's mind. The principle on which Joyce is operating may evidently be stated as follows. If the artist is to render directly all the feelings and fancies of a sleeper, primitive, inarticulate, infinitely imprecise as they are, he must create a literary medium of unexampled richness and freedom. Now it is also Joyce's purpose in *Finnegans Wake* to bring out in Earwicker's consciousness the processes of universal history: the languages, the cycles of society, the typical relationships of legend, are, he is trying to show us, all implicit in every human being. He has, as I have indicated, been careful to hook up his hero realistically with the main themes of his universal fantasia: the Bible stories, the Battle of Waterloo, Tristram and Iseult, and so forth. But since Earwicker's implications *are* shown to be universal, the author has the right to summon all the resources of his superior knowledge in order to supply a vehicle which will carry this experience of sleep. He has the same sort of justification for making the beings in Earwicker's dream speak Russian in fighting the siege of Sebastopol (which has got in by way of a picture hanging in Earwicker's house) as Thomas Hardy has, for example, to describe in his own literary vocabulary a landscape seen by an ignorant person. If it is objected that in *Finnegans Wake* the author is supposed to be not *describing,* but presenting the hero's consciousness directly, Joyce might reply that his procedure had precedent not only in

poetry, but also in pre-naturalistic fiction: even the characters of Dickens were allowed to make speeches in blank
verse, even the characters of Meredith were allowed to
converse in apothegms. Why shouldn't H. C. Earwicker
be allowed to dream in a language which draws flexibility
and variety from the author's enormous reservoir of colloquial and literary speech, of technical jargons and foreign tongues?

Yet here is where the reader's trouble begins, because
here, in spite of the defense just suggested, a convention
that seems indispensable has been disconcertingly violated.
What Joyce is trying to do is to break out of the Flaubert-
ian naturalism into something that moves more at ease
and that commands a wider horizon, something that is not
narrowly tied down to the data about a certain man living
in a certain year on a certain street of a certain city; and
the reaction is of course quite natural: it was inevitable
that the symbol and the myth, the traditional material of
poetry, should have asserted themselves again against the
formulas of scientific precision which had begun to prove
so cramping. But here the act of escaping from them
shocks, just as it sometimes did in Proust. Proust argues
in an impressive way, in the final section of his novel, the
case against nineteenth-century naturalism; yet who has
not been made uncomfortable at finding that Proust's personal manias have been allowed to affect the structure of
his book: that a story which has been presented as happening to real people should not maintain a consistent
chronology, that it should never be clear whether the narrator of the story is the same person as the author of the
book, and that the author, who ought to know everything,
should in some cases leave us in doubt as to the facts
about his hero? One had felt, in reading *Ulysses*, a touch
of the same uneasiness when the phantasmagoria imagined by Bloom in the drunken Night Town scene was en-
riched by learned fancies which would seem to be more

appropriate to Dedalus. And now in *Finnegans Wake* the balloon of this new kind of poetry pulls harder at its naturalistic anchor. We are in the first place asked to believe that a man like H. C. Earwicker would seize every possible pretext provided by his house and its location to include in a single night's dream a large number of historical and legendary characters. And is it not pretty farfetched to assume that Earwicker's awareness of the life of Swift or the Crimean War is really to be accurately conveyed in terms of the awareness of Joyce, who has acquired a special knowledge of these subjects? Also, what about the references to the literary life in Paris and to the book itself as Work in Progress, which take us right out of the mind of Earwicker and into the mind of Joyce?

There are not, to be sure, very many such winks and nudges as this, though the shadow of Joyce at his thankless task seems sometimes to fall between Earwicker and us. Joyce has evidently set himself limits as to how far he can go in this direction; and he may urge that since Earwicker is universal man, he must contain the implications of Joyce's destiny as he does those of Swift's and Napoleon's, though he has never heard of him as he has of them, and that to give these implications a personal accent is only to sign his canvas. Yet, even granting all this and recognizing the difficulty of the task and accepting without reservation the method Joyce has chosen for his purpose, the result still seems unsatisfactory, the thing has not quite come out right. Instead of the myths' growing out of Earwicker, Earwicker seems swamped in the myths. His personality is certainly created: we get to know him and feel sympathy for him. But he is not so convincing as Bloom was: there has been too much literature poured into him. He has exfoliated into too many arabesques, become hypertrophied by too many elements. And not merely has he to carry this load of myths; he has

also been all wound round by what seems Joyce's growing self-indulgence in an impulse to pure verbal play.

Here another kind of difficulty confronts us. There is
actually a special kind of language which people speak
in dreams and in which they sometimes even compose
poetry. This language consists of words and sentences
which, though they seem to be gibberish or nonsense
from the rational point of view, betray by their telescop-
ings of words, their combinations of incongruous ideas,
the involuntary preoccupations of the sleeper. Lewis Car-
roll exploited this dream language in *Jabberwocky,* and
it has been studied by Freud and his followers, from
whom Joyce seems to have got the idea of its literary possibilities. At any rate, *Finnegans Wake* is almost entirely
written in it.

The idea was brilliant in itself, and Joyce has in many
cases carried it out brilliantly. He has created a whole
new poetry, a whole new humor and pathos, of sentences
and words that go wrong. The special kind of equivocal
and prismatic effects aimed at by the symbolist poets have
here been achieved by a new method and on psychological principles which give them a new basis in humanity.
But the trouble is, it seems to me, that Joyce has somewhat overdone it. His method of giving words multiple
meanings allows him to go on indefinitely introducing
new ideas; and he has spent no less than seventeen years
embroidering *Finnegans Wake* in this way.

What has happened may be shown by the following
examples. First, a relatively simple one from a passage
about the Tree: 'Amengst menlike trees walking or trees
like angels weeping nobirdy aviar soar anywing to eagle
it!' It is quite clear in the last seven words how an ornitho-
logical turn has been given to 'nobody ever saw anything
to equal it.' Here is a more complex one: Earwicker, pic-

turing himself in the chapter in which he partially wakes
up, is made to designate his hair with the phrase 'beer wig.'
This has as its basis *bar wig*, which has rushed into the
breach as *beer wig* under the pressure of Earwicker's profession as a dispenser of drinks in his pub, of the fact that
his hair is yellow, and of his tendency to imagine that
his queer last name is being caricatured by his neighbors
as 'Earwigger' — a tendency which has led to his dream
being impishly haunted by earwigs. There are thus four
different ideas compressed in these two words. But let us
examine — with the aid of the hints provided by the *Exagmination* — an even more complicated passage. Here is
Earwicker-Joyce's depiction of the madness and eclipse of
Swift: 'Unslow, malswift, pro mean, proh noblesse, Atrahore, melancolores, nears; whose glauque eyes glitt bedimmed to imm; whose fingerings creep o'er skull: till
quench., asterr mist calls estarr and graw, honath Jon
raves homes glowcoma.' This passage, besides the more
or less obvious ones, contains apparently the following
ideas: Laracor, Swift's living in Ireland, combined with
the *atra cura, black care,* that rides behind the horseman
in the first poem of Book Three of Horace's *Odes;* the
Horatian idea that death comes to the mean and the noble
alike; *proh,* the Latin interjection of regret, and *pro,* perhaps referring to Swift's championship of the impoverished Irish; *melancolores, melancholy* plus *black-colored;*
glauque, French *gray-blue,* plus, Greek *glaux, owl* — gray
evening plus Swift's blue eyes, which also had an owlish
appearance; in *glitt bedimmed to imm,* the double con-
sonants evidently represent a deadening of the senses;
creep o'er skull, French *crépuscule, twilight; asterr,* Greek
aster, star, Swift's Stella, whose real name was Esther;
Vanessa's real name was Hester — so Stella calls Hester a
(q)wench; perhaps German *mist, dung, trash,* plays some
part here, too — as well as German *starr, rigid; graw* evidently contains German *grau,* gray; *honath Jon* is *honest*

John and *Jonathan; glowcoma* is *glaucoma,* a kind of blindness, plus the idea of a pale glow of life persisting in a coma. This passage has some beauty and power; but isn't it overingenious? Would anyone naturally think of Horace when he was confronted with 'Atrahore'? And, even admitting that it may be appropriate to associate Latin with Swift, how does the German get in? Swift did not know German nor had he any German associations.[1]

In some cases, this overlaying of meanings has had the result of rendering quite opaque passages which at an earlier stage — as we can see by comparing the finished text with some of the sections as they first appeared — were no less convincingly dreamlike for being more easily comprehensible. You will find three versions of a passage in *Anna Livia Plurabelle* on page 164 of the *Exagmination;* and on page 213 of the book you will see that Joyce has worked up still a fourth. My feeling is that he ought to have stopped somewhere between the second and the third. Here is Version I of 1925: 'Look, look, the dusk is growing. What time is it? It must be late. It's ages now since I or anyone last saw Waterhouse's clock. They took it asunder, I heard them say. When will they reassemble it?' And here is Version 4 of 1939: 'Look, look, the dusk is growing. My branches lofty are taking root. And my cold cher's gone ashley. Fieluhr? Filou! What age is at? It saon is late. 'Tis endless now senne eye or erewone last saw Waterhouse's clogh. They took it asunder, I hurd thum sigh. When will they reassemble it?' There is a gain

[1] I chose this passage because a partial exposition of it, which I take to be more or less authoritative, had appeared in the *Exagmination* (in the paper by Mr. Robert McAlmon). I did not remember to have read it in its place in *Finnegans Wake,* and was unable to find it when I looked for it. Since then I have been told by another reader who has been over and over the book that this sentence about Swift is not included. This is interesting because it indicates the operation of a principle of selection. Joyce suffered himself from glaucoma, and it may be that he eliminated the reference because he felt that it was too specifically personal.

in poetry, certainly; but in the meantime the question and the answer have almost disappeared. Has it really made Anna Livia any more riverlike to introduce the names of several hundred rivers (*saon* is *Saône* doing duty as *soon,* and *cher* is the *Cher* for French *chair*) — as he also introduces in other sections the names of cities, insects, trees? And why drag in *Erewhon?* In the same way, the talk of the Old Men, which, when it first came out in *Navire d'Argent,* seemed almost equal in beauty to the Anna Livia Plurabelle chapter, has now been so crammed with other things that the voices of the actual speakers have in places been nearly obliterated.

Joyce has always been rather deficient in dramatic and narrative sense. *Ulysses* already dragged; one got lost in it. The moments of critical importance were so run in with the rest that one was likely to miss them on first reading. One had to think about the book, read chapters of it over, in order to see the pattern and to realize how deep the insight went. And *Finnegans Wake* is much worse in this respect. The main outlines of the book are discernible, once we have been tipped off as to what it is all about. It is a help that, in forming our hypothesis, the principle of Occam's razor applies; for it is Joyce's whole design and point that the immense foaming-up of symbols should be reducible to a few simple facts. And it must also be conceded by a foreigner that a good deal which may appear to him mysterious would be plain enough to anyone who knew Dublin and something about Irish history, and that what Joyce has done here is as legitimate as it would be for an American writer to lay the scene of a similar fantasy somewhere on Riverside Drive in New York and to assume that his readers would be able to recognize Grant's Tomb, green buses, Columbia University and the figure of Hendrik Hudson. A foreign reader of *Finnegans Wake* should consult a map of Dublin, and look up the articles on Dublin and Ireland in the *Encyclopædia Britannica*.

Yet it seems to me a serious defect that we do not really understand what is happening till we have almost finished the book. *Then* we can look back and understand the significance of Earwicker's stuttering over the word *father* on page 45; we can see that 'Peder the Greste, altipaltar' on page 344 combines, along with Peter the Great and *agreste*, *pederast* and *pater*; we can conclude that the allusion on page 373 about 'begetting a wife which begame his niece by pouring her young-things into skintighs' refers back to the little story on pages 21-23, and that this whole theme is a device of the 'dream-work' to get over the incest barrier by disguising Earwicker's own children as the children of a niece.

But in the meantime we have had to make our way through five hundred and fifty-four pages; and there is much that is evidently important that we still do not understand. How, for example, is the story of the 'prankquean' just mentioned related to the motif of the letter scratched up by the chicken from the dump heap; and what is the point about this letter? The theme is developed at prodigious length in the chapter beginning on page 104; and it flickers all through the book. It turns up near the end — pages 623-624 — with new emotional connotations. The idea of letters and postmen plays a prominent part all through. Little Kevin is represented as giving the postman's knock; and Earwicker — though he here seems to be identifying himself with the other son, Jerry — is caught up into a long flight of fantasy in which he imagines himself a postman. The letter comes from Boston, Massachusetts, and seems to have been written by some female relation, perhaps the niece mentioned above. One feels that there is a third woman in the story, and that something important depends on this. Yet a consid-

erable amount of rereading has failed, in the case of the
present writer, to clear the matter up.

Finnegans Wake, in the actual reading, seems to me
for two thirds of its length not really to bring off what
it attempts. Nor do I think it possible to defend the procedure of Joyce on the basis of an analogy with music. It
is true that there is a good deal of the musician in Joyce:
his phonograph record of *Anna Livia* is as beautiful as a
fine tenor solo. But nobody would listen for half an hour
to a composer of operas or symphonic poems who went
on and on in one mood as monotonously as Joyce has done
in parts of *Finnegans Wake*, who scrambled so many motifs in one passage, or who returned to pick up a theme a
couple of hours after it had first been stated, when the
listeners would inevitably have forgotten it.[1]

[1] This essay was written in the summer of 1939, just after *Finnegans Wake* came out, and I have reprinted it substantially as it first
appeared. Since then an article by Mr. John Peale Bishop in *The
Southern Review* of summer, 1939, and studies by Mr. Harry Levin
in *The Kenyon Review* of Autumn, 1939, and in *New Directions*
of 1939, have thrown further light on the subject; and I have also
had the advantage of discussions with Mr. Thornton Wilder, who
has explored the book more thoroughly than anyone else I have
heard of. It is to be hoped that Mr. Wilder will some day publish
something about *Finnegans Wake;* and in the meantime those interested in the book should consult the essays mentioned, upon
which I have sometimes drawn in revising the present study.

One suggestion of Mr. Bishop's should certainly be noted here.
He believes that the riddle of the letter is the riddle of life itself.
This letter has been scratched up from a dung-heap and yet it has
come from another world; it includes in its very brief length marriage, children and death, and things to eat and drink – all the pri-
mary features of life, beyond which the ideas of the illiterate writer
evidently do not extend; and Earwicker can never really read it,
though the text seems exceedingly simple and though he confronts
it again and again.

I ought to amend what is said in this essay on the basis of a first
reading by adding that *Finnegans Wake*, like *Ulysses*, gets better
the more you go back to it. I do not know of any other books of
which it is true as it is of Joyce's that, though parts of them may
leave us blank or repel us when we try them the first time, they
gradually build themselves up for us as we return to them and think

I believe that the miscarriage of *Finnegans Wake,* in so far as it does miscarry, is due primarily to two tendencies of Joyce's which were already in evidence in *Ulysses:* the impulse, in the absence of dramatic power, to work up an epic impressiveness by multiplying and complicating detail, by filling in abstract diagrams and laying on intellectual conceits, till the organic effort at which he aims has been spoiled by too much that is synthetic; and a curious shrinking solicitude to conceal from the reader his real subjects. These subjects are always awkward and distressing: they have to do with the kind of feelings which people themselves conceal and which it takes courage in the artist to handle. And the more daring Joyce's subjects become, the more he tends to swathe them about with the fancywork of his literary virtuosity. It is as if it were not merely Earwicker who was frightened by the state of his emotions but as if Joyce were embarrassed, too.

Yet, with all this, *Finnegans Wake* has achieved certain amazing successes. Joyce has caught the psychology of sleep as no one else has ever caught it, laying hold on states of mind which it is difficult for the waking intellect to re-create, and distinguishing with marvelous delicacy between the different levels of dormant consciousness.

---

about them. That this should be true is due probably to some special defect of *rapport* between Joyce and the audience he is addressing, to some disease of his architectural faculty; but he compensates us partly for this by giving us more in the long run than we had realized at first was there, and he eventually produces the illusion that this fiction has a reality like life's, because, behind all the antics, the pedantry, the artificial patterns, something organic and independent of these is always revealing itself; and we end by recomposing a world in our mind as we do from the phenomena of experience. Mr. Max Eastman reports that Joyce once said to him, during a conversation on *Finnegans Wake,* when Mr. Eastman had suggested to Joyce that the demands made on the reader were too heavy and that he perhaps ought to provide a key: 'The demand that I make of my reader is that he should devote his whole life to reading my works.' It is in any case probably true that they will last you a whole lifetime.

There are the relative vividness of events reflected from
the day before; the nightmare viscidity and stammering of
the heavy slumbers of midnight; the buoyance and self-
assertive vitality which gradually emerge from this; the
half-waking of the early morning, which lapses back into
the rigmaroles of dreams; the awareness, later, of the light
outside, with its effect as of the curtain of the eyelids
standing between the mind and the day. Through all
this, the falling of twilight, the striking of the hours by the
clock, the morning fog and its clearing, the bell for early
mass, and the rising sun at the window, make themselves
felt by the sleeper. With what brilliance they are rendered
by Joyce! And the voices that echo in Earwicker's dream
— the beings that seize upon him and speak through him:
the Tree and the River, the eloquence of Shaun, the mum-
bling and running-on of the Old Men; the fluttery girl
sweetheart, the resigned elderly wife; the nagging and
jeering gibberish — close to madness and recalling the
apparition of Virag in the Walpurgisnacht scene of
Ulysses, but here identified with the Devil — which comes
like an incubus with the darkness and through which the
thickened voices of the Earwicker household occasionally
announce themselves startlingly: 'Mawmaw, luk, your
beeftay's fizzin' over' or 'Now a muss wash the little face.'
Joyce has only to strike the rhythm and the timbre, and
we know which of the spirits is with us.

Some of the episodes seem to me wholly successful: the
Anna Livia chapter, for example, and the end of *Haveth
Childers Everywhere,* which has a splendor and a high-
spirited movement of a kind not matched elsewhere in
Joyce. The passage in a minor key which precedes this
major *crescendo* and describes Earwicker's real habita-
tions — 'most respectable . . . thoroughly respectable . . .
partly respectable,' and so forth — is a masterpiece of hu-
morous sordidity (especially 'copious holes emitting mice');
and so is the inventory — on pages 183-184 — of all the use-

less and rubbishy objects in the house where Shem the Penman lives. The *Ballad of Persse O'Reilly* (*perce-oreille, earwig*) — which blazons the shame of Earwicker — is real dream literature and terribly funny; as is also the revelation — pages 572-573 — of the guilty and intricate sex relationships supposed to prevail in the Earwicker family, under the guise of one of those unintelligible summaries of a saint's legend or a Latin play. The waking-up chapter is charming in the passage — page 565 — in which the mother comforts the restless boy and in the summing-up — page 579 — of the married life of the Earwickers; and it is touchingly and thrillingly effective in throwing back on all that has gone before the shy impoverished family pathos which it is Joyce's special destiny to express.

Where he is least happy, I think, is in such episodes as the voyage, 311 ff., the football game, 373 ff, and the siege of Sebastopol, 338 ff. (all in the dense nightmarish part of the book, which to me is, in general, the dullest). Joyce is best when he is idyllic, nostalgic, or going insane in an introspective way; he is not good at energetic action. There is never any direct aggressive clash between the pairs of opponents in Joyce, and there is consequently no real violence (except Dedalus' smashing the chandelier in self-defense against the reproach of his dead mother). All that Joyce is able to do when he wants to represent a battle is to concoct an uncouth gush of language. In general one feels, also, in *Finnegans Wake* the narrow limitations of Joyce's interests. He has tried to make it universal by having Earwicker take part in his dream in as many human activities as possible: but Joyce himself has not the key either to politics, to sport or to fighting. The departments of activity that come out best are such quiet ones as teaching and preaching.

The finest thing in the book, and one of the finest things Joyce has done, is the passage at the end where

Ann, the wife, is for the first time allowed to speak with her full and mature voice. I have noted that Joyce's fiction usually deals with the tacit readjustment in the relationships between members of a family, the almost imperceptible moment which marks the beginning of a phase. In *Finnegans Wake,* the turning-point fixed is the moment when the husband and wife know definitely – they will wake up knowing it – that their own creative sexual partnership is over. That current no longer holds them polarized – as man and woman – toward one another; a new polarization takes place: the father is pulled back toward the children. 'Illas! I wisht I had better glances,' he thinks he hears Ann-Anna saying (page 626) 'to peer to you through this baylight's growing. But you're changing, acoolsha, you're changing from me, I can feel. Or is it me is? I'm getting mixed. Brightening up and tightening down. Yes, you're changing, sonhusband, and you're turning, I can feel you, for a daughterwife from the hills again. Imlamaya. And she is coming. Swimming in my hindmoist. Diveltaking on me tail. Just a whisk brisk sly spry spink spank sprint of a thing theresomere, saultering. Saltarella come to her own. I pity your oldself I was used to. Now a younger's there.' It is the 'young thin pale soft shy slim slip of a thing, sauntering by silvamoonlake' (page 202 in the Anna Livia Plurabelle section) that she herself used to be, who now seems to her awkward and pert, and the wife herself is now the lower river running into the sea. The water is wider here; the pace of the stream is calmer: the broad day of experience has opened. 'I thought you were all glittering with the noblest of carriage. You're only a bumpkin. I thought you the great in all things, in guilt and in glory. You're but a puny. Home!' She sees him clearly now: he is neither Sir Tristram nor Lucifer; and he is done with her and she with him. 'I'm loothing them that's here and all I lothe. Loonely in me loneness. For all their faults. I am passing out. O bitter ending! I'll slip away before they're up. They'll never see me. Nor know. Nor miss me. And it's old and old it's sad and old it's sad and weary I go back to you, my cold father, my cold mad father, my cold mad feary father.' . . . The helpless and heartbreaking voices of the Earwicker children recur: 'Carry me along, taddy, like you done through the toy fair' — for now she is herself the child entrusting herself to the sea, flowing out into the daylight that is to be her annihilation . . . 'a way a lone a last a loved a long the' . . .

The Viconian cycle of existence has come full circle again. The unfinished sentence which ends the book is to find its continuation in the sentence without a beginning with which it opens. The river which runs into the sea must commence as a cloud again; the woman must give up life to the child. The Earwickers will wake to another day, but the night has made them older: the very release of the daylight brings a weariness that looks back to life's source.

In these wonderful closing pages, Joyce has put over all he means with poetry of an originality, a purity and an emotional power, such as to raise *Finnegans Wake,* for all its excesses, to the rank of a great work of literature.

1964. This essay was written in 1939, not long, as I have said, after the book's publication. Though I had read the instalments in *transition,* I had been through the whole book only once and had not become aware of its architecture, as solid and simple and monumental as the surface is complicated. I had not even grasped the full significance of the antithetical roles of Shem and Shaun, Earwicker's twin sons, who are reflected in all the other pairs of opposites: Mutt and Jute, the two washerwomen, the Mookse and the Gripes, the Ondt and the Gracehoper, etc.; nor that the first part of the book is dominated by the sensitive and poetic and mother-protected Shem, that the brothers struggle and merge in the darkness of deepest night, and that, emerging from this struggle, the sensual and practical, the conventional, rather boring Shaun grows into a giant figure who dominates the remaining episodes. The longer one reads the book, the more of it comes to life and the more it communicates emotion, and I should by no means say today as I have above that two-thirds of it is unsuccessful.

I should note also that from one of Joyce's published letters it appears that I was mistaken in supposing that old Johnny MacDougall was Ulster. I do not know whether anyone has suggested that — since the four old men in one of their aspects are supposed to represent the four gospels — one of the reasons for old Johnny's belatedness may be the very much later date than those of the other three gospels which used to be assigned to John.

PHILOCTETES: THE WOUND AND THE BOW

THE *Philoctetes* of Sophocles is far from being his most popular play. The myth itself has not been one of those which have excited the modern imagination. The idea of Philoctetes' long illness and his banishment to the bleak island is dreary or distasteful to the young, who like to identify themselves with men of action — with Heracles or Perseus or Achilles; and for adults the story told by Sophocles fails to set off such emotional charges as are liberated by the crimes of the Atreidai and the tragedies of the siege of Troy. Whatever may have been dashing in the legend has been lost with the other plays and poems that dealt with it. Philoctetes is hardly mentioned in Homer; and we have only an incomplete account of the plays by Aeschylus and Euripides, which hinged on a critical moment of the campaign of the Greeks at Troy and which seem to have exploited the emotions of Greek patriotism. We have only a few scattered lines and phrases from that other play by Sophocles on the subject, the *Philoctetes at Troy*, in which the humiliated hero was presumably to be cured of his ulcer and to proceed to his victory over Paris.

There survives only this one curious drama which presents Philoctetes in exile — a drama which does not supply us at all with what we ordinarily expect of Greek tragedy, since it culminates in no catastrophe, and which indeed resembles rather our modern idea of a comedy (though the record of the lost plays of Sophocles show that there must have been others like it). Its interest depends almost as much on the latent interplay of character, on a gradual psychological conflict, as that of *Le Misan-thrope*. And it assigns itself, also, to a category even more special and less generally appealing through the fact (though this, again, was a feature not uncommon with Sophocles) that the conflict is not even allowed to take place between a man and a woman. Nor does it even put before us the spectacle — which may be made exceedingly thrilling — of the individual in conflict with his social group, which we get in such plays devoid of feminine interest as *Coriolanus* and *An Enemy of the People*. Nor is the conflict even a dual one, as most dramatic conflicts are — so that our emotions seesaw up and down between two opposed persons or groups: though Philoctetes and Odysseus struggle for the loyalty of Neoptolemus, he himself emerges more and more distinctly as representing an independent point of view, so that the contrast becomes a triple affair which makes more complicated demands on our sympathies.

A French dramatist of the seventeenth century, Chateaubrun, found the subject so inconceivable that, in trying to concoct an adaptation which would be acceptable to the taste of his time, he provided Philoctetes with a daughter named Sophie with whom Neoptolemus was to fall in love and thus bring the drama back to the reliable and eternal formula of Romeo and Juliet and the organizer who loves the factory-owner's daughter. And if we look for the imprint of the play on literature since the Renaissance, we shall find a very meager record: a chapter of Fénelon's *Télémaque*, a discussion in Lessing's *Laocoön*, a sonnet of Wordsworth's, a little play by André Gide, an adaptation by John Jay Chapman — this is all, so far as I know, that has any claim to interest.

And yet the play itself *is* most interesting, as some of these writers have felt; and it is certainly one of Sophocles'

PHILOCTETES: THE WOUND AND THE BOW   225

masterpieces. If we come upon it in the course of reading
him, without having heard it praised, we are surprised to
be so charmed, so moved — to find ourselves in the presence of something that is so much less crude in its subtlety
than either a three-cornered modern comedy like *Candida*
or *La Parisienne* or an underplayed affair of male loyalty
in a story by Ernest Hemingway, to both of which it has
some similarity. It is as if having the three men on the
lonely island has enabled the highly sophisticated Sophocles to get further away from the framework of the old
myths on which he has to depend and whose barbarities,
anomalies and absurdities, tactfully and realistically
though he handles them, seem sometimes almost as much
out of place as they would in a dialogue by Plato. The
people of the *Philoctetes* seem to us more familiar than
they do in most of the other Greek tragedies;[1] and they
take on for us a more intimate meaning. Philoctetes remains in our mind, and his incurable wound and his invincible bow recur to us with a special insistence. But
what is it they mean? How is it possible for Sophocles to
make us accept them so naturally? Why do we enter with
scarcely a stumble into the situation of people who are
preoccupied with a snake-bite that lasts forever and a
weapon that cannot fail?

Let us first take account of the peculiar twist which
Sophocles seems to have given the legend, as it had come
to him from the old epics and the dramatists who had
used it before him.

The main outline of the story ran as follows: The demi-
god Heracles had been given by Apollo a bow that never
missed its mark. When, poisoned by Deianeira's robe, he
had had himself burned on Mount Oeta, he had per-

[1] 'Apropos of the rare occasions when the ancients seem just like us,
it always has seemed to me that a wonderful example was the repentance of the lad in the (*Philoctetes?*) play of Sophocles over his
deceit, and the restoration of the bow.' — Mr. Justice Holmes to Sir
Frederick Pollock, October 2, 1921.

suaded Philoctetes to light the pyre and had rewarded him
by bequeathing to him this weapon. Philoctetes had thus
been formidably equipped when he had later set forth
against Troy with Agamemnon and Menelaus. But on the
way they had to stop off at the tiny island of Chrysè to
sacrifice to the local deity. Philoctetes approched the
shrine first, and he was bitten in the foot by a snake. The
infection became peculiarly virulent; and the groans of
Philoctetes made it impossible to perform the sacrifice,
which would be spoiled by ill-omened sounds; the bite
began to suppurate with so horrible a smell that his companions could not bear to have him near them. They removed him to Lemnos, a neighboring island which was
much larger than Chrysè and inhabited, and sailed away
to Troy without him.

Philoctetes remained there ten years. The mysterious
wound never healed. In the meantime, the Greeks, hard
put to it at Troy after the deaths of Achilles and Ajax and
baffled by the confession of their soothsayer that he was
unable to advise them further, had kidnapped the soothsayer of the Trojans and had forced him to reveal to them
that they could never win till they had sent for Neoptolemus, the son of Achilles, and given him his father's armor,
and till they had brought Philoctetes and his bow.

Both these things were done. Philoctetes was healed at
Troy by the son of the physician Asclepius; and he fought
Paris in single combat and killed him. Philoctetes and
Neoptolemus became the heroes of the taking of Troy.

Both Aeschylus and Euripides wrote plays on this subject long before Sophocles did; and we know something
about them from a comparison of the treatments by the
three different dramatists which was written by Dion
Chrysostom, a rhetorician of the first century A.D. Both
these versions would seem to have been mainly concerned
with the relation of Philoctetes to the success of the Greek
campaign. All three of the plays dealt with the same epi-

sode: the visit of Odysseus to Lemnos for the purpose of getting the bow; and all represented Odysseus as particularly hateful to Philoctetes (because he had been one of those responsible for abandoning him on the island), and obliged to resort to cunning. But the emphasis of Sophocles' treatment appears fundamentally to have differed from that of the other two. In the drama of Aeschylus, we are told, Odysseus was not recognized by Philoctetes, and he seems simply to have stolen the bow. In Euripides, he was disguised by Athena in the likeness of another person, and he pretended that he had been wronged by the Greeks as Philoctetes had been. He had to compete with a delegation of Trojans, who had been sent to get the bow for their side and who arrived at the same time as he; and we do not know precisely what happened. But Dion Chrysostom regarded the play as 'a masterpiece of declamation' and 'a model of ingenious debate,' and Jebb thinks it probable that Odysseus won the contest by an appeal to Philoctetes' patriotism. Since Odysseus was pretending to have been wronged by the Greeks, he could point to his own behavior in suppressing his personal resentments in the interests of saving Greek honor. The moral theme thus established by Aeschylus and Euripides both would have been simply, like the theme of the wrath of Achilles, the conflict between the passions of an individual — in this case, an individual suffering from a genuine wrong — and the demands of duty to a common cause.

This conflict appears also in Sophocles; but it takes on a peculiar aspect. Sophocles, in the plays of his we have, shows himself particularly successful with people whose natures have been poisoned by narrow fanatical hatreds. Even allowing for the tendency of Greek heroes, in legend and history both, to fly into rather childish rages, we still feel on Sophocles' part some sort of special point of view, some sort of special sympathy, for these cases. Such people — Electra and the embittered old Oedipus — suffer as much as they hate: it is because they suffer they hate. They horrify, but they waken pity. Philoctetes is such another: a man obsessed by a grievance, which in his case he is to be kept from forgetting by an agonizing physical ailment; and for Sophocles his pain and hatred have a dignity and an interest. Just as it is by no means plain to Sophocles that in the affair of Antigone *versus* Cleon it is the official point of view of Cleon, representing the interests of his victorious faction, which should have the last word against Antigone, infuriated by a personal wrong; so it is by no means plain to him that the morality of Odysseus, who is lying and stealing for the fatherland, necessarily deserves to prevail over the animus of the stricken Philoctetes.

The contribution of Sophocles to the story is a third person who will sympathize with Philoctetes. This new character is Neoptolemus, the young son of Achilles, who, along with Philoctetes, is indispensable to the victory of the Greeks and who has just been summoned to Troy. Odysseus is made to bring him to Lemnos for the purpose of deceiving Philoctetes and shanghai-ing him aboard the ship.

The play opens with a scene between Odysseus and the boy, in which the former explains the purpose of their trip. Odysseus will remain in hiding in order not to be recognized by Philoctetes, and Neoptolemus will go up to the cave in which Philoctetes lives and win his confidence by pretending that the Greeks have robbed him of his father's armor, so that he, too, has a grievance against them. The youth in his innocence and candor objects when he is told what his rôle is to be, but Odysseus persuades him by reminding him that they can only take Troy through his obedience and that once they have taken Troy, he will be glorified for his bravery and wisdom. 'As soon as we have won,' Odysseus assures him, 'we shall conduct ourselves with perfect honesty. But for one short day of dishonesty, allow me to direct you what to do — and then forever after you will be known as the most righteous of men.' The line of argument adopted by Odysseus is one with which the politics of our time have made us very familiar. 'Isn't it base, then, to tell falsehoods?' Neoptolemus asks. 'Not,' Odysseus replies, 'when a falsehood will bring our salvation.'

Neoptolemus goes to talk to Philoctetes. He finds him in the wretched cave —described by Sophocles with characteristic realism: the bed of leaves, the crude wooden bowl, the filthy bandages drying in the sun — where he has been living in rags for ten years, limping out from time to time to shoot wild birds or to get himself wood and water. The boy hears the harrowing story of Philoctetes' desertion by the Greeks and listens to his indignation. The ruined captain begs Neoptolemus to take him back to his native land, and the young man pretends to consent. (Here and elsewhere I am telescoping the scenes and simplifying a more complex development.) But just as they are leaving for the ship, the ulcer on Philoctetes' foot sets up an ominous throbbing in preparation for one of its periodical burstings: 'She returns from time to time,' says the invalid, 'as if she were sated with her wanderings.' In a moment he is stretched on the ground, writhing in abject anguish and begging the young man to cut off his foot. He gives Neoptolemus the bow, telling him to take care of it till the seizure is over. A second spasm, worse than the first, reduces him to imploring the boy to throw him into the crater of the Lemnian volcano: so he himself, he says, had lit the fire which consumed the tormented Heracles and had got in return these arms, which he is now handing on to Neoptolemus. The pain abates a little; 'It comes and goes,' says Philoctetes; and he entreats the young man not to leave him. 'Don't worry about

that. We'll stay.' 'I shan't even make you swear it, my son.'
'It would not be right to leave you' (it would not be right,
of course, even from the Greeks' point of view). They
shake hands on it. A third paroxysm twists the cripple;
now he asks Neoptolemus to carry him to the cave, but
shrinks from his grasp and struggles. At last the abscess
bursts, the dark blood begins to flow. Philoctetes, faint and
sweating, falls asleep.

The sailors who have come with Neoptolemus urge him
to make off with the bow. 'No,' the young man replies.
'He cannot hear us; but I am sure that it will not be
enough for us to recapture the bow without him. It is he
who is to have the glory — it was he the god told us to
bring.'

While they are arguing, Philoctetes awakes and thanks
the young man with emotion: 'Agamemnon and Menelaus were not so patient and loyal.' But now they must get
him to the ship, and the boy will have to see him unde-
ceived and endure his bitter reproaches. 'The men will
carry you down,' says Neoptolemus. 'Don't trouble them:
just help me up,' Philoctetes replies. 'It would be too disagreeable for them to take me all the way to the ship.' The
smell of the suppuration has been sickening. The young
man begins to hesitate. The other sees that he is in doubt
about something: 'You're not so overcome with disgust at
my disease that you don't think you can have me on the
ship with you?' —

οὐ δή σε δυσχέρεια τοῦ νοσήματος
ἔπεισεν ὥστε μή μ' ἄγειν ναύτην ἔτι;

The answer is one of the most effective of those swift and
brief speeches of Sophocles which for the first time make
a situation explicit (my attempts to render this dialogue
colloquially do no justice to the feeling and point of the
verse):

ἅπαντα δυσχέρεια, τὴν αὐτοῦ φύσιν

ὅταν λιπών τις δρᾷ τὰ μὴ προσεικότα.

'Everything becomes disgusting when you are false to your own nature and behave in an unbecoming way.'

He confesses his real intentions; and a painful scene occurs. Philoctetes denounces the boy in terms that would be appropriate for Odysseus; he sees himself robbed of his bow and left to starve on the island. The young man is deeply worried: 'Why did I ever leave Scyros?' he asks himself. 'Comrades, what shall I do?'

At this moment, Odysseus, who has been listening, pops out from his hiding place. With a lash of abuse at Neoptolemus, he orders him to hand over the arms. The young man's spirit flares up: when Odysseus invokes the will of Zeus, he tells him that he is degrading the gods by lending them his own lies. Philoctetes turns on Odysseus with an invective which cannot fail to impress the generous Neoptolemus: Why have they come for him now? he demands. Is he not still just as ill-omened and loathsome as he had been when they made him an outcast? They have only come back to get him because the gods have told them they must.

The young man now defies his mentor and takes his stand with Philoctetes. Odysseus threatens him: if he persists, he will have the whole Greek army against him, and they will see to it that he is punished for his treason. Neoptolemus declares his intention of taking Philoctetes home; he gives him back his bow. Odysseus tries to intervene; but Philoctetes has got the bow and aims an arrow at him. Neoptolemus seizes his hand and restrains him. Odysseus, always prudent, beats a quiet retreat.

Now the boy tries to persuade the angry man that he should, nevertheless, rescue the Greeks. 'I have proved my good faith,' says Neoptolemus; 'you know that I am not going to coerce you. Why be so wrong-headed? When the gods afflict us, we are obliged to bear our misfortunes; but must people pity a man who suffers through his own choice? The snake that bit you was an agent of the gods, it was the guardian of the goddess's shrine, and I swear to you by Zeus that the sons of Asclepius will cure you if you let us take you to Troy.' Philoctetes is incredulous, refuses. 'Since you gave me your word,' he says, 'take me home again.' 'The Greeks will attack me and ruin me.' 'I'll defend you.' 'How can you?' 'With my bow.' Neoptolemus is forced to consent.

But now Heracles suddenly appears from the skies and declares to Philoctetes that what the young man says is true, and that it is right for him to go to Troy. He and the son of Achilles shall stand together like lions and shall gloriously carry the day. — The *deus ex machina* here may of course figure a change of heart which has taken place in Philoctetes as the result of his having found a man who recognizes the wrong that has been done him and who is willing to champion his cause in defiance of all the Greek forces. His patron, the chivalrous Heracles, who had himself performed so many generous exploits, asserts his influence over his heir. The long hatred is finally exorcised.

In a fine lyric utterance which ends the play, Philoctetes says farewell to the cavern, where he has lain through so many nights listening to the deep-voiced waves as they crashed against the headland, and wetted by the rain and the spray blown in by the winter gales. A favorable wind has sprung up; and he sails away to Troy.

It is possible to guess at several motivations behind the writing of the *Philoctetes*. The play was produced in 409, when — if the tradition of his longevity be true — Sophocles would have been eighty-seven; and it is supposed to have been followed by the *Oedipus Coloneus,* which is assigned to 405 or 406. The latter deals directly with old age; but it would appear that the *Philoctetes* anticipates this theme in another form. Philoctetes, like the outlawed

Oedipus, is impoverished, humbled, abandoned by his people, exacerbated by hardship and chagrin. He is accursed: Philoctetes' ulcer is an equivalent for the abhorrent sins of Oedipus, parricide and incest together, which have made of the ruler a pariah. And yet somehow both are sacred persons who have acquired superhuman powers, and who are destined to be purged of their guilt. One passage from the earlier play is even strikingly repeated in the later. The conception of the wave-beaten promontory and the sick man lying in his cave assailed by the wind and rain turns up in the *Oedipus Coloneus* (Coloneus was Sophocles' native deme) with a figurative moral value. So the ills of old age assail Oedipus. Here are the lines, in A. E. Housman's translation:

> This man, as me, even so,
> Have the evil days overtaken;
> And like as a cape sea-shaken
> With tempest at earth's last verges
> And shock of all winds that blow,
> His head the seas of woe,
> The thunders of awful surges
> Ruining overflow:
> Blown from the fall of even,
>   Blown from the dayspring forth,
> Blown from the moon in heaven,
>   Blown from night and the North.

But Oedipus has endured as Philoctetes has endured in the teeth of all the cold and the darkness, the screaming winds and the bellowing breakers: the blind old man is here in his own person the headland that stands against the storm.

We may remember a widely current story about the creator of these two figures. It is said that one of Sophocles' sons brought him into court in his advanced old age on the complaint that he was no longer competent to man-

age his property. The old poet is supposed to have recited
a passage from the play which he had been writing: the
chorus in praise of Coloneus, with its clear song of night-
ingales, its wine-dark ivy, its crocus glowing golden and
its narcissus moist with dew, where the stainless stream of
the Cephisus wanders through the broad-swelling plain
and where the gray-leaved olive grows of itself beneath
the gaze of the gray-eyed Athena — shining Colonus,
breeder of horses and of oarsmen whom the Nereids lead.
The scene had been represented on the stage and Sophocles had been made to declare: 'If I am Sophocles, I am
not mentally incapable; if I am mentally incapable, I am
not Sophocles.' In any case, the story was that the tribunal,
composed of his fellow clansmen, applauded and acquitted
the poet and censored the litigating son. The ruined and
humiliated heroes of Sophocles' later plays are still persons of mysterious virtue, whom their fellows are forced
to respect.

There is also a possibility, even a strong probability,
that Sophocles intended Philoctetes to be identified with
Alcibiades. This brilliant and unique individual, one of
the great military leaders of the Athenians, had been ac-
cused by political opponents of damaging the sacred sta-
tues of Hermes and burlesquing the Eleusinian mysteries,
and had been summoned to stand trial at Athens while
he was away on his campaign against Sicily. He had at
once gone over to the Spartans, commencing that insolent
career of shifting allegiances which ended with his returning to the Athenian side. At a moment of extreme danger,
he had taken over a part of the Athenian fleet and had defeated the Spartans in two sensational battles in 411 and
410, thus sweeping them out of the Eastern Aegean and
enabling the Athenians to dominate the Hellespont. The
Philoctetes was produced in 409, when the Athenians already wanted him back and were ready to cancel the
charges against him and to restore him to citizenship. Al-

cibiades was a startling example of a bad character who was indispensable. Plutarch says that Aristophanes well describes the Athenian feeling about Alcibiades when he writes: 'They miss him and hate him and long to have him back.' And the malady of Philoctetes may have figured his moral defects: the unruly and unscrupulous nature which, even though he seems to have been innocent of the charges brought against him, had given them a certain plausibility. It must have looked to the Athenians, too, after the victories of Abydos and Cyzicus, as if he possessed an invincible bow. Plutarch says that the men who had served under him at the taking of Cyzicus did actually come to regard themselves as undefeatable and refused to share quarters with other soldiers who had fought in less successful engagements.

Yet behind both the picture of old age and the line in regard to Alcibiades, one feels in the *Philoctetes* a more general and fundamental idea: the conception of superior strength as inseparable from disability.

For the superiority of Philoctetes does not reside merely in the enchanted bow. When Lessing replied to Winckelmann, who had referred to Sophocles' cripple as if he were an example of the conventional idea of impassive classical fortitude, he pointed out that, far from exemplifying impassivity, Philoctetes becomes completely demoralized every time he has one of his seizures, and yet that this only heightens our admiration for the pride which prevents him from escaping at the expense of helping those who have deserted him. 'We despise,' say the objectors, 'any man from whom bodily pain extorts a shriek. Ay, but not always; not for the first time, nor if we see that the sufferer strains every nerve to stifle the expression of his pain; not if we know him otherwise to be a man of firmness; still less if we witness evidences of his firmness in the very midst of his sufferings, and observe that, although pain may have extorted a shriek, it has extorted nothing else from him, but that on the contrary he submits to the prolongation of his pain rather than renounce one iota of his resolutions, even where such a concession would promise him the termination of his misery.'

André Gide, in his *Philoctète*, the obstinacy of the invalid hermit takes on a character almost mystical. By persisting in his bleak and lonely life, the Philoctetes of Gide wins the love of a more childlike Neoptolemus and even compels the respect of a less hard-boiled Odysseus. He is practicing a kind of virtue superior not only to the virtue of the latter, with his code of obedience to the demands of the group, but also to that of the former, who forgets his patriotic obligations for those of a personal attachment. There is something above the gods, says the Philoctetes of Gide; and it is virtue to devote oneself to this. But what is it? asks Neoptolemus. I do not know, he answers; oneself! The misfortune of his exile on the island has enabled him to perfect himself: 'I have learned to express myself better,' he tells them, 'now that I am no longer with men. Between hunting and sleeping, I occupy myself with thinking. My ideas, since I have been alone so that nothing, not even suffering, disturbs them, have taken a subtle course which sometimes I can hardly follow. I have come to know more of the secrets of life than my masters had ever revealed to me. And I took to telling the story of my sufferings, and if the phrase was very beautiful, I was by so much consoled; I even sometimes forgot my sadness by uttering it. I came to understand that words inevitably become more beautiful from the moment they are no longer put together in response to the demands of others. . . .' The Philoctetes of Gide is, in fact, a literary man: at once a moralist and an artist, whose genius becomes purer and deeper in ratio to his isolation and outlawry. In the end, he lets the intruders steal the bow after satisfying himself that Neoptolemus can handle it, and subsides into a blissful tranquillity, much relieved that there is no longer any reason for people to seek him out.

With Gide we come close to a further implication, which even Gide does not fully develop but which must occur to the modern reader: the idea that genius and disease, like strength and mutilation, may be inextricably bound up together. It is significant that the only two writers of our time who have especially interested themselves in Philoctetes — André Gide and John Jay Chapman — should both be persons who have not only, like the hero of the play, stood at an angle to the morality of society and defended their position with stubbornness, but who have suffered from psychological disorders which have made them, in Gide's case, ill-regarded by his fellows; in Chapman's case, excessively difficult. Nor is it perhaps accidental that Charles Lamb, with his experience of his sister's insanity, should in his essay on *The Convalescent* choose the figure of Philoctetes as a symbol for his own 'nervous fever.'

And we must even, I believe, grant Sophocles some special insight into morbid psychology. The tragic themes of all three of the great dramatists — the madnesses, the murders and the incests — may seem to us sufficiently morbid. The hero with an incurable wound was even a stock subject of myth not confined to the Philoctetes legend: there was also the story of Telephus, also wounded and also indispensable, about which both Sophocles and Euripides wrote plays. But there is a difference between the treatment that Sophocles gives to these conventional epic subjects and the treatments of the other writers. Aeschylus is more religious and philosophical; Euripides more romantic and sentimental. Sophocles by comparison is clinical. Arthur Platt, who had a special interest in the scientific aspect of the classics, says that Sophocles was scrupulously up-to-date in the physical science of his time. He was himself closely associated by tradition with the cult of the healer Asclepius, whose son is to cure Philoctetes: Lucian had read a poem which he had dedicated to the doctor-god; and Plutarch reports that Asclepius was supposed to have visited his hearth. He is said also to have been actually a priest of another of the medical cults. Platt speaks particularly of his medical knowledge — which is illustrated by the naturalism and precision of his description of Philoctetes' infected bite.

But there is also in Sophocles a cool observation of the behavior of psychological derangements. The madness of Ajax is a genuine madness, from which he recovers to be horrified at the realization of what he has done. And it was not without good reason that Freud laid Sophocles under contribution for the naming of the Oedipus complex — since Sophocles had not only dramatized the myth that dwelt with the violation of the incest taboo, but had exhibited the suppressed impulse behind it in the speech in which he makes Jocasta attempt to reassure Oedipus by reminding him that it was not uncommon for men to dream about sleeping with their mothers — 'and he who thinks nothing of this gets through his life most easily.' Those who do not get through life so easily are presented by Sophocles with a very firm grasp on the springs of their abnormal conduct. Electra is what we should call nowadays schizophrenic: the woman who weeps over the urn which is supposed to contain her brother's ashes is not 'integrated,' as we say, with the fury who prepares her mother's murder. And certainly the fanaticism of Antigone — 'fixated,' like Electra, on her brother — is intended to be abnormal, too. The banishment by Jebb from Sophocles' text of the passage in which Antigone explains the unique importance of a brother and his juggling of the dialogue in the scene in which she betrays her indifference to the feelings of the man she is supposed to marry are certainly among the curiosities of Victorian scholarship — though he was taking his cue from the complaint of Goethe that

Antigone had been shown by Sophocles as acting from trivial motives and Goethe's hope that her speech about her brother might some day be shown to be spurious. Aristotle had cited this speech of Antigone's as an outstanding example of the principle that if anything peculiar occurs in a play the cause must be shown by the dramatist. It was admitted by Jebb that his rewriting of these passages had no real textual justification; and in one case he violates glaringly the convention of the one-line dialogue. To accept his emendation would involve the assumption that Aristotle did not know what the original text had been and was incapable of criticizing the corrupted version. No: Antigone forgets her fiancé and kills herself for her brother. Her timid sister (like Electra's timid sister) represents the normal feminine point of view. Antigone's point of view is peculiar, as Aristotle says. (The real motivation of the Antigone has been retraced with unmistakable accuracy by Professor Walter R. Agard in *Classical Philology* of July, 1937.)

These insane or obsessed people of Sophocles all display a perverse kind of nobility. I have spoken of the authority of expiation which emanates from the blasted Oedipus. Even the virulence of Electra's revenge conditions the intensity of her tenderness for Orestes. And so the maniacal fury which makes Ajax run amok, the frenzy of Heracles in the Nessus robe, terribly though they transform their victims, can never destroy their virtue of heroes. The poor disgraced Ajax will receive his due of honor after his suicide and will come to stand higher in our sympathies than Menelaus and Agamemnon, those obtuse and brutal captains, who here as in the *Philoctetes* are obviously no favorites of Sophocles'. Heracles in his final moments bids his spirit curb his lips with steel to keep him from crying out, and carry him through his self-destructive duty as a thing that is to be desired.

Some of these maladies are physical in origin, others are

psychological; but they link themselves with one another.
The case of Ajax connects psychological disorder as we get
it in Electra, for example, with the access of pain and rage
that causes Heracles to kill the herald Lichas; the case of
Heracles connects a poisoning that produces a murderous
fury with an infection that, though it distorts the personality, does not actually render the victim demented: the
wound of Philoctetes, whose agony comes in spasms like
that of Heracles. All these cases seem intimately related.

It has been the misfortune of Sophocles to figure in
academic tradition as the model of those qualities of coolness and restraint which that tradition regards as classical.
Those who have never read him — remembering the familiar statue — are likely to conceive something hollow
and marmoreal. Actually, as C. M. Bowra says, Sophocles
is 'passionate and profound.' Almost everything that we are
told about him by the tradition of the ancient world suggests equanimity and amiability and the enjoyment of un-
usual good fortune. But there is one important exception:
the anecdote in Plato's *Republic* in which Sophocles is
represented as saying that the release from amorous desire
which had come to him in his old age had been like a
liberation from an insane and cruel master. He *has* balance and logic, of course: those qualities that the classicists
admire; but these qualities only count because they master
so much savagery and madness. Somewhere even in the
fortunate Sophocles there had been a sick and raving
Philoctetes.

And now let us go back to the *Philoctetes* as a parable
of human character. I should interpret the fable as follows. The victim of a malodorous disease which renders
him abhorrent to society and periodically degrades him
and makes him helpless is also the master of a superhuman art which everybody has to respect and which the
normal man finds he needs. A practical man like Odysseus,
at the same time coarse-grained and clever, imagines that

PHILOCTETES: THE WOUND AND THE BOW   241

he can somehow get the bow without having Philoctetes
on his hands or that he can kidnap Philoctetes the bowman without regard for Philoctetes the invalid. But the
young son of Achilles knows better. It is at the moment
when his sympathy for Philoctetes would naturally inhibit
his cheating him — so the supernatural influences in Sophocles are often made with infinite delicacy to shade into
subjective motivations — it is at this moment of his natural
shrinking that it becomes clear to him that the words of
the seer had meant that the bow would be useless without
Philoctetes himself. It is in the nature of things — of this
world where the divine and the human fuse — that they
cannot have the irresistible weapon without its loathsome
owner, who upsets the processes of normal life by his
curses and his cries, and who in any case refuses to work
for men who have exiled him from their fellowship.

It is quite right that Philoctetes should refuse to come
to Troy. Yet it is also decreed that he shall be cured when
he shall have been able to forget his grievance and to devote his divine gifts to the service of his own people. It is
right that he should refuse to submit to the purposes of
Odysseus, whose only idea is to exploit him. How then is
the gulf to be got over between the ineffective plight of
the bowman and his proper use of his bow, between his
ignominy and his destined glory? Only by the intervention
of one who is guileless enough and human enough to treat
him, not as a monster, nor yet as a mere magical property
which is wanted for accomplishing some end, but simply
as another man, whose sufferings elicit his sympathy and
whose courage and pride he admires. When this human
relation has been realized, it seems at first that it is to have
the consequence of frustrating the purpose of the expedition and ruining the Greek campaign. Instead of winning
over the outlaw, Neoptolemus has outlawed himself as
well, at a time when both the boy and the cripple are des-
perately needed by the Greeks. Yet in taking the risk to

his cause which is involved in the recognition of his common humanity with the sick man, in refusing to break his word, he dissolves Philoctetes' stubbornness, and thus cures him and sets him free, and saves the campaign as well.